The Bridger Pass
OVERLAND TRAIL
1862-1869
Through
Colorado and Wyoming
and
Cross Roads
at the
Rawlins-Baggs Stage Road
in
Wyoming

Stories and History with Rare Photographs
Revised WAGON TRAILS & FOLK TALES to include the full length of the Overland Trail
Researched, compiled and written by:

Louise Bruning Erb
Ann Bruning Brown
Gilberta Bruning Hughes

FOREWORD

All the famous transcontinental routes westward - notably the Oregon, California, Mormon or Council Bluffs, and Santa Fe Trails - were themselves bona fide "overland trails," a term differentiating them categorically from the sea route to California around Cape Horn and the sea-land combination routes involving traverses of Mexico or Central America. However, among trail historians the capitalized "Overland Trail" by itself seems to have been tacitly adopted for the specific route described by the authors of this book - from Julesburg, Colorado to Salt Lake City via the South Platte and Cache-la-Poudre Rivers and then across southern Wyoming via Bridger Pass and Fort Bridger. It appears that the "Overland" name bestowed on this trail has been inspired and legitimized by the fact that among all historic western trails it was the one most heavily used by the famed "Overland" stage lines of Ben Holladay and associates, immortalized by images of swaying Concord coaches drawn by six-horse teams.

With poetic justice, and to their great credit, the authors - three grand-daughters of Wyoming pioneers - have written here the first book exclusively devoted to this particular trail, a subject too long neglected except in obscure and ephemeral articles and foot-notes. These authors are eminently qualified to write knowledgeably about this trail, not only as descendants of pioneers who ranched along it, but as avid latter-day trail followers who have spent years searching for and recording evidence of landmarks, military posts, stage stations, early ranches, and surviving trail remains - the actual wagon and stagecoach tracks of over a century ago. Such dedication is rare, and this book, the result of that dedication, will itself become a landmark of transcontinental trail literature.

In the interest of reinforcing the authors' clarification of often confusing trail terminology, it must be stressed here that the Overland Trail to Bridger Pass was a late period offspring of the great Oregon-California migration corridor via the main Platte and North Platte Rivers and South Pass, also known as the Central Overland Route or the Great Platte River Road. It departed from that primary route at Julesburg and rejoined it at or near Fort Bridger. Along the South Platte it coincided in part with the primary southwest-bearing migration route to Denver - identified historically as the Pikes Peak Trail, the South Platte Trail, or the Denver Road - then veered northwestward, merging with the old Cherokee Trail to skirt the Rocky Mountains before heading due west once more over the Wyoming plains.

Merrill J. Mattes, Director
Oregon-California Trails Association

INTRODUCTION

The events of history have a way of quietly slipping away until suddenly the few people left who remember, realize nothing has been written down for those who follow them. Such is the case of us three grandaughters of John and Ann Robertson, who in 1900 purchased, then lived on and operated until 1940, the old Sulphur Springs stage station ranch at the cross roads of the Overland Trail and the Rawlins-Meeker freight and stage road 30 miles southwest of Rawlins, Wyoming. We have chosen to deal only with that part of the freight-stage route that is in Carbon County in the state of Wyoming, thus from Rawlins to Baggs.

We have realized that a history of the complete Holladay's Overland Mail Route or The Overland Trail through Northern Colorado and Southern Wyoming over Bridger's Pass has never been put together in one volume. Our Aunt Jean Tallman's research--in the 1930s inspired us to do more extensive research--and the fact that we lived on part of the trail--gives us pleasure to bring you an accurate account of the trail and stage stations from Julesburg, Colorado, where the trail began, to Ft. Bridger, Wyoming where the trail again joined the Salt Lake City and California trail.

The three of us with our parents, Herman and Elizabeth Robertson Bruning, lived our young lives at Sulphur and on the Bruning homestead at Hay Gulch adjoining Sulphur to the north.

Recent photographs of what remains of some of the stations and our collection of old and rare photos are the only concrete records left of how the stations looked during the days when they were used, also many family letters and documents dating back to 1880.

In addition to this we are indebted to several men and women who lived in the area at the same time we did and graciously gave us their time, material and pictures which contribute greatly to the authenticity and completeness of our account.

© Copyright 1989 by the authors, Louise B. Erb, Ann B. Brown, and Gilberta B. Hughes.

Please do not copy in any form the material in this publication without permission.

The photographs and documents are strictly the property of the three authors or Mr. and Mrs. John Hansen, Roy Rasmussen, Millicent Goffar or Ed Tierney of Rawlins, Wyoming, and are not to be used elsewhere.

Some pen and ink drawings were executed by Ann Bruning Brown or W.R. Brown. Others borrowed with permission from the *Wyoming Wild Life Magazine*.

Typesetting and Printing by Journal Publishing Company, Inc., Greeley, Colorado, USA.

ISBN 0-9626193-0-2

ERBGEM Publishing Co.
5727 S. Hickory Way
Littleton, Colorado 80120-2315
(303) 794-0127

DEDICATION

We dedicate this historic record to the memory of our courageous pioneer grandparents, John and Ann Robertson and their children, our aunts and uncle, Jean Stewart Robertson Tallman, Ann Robertson Leap, James Robertson, our mother Elizabeth Robertson Bruning, who spent forty years at the Sulphur Springs Stage Station Ranch on the Overland Trail and to our father, Herman H. Bruning, Jr.

Now to our children, Robertson's great-grandchildren and the great, great-grandchildren.

Ann Bruning Brown

Gilberta Bruning Hughes

Louise Bruning Erb

TABLE OF CONTENTS

Maps
- Historic Trails of Wyoming 3
- Overland Trail Stations in Colorado - 1862-1869 15
- Holladay's Mail Stations From Denver to Laporte 16
- Cherokee-Overland and Trails - Ft. Collins North 32
- Overland Trail Stations in Wyoming - 1862-1869 38
- Cooper Creek Stage Station 44
- Rawlins to Baggs Stage Freight Road - 1868-1900 108
- In Between Canyons and Gulches - 1979 149
- Union Pacific Railroad in Wyoming - 1868 101

Documents
- Civil War Volunteer Enlistment (2 parts) - 1864 169-170
- Dacotah Territory Envelope - 1868 88
- Plat of Sulphur Springs Ranch 125
- Claim to Water Rights on Boner Ditch - 1886 123
- Liquor License from Sulphur Saloon - 1883-1884 131
- Leander Boner Deed to John Robertson for Sulphur Ranch - 1900 122
- Letter Edged in Black - 1888 135
- Parmelee and Weld Assay Report - 1903 183
- Larsen Oil Company Prospectus - 1911 132
- Constables Sale - 1911 133
- Registration and Poll Book for 1918 Election 136
- Deed to Hay Gulch Homestead - 1920 159
- The "Great Price Maker" - Sears Roebuck Catalog - 1908 177

Early Exploration of Bridger Pass Country 4
The Overland Trail or Holladay's Overland Mail Road 10
Mileage Between Stations in Colorado and Wyoming 14
Ben Holladay's Mail Stations in Colorado 16
Ben Holladay's Mail Stations in Wyoming 38
Forts on the Overland Trail
- Fort Sedgwick 18
- Camp Collins 27
- Fort Collins 27
- Fort Halleck 50
- Fort Sanders 59
- Fort LaClede 94
- Fort Bridger 101

Historical Review of Rawlins
- Baggs Stage & Freight Road 104

Canyons and Ranches 149
Summation of John Robertson and
- Herman H. Bruning Families 165

Personal Accounts of the Authors 173-185
Personal Account of Richard Robertson 186
Diary of Ann Leap 188

HISTORY OF THE OVERLAND TRAIL AND THE SULPHUR SPRINGS RANCH

Building built in the mid 1800s
Jim Robertson shown here

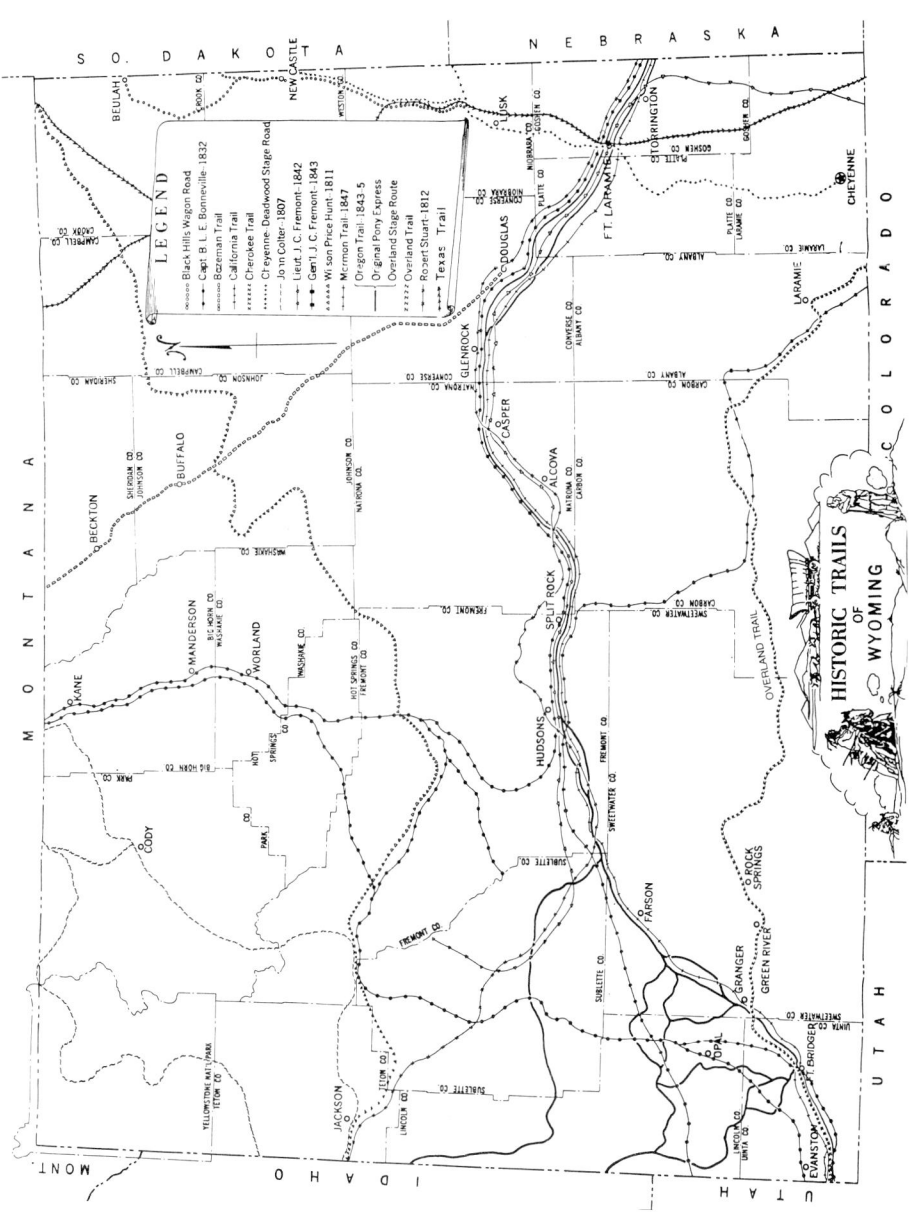

Overland Trail

EARLY EXPLORATION OF BRIDGER PASS COUNTRY

The lowly beaver and the tall hat made from the furry hide may be said to have opened the central Rocky Mountain region to the white man. This style of hat was the height of fashion for men for years in the first part of the 19th century. It went out of fashion about the year 1842 which is generally conceded, by historians, to be the end of the fur trade proper and the beginning of colonization. Kit Carson retired from trapping at this time and said, "There was no longer any money in it." Jim Bridger established his fort, trading post and blacksmith shop on Black's Fork of the Green River "in the road of the emigrants",[1] so he wrote at this time to Pierre Choteau, Jr. and Co. of St. Louis, one of the financial heads of the great fur business.[2]

Be that as it may, this had filled the demand of a greatly accelerated and remunerative market for beaver fur that caused the fur companies of the early 19th century to venture far afield into the very heart of the most hostile Indian country, and it was to find new and untrapped streams that made Major Andrew Henry and General William H. Ashley of St. Louis, Missouri, form a partnership in April, 1822, and advertise in a St. Louis newspaper for "enterprising young men to go into the fur country" with them to hunt and trap beaver. This "ad" drew a collection of famous names. Among them we see James Bridger (about 20 years old), Thomas Fitzpatrick, William and Milton Sublette and others. Names, together with their employers--Ashley and Henry--are written all over the early history of the central Rocky Mountain area because of the power and personality of their owners. A year later in 1823, we see three other famous kindred spirits gathered into their band, namely Jedediah S. Smith, David E. Jackson and Louis Vasquez. Ashley and Henry had reason to feel proud of the personnel of their party.[3]

By 1823 the streams of the upper Missouri were old in trapping history, as far up their courses as the Sioux and the Blackfeet Indians would permit white men to go. After one year of trapping in this territory, Henry and party, in September 1823, turned southward along the Powder River into the heart of what is now Wyoming--a new territory to the white man. They drifted along exploring, trapping and hunting, and keeping a wary eye out for Indians. The trappers found the Sioux, Crow, Snake, Arikara and Blackfoot Indians and grizzly bears formidable and treacherous foes. Somewhere on the Powder River they wintered. Henry decided to divide his brigade so as to better explore the country. He placed Fitzpatrick in charge of one group, in which was young Bridger, and retained the leadership of the other group himself.[4]

From the beginning, Jim Bridger had an insatiable love for exploring. He was constantly alert to the ways of nature; in his mind trapping and storing all the details down to the merest nook and cranny of every place he saw. His safety and livelihood, and those of his associates, depended upon his knowledge. Bridger's friendly association with the Indians gave him the advantage of learning more of the topography of the land.[5]

In the spring of 1824 Crow hunters told Fitzpatrick that if the trappers wanted many beaver they should follow one of their well known Indian trails to lucrative mountain streams. As quickly as they could, Tom Fitzpatrick, Jim Bridger and also possibly Jedediah Smith and party crossed from the Powder River, Wyoming, into the Sweetwater country from the east and there one of the greatest discoveries was attributed to them. They traversed a flat section of the land that had such an easy grade it was hardly discernable but suddenly realized the water was flowing west. Then and there the Great South Pass was discovered. The Continental Divide was crossed. This easy pass would allow for wagon traffic and connect the east and west coasts. In two decades from that moment the pass was to resound with the shouts of the land-hungry, gold-hungry, advance guard of the Pioneers on "The Great Medicine Way of the Whites", as the Indians termed the Oregon Trail. Major Fitzpatrick never dreamed that 20 years later he would be piloting the first emigrant train across the pass.[6]

Other historians gave Robert Stuart, of the Astorians, the credit for crossing the South Pass route in 1812 on their way back to St. Louis from exploration in the northwest part of the country. Perhaps Stuart did not recognize it as being an important find. His journal does not state the crossing.

The Fitzpatrick-Bridger party of Henry's Brigade continued on to the Siskadee, the Indian name for Green River, getting the lay of the land in mind as they trapped and hunted their way along. A "Beaver's Paradise" it was, on this new river and its tributaries. It is supposed that Henry and his part of the original party on this expedition explored and trapped in the Jackson's Hole country.[7]

Henry's entire Brigade including Jim Bridger spent all the spring and summer of 1824 exploring and trapping on the Green River and its tributaries in Wyoming.

In the autumn of this year we find the trappers in one of their favorite places, the Cache or Willow Valley in the Utah-Idaho area on the Bear River. They had always wondered where the mouth of the Bear River was since no one had explored it.

A wager was made between Bridger and another member of the party on this question. Bridger was the one to go. He followed the Bear River south thru mountains and a large canyon and found that it emptied into a large lake that tasted very salty. At that time it was thought to be an arm of the Pacific Ocean. Thus James Bridger is given the distinction of discovering the Great Salt Lake. A letter, of April 4, 1857, from Robert Campbell, an Ashley fur trader, to G.K. Warren, U.S. government geographer, verifies this fact.[8] In 1826 the lake was explored by other men and found to have no outlet.

After the Henry Brigade trappers had trapped to their satisfaction, Fitzpatrick left for St. Louis over the new route, namely South Pass, Sweetwater River and North Platte River to the Missouri. It is related that Fitzpatrick undertook a new system of transportation when he reached the Sweetwater. The party made a number of bull boats, loaded them with furs and started the cargo down the river. All went well until the junction of the Sweetwater and the North Platte was reached, where the swirling waters sank many of the boats; however, enough were salvaged to make the journey worthwhile for himself and men when he reached St. Louis.[9]

Bull boats were large rounded, open work baskets, made of stout, thick willows, which had been propped on posts fastened in the ground. Over this was stretched the fresh hide of one or more large buffalo and securely fastened with thongs of green hide. A slow fire was then built under the boat to dry it out and melt the tallow to be absorbed into the seams. This hardened the structure to keep it water tight.

Major Henry and a small part of his party returned to St. Louis. Henry did not return to the mountains again but his partner did. The Ashley-Henry partnership was dissolved and the Ashley-Jedediah Smith Co. was organized. Thomas Fitzpatick then became captain of Henry's Brigade.

Exactly when Bridger Pass got its name or even when Bridger scouted it out is pure speculation but it must have been in the year 1824. Regardless, he championed his pass.[10]

Scouting and exploring by Bridger and the other Mountain Men was truly extensive in what was so short a time. Charlie Russell, the famous cowboy artist, paid tribute to "Such people as Colter, Bridger and men of their stamp, these fellers were not out for gold or great wealth--they asked for little but life and adventure."

Bridger's Pass is in south-central Wyoming, 28 miles south of the present city of Rawlins and the Union Pacific Railroad. About two miles north and east of the head of the Muddy Creek Canyon, which runs east of Sulphur Springs Ranch, the trail slips through a notch, approximately 7350 feet in elevation, in the long barrier of hills, now called Atlantic Rim, which rises in places to 8400 feet. The trail continues in a north-easterly direction and approximately two miles from the Pass, the 7550 foot easement over the Continental Divide where the Muddy Creek runs west and the Sage creek runs east, would not have been readily recognized. Emigrants learned of the divide and looked forward to crossing it. Now a good dirt road (summertime only) follows along the valley and slips up over this pass in the hills. Emigrant days saw countless wagons, mail, coaches and animals crossing here. The beautiful days and quiet living that the authors experienced in their formative years in this post-pioneer country belies the horrors and tragedies that befell so many unfortunate emigrants all along the trail.

Bridger's Pass Photo by Louise B. Erb
This present road is on the Overland Trail

Ashley's return trip to the Green River was made in the bitter cold and stormy winter of 1824-25 in order to be there for the first trappers' Rocky Mountain Rendezvous, that was of his planning, in the spring of 1825. Departing from St. Louis by way of Ft. Atkinson the latter part of October with 50 head of heavily laden pack horses and mules, and a packed wagon, he traveled west up the Platte River. His party consisted of Tom Fitzpatrick, Jim Clyman, Zacharias Ham (Ham's Fork namesake), Jedediah Smith, Jim Beckwourth, "The gaudy liar!" and possibly Robert Campbell. Jim Bridger was not listed. They experienced exceedingly difficult and dangerous winter conditions, horses died from the severe cold but the men kept on trapping beaver as they went along. At the forks of the North and South Platte Rivers, where the friendly Loupe Pawnee Indians wintered, they were able to trade, for 23 horses, some buffalo robes and dried meat. Ashley could have gone on up the North Platte and across the South Pass but his desire to find a shorter way to the Green River, and the lure of exploration led him to scout out the South Platte route. He abandoned his wagon here. From the mouth of the Cache la Poudre River on the South Platte, he headed northwest over the Laramie Plains. Traveling was slow. It was stated the everything was "one mass of snow and ice". The Medicine Bow Mountains (Snowy Range) were too formidable--snow 5 feet deep in places. This led to their finding a way around the north tip of Elk Mountain which proved to be the accepted route for the emigrant trail later. On March 25 the party reached and crossed the North Platte then traveled west over Bridger's Pass. This accounting indicates they then went north to the Dry Sandy and the Sweetwater River. Whether Ashley already knew of Bridger's Pass or discovered it himself is unclear. By the 19th of April the Ashley party reached the Green.[11] They were still a great distance from the Rendezvous site. His desire to learn the Green River sent him on a hair-raising boat trip through the Flaming Gorge reaching approximately the present day location of Dinosaur National Monument area. He then traveled overland, skirting the Uinta Mountains on the west, then north to Henry's Fork.[12]

John Wesley Powell, who explored the Colorado River by boat in 1869, writes in his journal on June 1st, "...we came near to (some) falls, and tie up just above them. Here we shall be compelled to make a portage." June 2nd, "...we make a trail among the rocks, and transport the cargoes to a point below the falls. On a high rock by which the trail passes we find the inscription: "Ashley 18-5". The third figure is obscure--some of the party reading it 1835, some 1855. James Baker, an old-time mountaineer, once told me about a party of men starting down the river, and Ashley was named as one. The story runs that the boat was swamped, and some of the party drowned in one of the canyons below. The word "Ashley" is a warning to us, and we resolve on great caution. Ashley Falls is the name we give to the cataract."[13]

A second author has this Ashley party crossing the Laramie Plains--the same Elk Mountain route--and when they reached the North Platte descended it to the Sweetwater.[14]

A third author agrees with the others on the first part of Ashley's journey and has interpreted his diary as indicating the men crossed the Continental Divide near the present site of Rawlins, Wyoming, then crossed the Great Divide Basin "...valleys...most extensive and generally covered with water produced by melting snow and which appeared to have no outlet", then on northwest to the Sweetwater.[15] None of these groups went down Bitter Creek to the Green.

The first Rocky Mountain Rendezvous was held July 1, 1825 on Henry's Fork twenty miles from the confluence with the Green. Ashley records in his journal the presence of 120 men. Most were employed by a fur company but some were free trappers, or ones who worked for themselves. Also perhaps there were a few Indians and some deserters from the Hudson Bay Co.

Trappers bundled their skins together in packs of about 32 skins each. The average weight of a pack was 52 lbs. They would receive about $3.00 per pound. When arriving in St. Louis, the buyers put a $50,000 value on 100 packs, or $500 per pack.

Prices charged for merchandise bought from St. Louis was:

  Coffee & sugar--$1.50 per pound
  Tobacco--$3.00 per pound
  Powder--$2.00 per pound
  Flints--$1.00 per dozen
  Lead--$1.00 per pound
  Fish hooks--$1.50 per dozen
  Blue cloth--$5.00 per yard
  Scarlett cloth--$6.00 per yard
  Scissors--$2.00 each
  Knives--$2.50 each
  Buttons--$1.50 per dozen[16]

This first rendezvous lasted only one day although some of the men arrived a few days ahead. James Beckwourth writes in his journal: "...On arriving at the rendezvous, we found the main body of the Salt Lake party already there with the whole of their effects. The general would open none of his goods, except tobacco, until all had arrived, as he wished to make an equal distribution; for goods were very scarce in the mountains and hard to obtain.

"When all had come in, he opened his goods, and there was general jubilee among all at the rendezvous. We constituted quite a little town, numbering at least 800 souls, of whom one half were women and children. There were some among us who had not seen any groceries such as coffee, sugar, etc, for several months. The whisky went off as freely as water, even at the exorbitant price he sold it for. All kinds of sports were indulged in with a heartiness that would astonish more civilized societies." Beckwourth was known to take liberty with his statements, thus "800 souls" is quite a difference from Ashley's 120.

On May 13, 1989, a sign marking the 1825 Rocky Mountain Rendezvous Site was placed and dedicated at Henry's Fork in Sweetwater County, one mile east of the town of Burntfork, Wyoming on Highway 413. This is a Wyoming Centennial Event.

The Bridger Pass trail was well known and used by native Indians for many years prior to Jim Bridger's recognition of it as a negotiable pass through these hills in 1824. Trappers hunted its streams for the next two decades.

In 1842, John C. Fremont's vast exploration of the Rocky Mountains brought him into the Bridger Pass area but not over the pass itself.

In 1849, a group of migrating Cherokee Indians consisting of 130 men, women and children with 40 wagons and horses, and led by Capt. Lewis Evans for relocation to California, followed this trail to some extent. Historical references to this trek differ as to the location of their trail through this area. Their trail did go south around Elk Mountain. So far as is known, this is the first time wagons were used over this route. Previous transportation has been by pack animals. From this occurrence the route was often referred to as "The Cherokee Trail". The Cherokee

Trail came west out of Oklahoma along the Arkansas River Valley in Colorado to the mouth of Black Squirrel Creek, a tributary of Cherry Creek, following the latter to the South Platte River. It went on north along the eastern base of the Rockies to the Cache la Poudre in the vicinity of Laporte and Virginia Dale then over to the Laramie Plains.

In 1849-50 Captain Howard Stansbury of the Corps of Topographical Engineers of the U.S. Army was sent west to map old routes of travel and to find shorter ones. He was often in the vicinity of Fort Bridger, built by Jim Bridger in 1842 as a trading post on Black's Fork of the Green River. Bridger was invaluable to Stansbury. He acted as guide and gave first-hand information about the country. In 1850 when Stansbury was ready to return, Bridger assured him that he could guide him over a shorter route, 150 miles shorter than the Oregon Trail, whence he had come west. From the Green River this trail went eastward along Bitter Creek, skirting the Red Desert to Muddy Creek, following the Muddy Canyon to Bridger's Pass where the Continental Divide was crossed, then down Sage Creek, crossing the North Platte River and dropping down onto the Laramie Plains.[17]

In 1856, Lieutenant F.T. Bryan scouted from the east as far as Muddy Creek near Bridger's Pass and determined it to be a "practicable route for wagons", as stated in his diary.

In 1857 Army troops, commanded by Col. Albert Sidney Johnston, on an expedition to quell the Morman disturbances in Utah, suffered the burning of their army wagon trains and destruction of supplies along the Oregon Trail. At Col. Johnston's base near Ft. Bridger, he learned from Jim Bridger of the shorter southern trail across Wyoming. On December 9, 1857, Janis a trapper and Indian trader, Borderai a Spaniard and a Mr. Bartleson began an exploratory trip to the east from Ft. Bridger. According to Bartleson's journal, the conclusion was that the Muddy Creek Canyon up to Bridger's Pass would be utterly impossible to traverse in the winter and spring.[18]

1857 also found Lieutenant F.T. Bryan making a second trip across this route with some road improvements being done.

In 1858, Col. W.W. Loring, in command of reinforcements for the Mormon Expedition, with Captain R.B. Marcy, after having secured mules and horses from Ft. Union in New Mexico (northeast of Santa Fe) traveled back up the front range of the Rockies to the South Platte River where they built a flat boat to cross that stream and then transported it on a 20 mule team wagon to use it again to cross the North Platte at the site of the later Overland Trail. They found the river fordable so left the boat lying on the bank for others to use. The journal of Col. DuBois on this trip dwells on the difficult crossing of the streams and the desolate, forsaken desert west of the North Platte River.[19]

In 1858, Lt. F.T. Bryan, with a topographical party, made his third expedition across the Bridger Pass route, accompanying the 6th Infantry commanded by Lt. Col. George Andrew. William P. Seville, an Artificer in Company "A" Engineers, wrote a detailed diary of the trip telling of bridges being built, gullies filled in and roadways determined. Due to lack of large timber in this area, generally bridges were small and barely sufficient for wagons to cross. The skilled crew was a jovial group and took weather and adversities in stride. Lt. Bryan and his party certainly must be given credit for the extensive road and bridge building on the Overland Trail, especially through Carbon County in Wyoming. The authors had been across the Muddy Canyon road many times and wondered who made it!

Fitzhugh Ludlow, an emigrant in June of 1863, on his travels to Salt Lake City on the Overland Trail, wrote in his book *The Heart of the Continent:* "I was astonished at finding the art of the engineer so far anticipated for the purpose of a convenient transit route between the two coasts of our country, as everywhere appears in Bridger's Pass..."

Stansbury's report and to a lesser degree, Fremont's, were the main deciding forces for choosing the route of the Overland Trail and the transcontinental railroad.[20]

THE OVERLAND TRAIL
OR
HOLLADAY'S OVERLAND MAIL ROAD

When the 1849 cry of "GOLD!" echoed from California to the rest of the land, thousands of gold seekers, opportunists, and Mormons trudged along this Overland Trail. Evidence of this is the names and dates carved into the sandstone monoliths and cliffs along the way.

For a six week period in the spring and summer of 1849, the "jumping off" place at St. Joseph, on the Missouri River, reported 1500 wagons leaving. All the towns from Council Bluffs to Independence reported no less than 27,000 men and nearly 40,000 oxen and mules. In the years of 1850-52, traffic increased to 100,000 persons yearly[21]. Emigrants were traveling over the Oregon-California Trail.

In 1858 gold was being found in a few places along the foothills of the Rockies in Colorado. The small encampment of Auraria was established on the west side of Cherry Creek and soon Denver City was started on the east bank of the same stream. In April 1860, by act of the Legislature of Jefferson Territory they merged into just Denver. At this time the area of Colorado, plus most of the northwestern part of the United States, was under Jefferson Territory jurisdiction. Denver, from the Continental Divide and eastward to the present eastern boundary of Colorado, was in Kansas Territory and northeastern Colorado was in Nebraska Territory. The mines in the mountains were often called the Nebraska mines. In 1861 the area of the present Colorado was determined and officially declared the Territory of Colorado. On August 1, 1876 it became the 38th state of the Union--the Centennial State.

Eastern newspapers were spreading the gold word but with their limited knowledge of "The Great American Desert" lying between the Mississippi River and California, the only word they knew to place on the Colorado Mountains was "Pikes Peak", even though the actual mountain by that name is 65 miles down range south of Denver. Thus, the familiar slogan "Pikes Peak or Bust" stirred the second wave of gold seekers to go into the Denver foothills and mountains in 1859.

Migration began flooding down the South Plate River. Miners were also able to reach Denver by the Smoky Hill Trail which came across Kansas or by the Santa Fe Trail which came through southern Colorado along the Arkansas River then their route headed north along the Rocky Mountains. The Smoky Hill route, also known as the Butterfield Overland Dispatch Road, was more direct but lacked water and forage for the teams and there was no protection from Indians.

Denver, being in an isolated area and quite a distance from the Oregon-California Trail and the Pony Express, had sporadic mail and freight service.

From 1859, mail stages from Missouri were operating on the South Pass Oregon-California trail under the ownership, of first, the Leavenworth and Pike's

Peak Express. They had very few stations along the way. In 1860, this defunct company was bought by Russell, Majors and Waddell and renamed Central Overland California and Pike's Peak Express. More stations were built along the road. These new owners were soon having heavy financial difficulties and the C.O.C. & P.P. line was dubbed "Clean Out of Cash and Poor Pay". In 1860, a small line called Western Stage Co. operated a weekly coach service from Kansas City to Denver along the South Platte River road. In 1862 Ben Holladay bought the C.O.C. & P.P. and operated his mail service on the northern South Pass Oregon Trail for a few months. He restocked all the stations with men, horses and supplies, and operated through the winter and spring, when suddenly in early spring, the Shoshone Indians, who had been very friendly until now, made a broad attack on all stations from the Platte River Bridge at Casper to Bear River station beyond Ft. Bridger, capturing all horses and mules and inflicting heavy property damage.

The nomadic plains Indians were completely dependent upon the horse. The coming of the white men with their horse and mule herds was a joyful windfall for the red savage. All it took was their cunning thievery and bloody raids to reap a good harvest.

The increasing Indian depredations and Holladay's desire to serve the citizens of Denver City with freight, mail and transportation, and also to save 150 miles distance, convinced him and the Postmaster General to change mail service and emigrant travel to the Bridger Pass route through southern Wyoming. This southern route had not had much Indian activity and was thought to be safer--but that would soon change.

In the spring of 1862, Major John Kerr, an employee of Ben Holladay, and a party of men reconnoitered the Bridger Pass trail to determine the feasibility of a new route for the Overland Mail stages. He reported in the affirmative to Holladay and by July had determined the locations for the stations, laid out the buildings and corrals which were in the process of being erected. Kerr was promptly given the position of division superintendent between Denver and Salt Lake. Jack Slade, also an employee of Holladay, was greatly instrumental in moving men, stock and equipment from the northern route to the new Overland Trail. On July 21, 1862 Holladay's mail coaches began running west from Julesburg.

Holladay had been operating under the existing Kansas charter of Russell, Majors and Waddell, but it was not until February 5, 1866 that he received a charter from the Colorado Territorial legislature for his new corporation called the **HOLLADAY OVERLAND MAIL AND EXPRESS CO**, to operate in Colorado Territory and beyond its limits.[22]

Stations were located approximately every 10 to 15 miles apart and stocked with the finest horses, mules, tack and coaches. The larger places, called Home Stations, located approximately every 50 miles, where the driver's route ended, were built to accomodate travelers with meals and overnight lodging, and had a telegraph station. The smaller, or swing stations, built on one-quarter to one-half acre plots, just provided fresh teams for the coaches.

This standard repeatable design of small two room sod or log cabins served the necessity of rapid construction and offered the bare necessities. They were chinked with mud and had a pole and dirt roof and dirt floor, and were big enough for two men. Adjoining this, and often attached to the cabin, was a sod corral large enough to accomodate about 25 horses. The cabin had only a small window and/or small loopholes through which to site a rifle. The sod walls were fire and bullet-proof but when the Indians raided they would pillage and burn the contents. If there happened to be a house already built at the site of the station, it probably was owned by the keeper but barns and corrals built by Holladay were his property. Or Holladay could build and own the entire station. The majority of stations in Wyoming were thusly built and owned. Very few, if any, established "ranches" existed along the Overland Trail in Wyoming in 1862.

The stage coaches Holladay used for his mail and passenger service were built by the Abbot-Downing Company in Concord, New Hampshire. These one ton conveyances were strongly built of oak wood, braced with iron bands and slung upon stout leather through-braces. The latter acted as shock absorbers and supported the body of the coach in a hammock like way. The wheels were heavy with wide thick tires. The coach had adjustable leather curtains that covered the "windows" of the doors and sides of the coach but they weren't the most efficient in keeping out wind, dust, snow and rain. The locked strong box carrying all the valuable mails was kept under the driver's seat. Holladay's coaches were equiped with sand boxes placed under the body and over the brake pads and sand could be released when more positive braking was needed. The inside of the coach had three seats to accomodate nine passengers. The three unlucky late-comers had to sit on the middle seat with no back and were subject to some tossing about on rough stretches. Outside one person could sit alongside the driver. More passengers could be carried if they were willing to ride outside on top and if the space was not needed for mail sacks. Mail sacks were also carried in the boot along with the passengers' luggage. The coaches were drawn by six of the finest and swiftest horses or mules. The tough mules were most often used for the long hard pulls. Their average speed of travel was 8 miles per hour, which varied up and down.

CONCORD COACH

Holladay's Mail and Stage route extended from Atchison, Kansas to Salt Lake City and California. As the trail entered the northeast corner of Colorado along the South Platte River at Old Julesburg, it departed from the Oregon -California trail, which continued on north to the North Platte and Ft. Laramie and over South Pass, while the new mail route continued to the west and became known as the Overland Stage and Mail Line, or simply the **OVERLAND TRAIL.**

The copper wire Western Union Telegraph line, was quickly installed along the Overland Trail by Edward Creighton, to ensure communication. These lines were the victims of many Indian attacks.

Building the Western Union Telegraph Line
Courtesy Colorado State Historical Society

ROOT & CONNELLEY, THE OVERLAND STAGE TO CALIFORNIA
1950 reprint pgs. 102-103.

Miles Between Stations	Station
*	Julesburg (Colorado terr.)
12	Antelope
*13	Spring Hill
13	Dennison's
*12	Valley
15	Kelley's
12	Beaver Creek
20	Bijou
16	Fremont's Orchard
16	Eagle's Nest
*12	Latham
*35	Laporte
10	Bonner
12	Cherokee or Stonewall
*12	Virginia Dale
15	Willow Springs (Dakota terr.)
*15	Big Laramie
14	Little Laramie
17	Cooper Creek
11	Rock Creek
17	Medicine Bow
8	Elk Mountain (Ft. Halleck)
14	Pass Creek
*16	North Platte
14	Sage Creek
10	Pine Grove
9	Bridger's Pass
*10	Sulphur Springs
11	Washakie
13	Duck Lake
12	Dug Springs
*15	LaClede
12	Big Pond
14	Black Buttes
14	Point of Rocks
14	Salt Wells
14	Rock Springs
*15	Green River
14	Lone Tree
*18	Ham's Fork
12	Church Buttes
8	Millerville
*13	Fort Bridger

* Denotes Home Stations and Telegraph

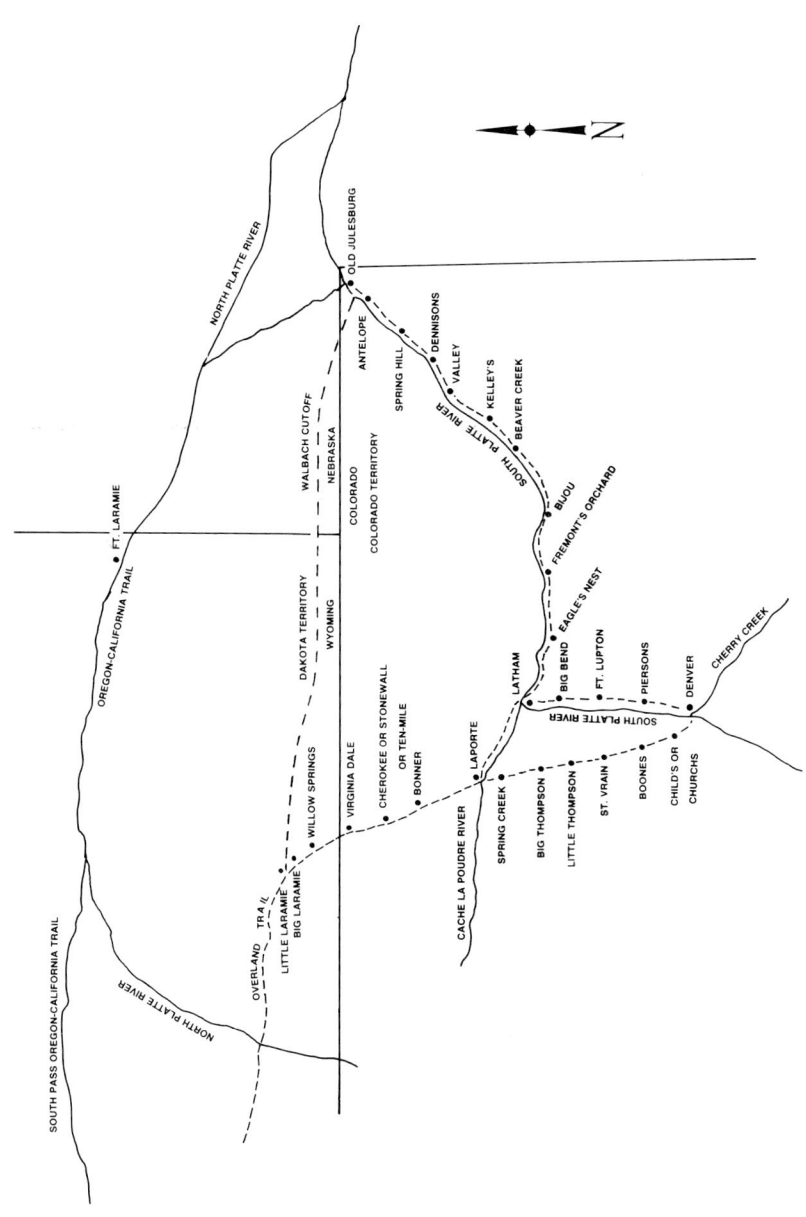

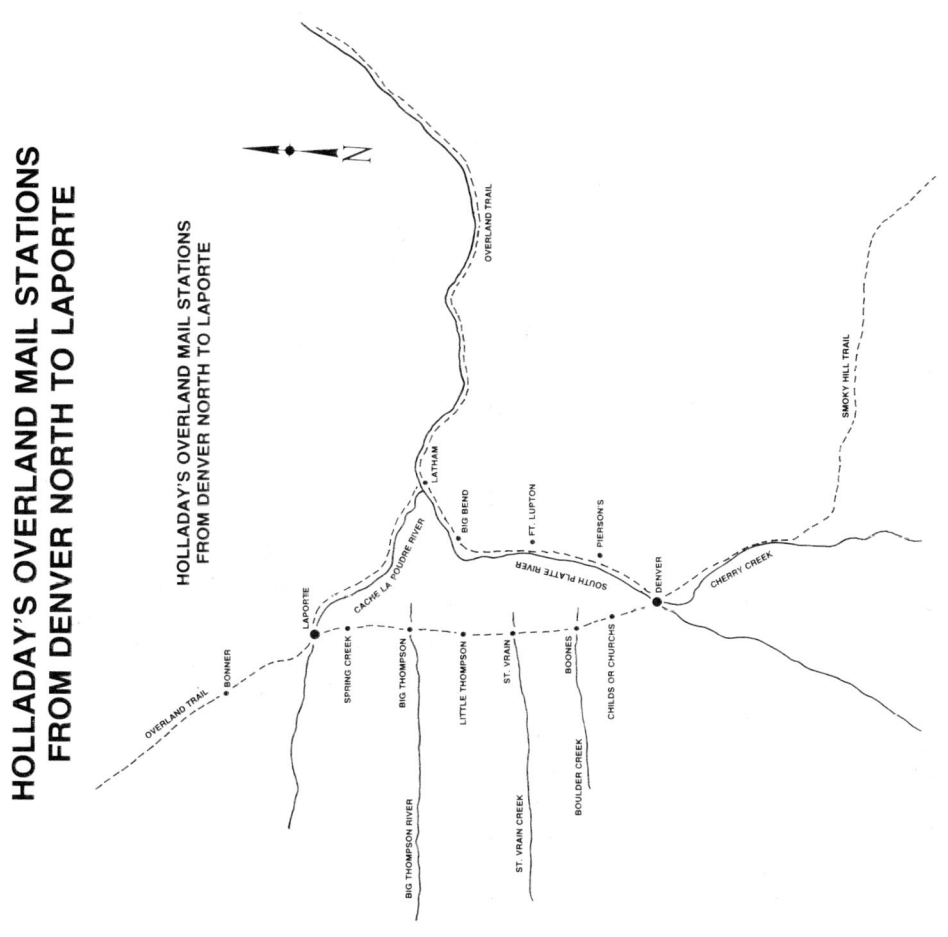

The stations on the Bridger Pass Overland Trail, from 1862 to 1869, to be covered in this book are those listed in both *"Ben Holladay the Stagecoach King"* by J.V. Frederick (Appendix F, pp 291-2) and the *"Overland Stage to California"* by Root and Connelley (1950 reprint pp 102-3). Apparently there were also many more small places, especially on the South Platte River, that must have been under his jurisdiction, as shown in his claims submitted to the government, for losses in Indian raids. ("Ben Holladay The Stagecoach King" - Appendix G, pp 295-301).

The established road paralleled the South Platte, on the south side, to the Latham station near the present city of Greeley, Colorado. Latham was a junction point, from which Denver bound traffic went south. In 1864 this Denver cut-off was changed to depart from the Bijou station. Westbound travelers crossed the river and continued northwest to Laporte on the Cache la Poudre River, thence to Wyoming.

The length of the Overland Trail from Julesburg to Fort Bridger was approximately 575 miles.

Sign of 1st Julesburg
Nothing remains of Old Julesburg today.

JULESBURG, established as a trading post in 1859 by a French trader, Jules Beni, who was also station keeper in 1862, was a vital home station on the great overland routes. Being a junction point at the Upper California Crossing of the South Platte River for the two trails, it experienced tremendous activity. The settlement consisted of the station building, telegraph office, a few cabins, a store, blacksmith shop, warehouse, stable, a billiard saloon, all made of hewn logs. The saloon was said to have sold "the vilest of liquor at two bits a glass". Julesburg was a rendezvous for gamblers, horse thieves and desparados with Old Jules as one of the leaders.[23] It was known as the toughest town between the Missouri and the Rocky Mountains. Cedar poles, used for the telegraph line and many buildings at Julesburg and the stations along the Platte, were obtained from Cottonwood Springs, 100 miles west of Ft. Kearney, in Nebraska. Thousands of emigrants and thousands more livestock passed through this post for the gold fields. Gold, the Lorelei of the Rockies lured the argonauts, like a fickle lover, to many a man's destruction. Disillusioned with not finding the ground and streams abounding in nuggets, and penniless, many turned around and went back home. The number of wagons going back east and sometimes men, women and children walking, was almost equal to those going west. Huge freight wagons, with tires 4 inches wide and one half inch thick, from St. Louis, each carrying from 3 to 6 thousand pounds of merchandise, and pulled by six yoke of sturdy oxen, supplied this station and others beyond.

When Ben Holladay, the dynamic tycoon, took over this mail line, he changed the name of Julesburg to Overland City in order to change the town's image, but not many acknowledged it. It was always Julesburg.

Mr. Frank Root, the Latham mail and station master, noted that there was a high hill called 'Pilot Knob', south of Julesburg that commanded a broad view of the surrounding area. Indians could see the North and South Platte rivers, for many miles including the confluence of the Lodgepole Creek, and the headwaters of the Republican River and used this for a signal tower. [24]

CAMP RANKIN one mile west of Julesburg, was an important military post, established August 21, 1864 for the protection of settlers, emigrant trains and the mail coaches along the South Platte River. The post was garrisoned by four companies of troops of the 5th U.S. Volunteers, 2nd U.S. Cavalry and 18th Regulars. Captain Neill of the 18th Regulars was in command.[25]

In September 1865 the name was changed to **FT. SEDGWICK.** The Surgeon General of the War Dept. in Washington, D.C., on Dec. 5, 1870 issued a description of Ft. Sedgwick. The post, comprising 64 square miles of land, was built on an established ranch that had a good well. Another well was dug and water was reached at 20 feet. Water percolated from the river and it was determined satisfactory for drinking.

The buildings were situated on the north side of the parade grounds. Barracks were made of sod and adobe; walls 2 feet thick and from 8 to 10 feet high and measured 28 x 120 feet. The roofs were made of poles and dirt. Buildings were heated by stoves, ventilated by doors and windows but had no bath or wash rooms or water closets. Barracks housed one company of soldiers. Personnel at any one time probably numbered between 150 to 175 men.

The guard house was a frame building, 48 x 24 feet with 10 foot high walls and contained no cells.

The barn was large enough for horses for one cavalry unit.

The adobe walled hospital stood 200 yards to the rear of the parade ground. It was an L shaped structure consisting of one building 28 x 100 feet with a wing 28 x 32 feet. The walls were 10 feet 6 inches high. This was sufficient for a 4 company post. Stoves were used for heating and doors and windows for ventilation. The dispensary was convenient and the well arranged wards contained 10 beds giving 656 cubic feet air space per man if all occupied. There was no bath or wash rooms or water closets connected with the hospital. The wing portion was erected as a ward but was occupied as surgeons' quarters. The hospital portion was occupied chiefly by patients from sub posts or citizens from the U.P. Railroad who were planning to build. Most cases on the Post were surgical. Rheumatism was prevalent from the sub posts. There was a small number of malaria cases. Disease of the lungs was unknown.

The bakery was 18 x 23 feet with 12 foot high and 3 foot thick walls. It had a 10 x 12 foot oven. Bread to the garrison was constant and sufficient.

The library was kept in the Adjutant's office under the care of a librarian. Novels, biographies and miscellaneous subjects comprised the 286 volumes.

The fort was enclosed by an 8 foot high sod stockade.[26]

Much Indian activity took place all along this stretch of the river on January 7, 1865 Indians attacked Julesburg killing soldiers and civilians. The fort weathered a raid by one thousand Indians on February 2, 1865, at which time Indians torched Julesburg and all stations. Their anger had reached its bloody pitch and they were desperately fighting to hold their land and their hunting grounds, and also to avenge

Copy of a painting of Indians burning
Old Julesburg, Feb. 2, 1865
Artist unknown.
Picture courtesy of Colorado State Historical Society

the massacre at Sand Creek. Citizens of Julesburg fled to Sedgwick. Cavalrymen fought valiantly. Lieutenant Ware, accompanied by a small squad of men, on returning from an expedition, made a heroic and successful ride to the safety of the Fort through the frenzied Indians and the smoke of the burning buildings.

On Feb. 5, 1865 Col. Robert Livingston reported that for about 75 miles to the west, 12 ranch and stations, 100 tons of government hay, a train of 22 wagons and the trans-continental telegraph line had been destroyed and 1500 head of stock run off.

This fort was active until May 31, 1871 when, after all Indian raids has ceased, it was abandoned. Today the buildings are all gone, but a flagpole, erected in 1988 by the Sedgwick County Historical Society, stands in the center of the parade ground. The mounds of dirt on each side of the flagpole were implacements for cannons when the fort was active.

The 1865 emigrants passing through this part of the trail noted that all ranches and stations had been destroyed by Indians.

The present city of Julesburg is located a few miles from the first Julesburg. It has changed locations three more times since its beginning.

The Sedgwick County Historical Society has placed markers at their historical sites and the Oregon-California Trail Association, (O.C.T.A.), in association with the Nebraska State Historical Society, has dedicated a marker at the Old California Trail Crossing just northeast of Julesburg where the Oregon-California Trail departs to the north. The Oregon-California Trail Association was given the California Hill trail rut land and the marker by Malcolm E. Smith, in memory of Irene Paden who dedicated much of her life to retracing and writing about the Oregon and California Trails.

Emigrant wagon ruts going up California Hill in Nebraska, north-east of Julesburg, Colorado

West, along the South Platte River, were ranches among which Ben Holladay planned to put his stations. 11 miles west of Old Julesburg was the station of **ANTELOPE**; 13 miles to **SPRING HILL**, a home station kept by Mr. A. Thorne; 13 miles to **DENNISON'S**; 12 miles to **VALLEY**, a home station; 15 miles to **KELLEY'S** or **AMERICAN RANCH,** where an amiable Irish station master greeted travelers; 12 miles to **BEAVER CREEK**, where, suddenly, travelers got their first breath taking view of the beautiful Rocky Mountains with majestic Long's Peak. Each day afterward they could see how far they had gone by how much closer they were to the mountains; 20 mile to **BIJOU**. This last distance was the longest drive without a change of teams because there was no suitable location between the last two for another station. This long difficult road was through deep sand, alkali and sloughs which greatly taxed even the strongest of teams. They often double teamed the wagons to make it. There was another difficult 16 miles with no wood or water, to **FREMONT'S ORCHARD**. The name Fremont was to honor the early explorer and the "Orchard" name came from the stunted cottonwood trees that reminded someone of an apple orchard back home in the east; 11 miles to small **EAGLE'S NEST**, which got its name from the circular route the Platte River took at that spot, and last, 12 miles to **LATHAM**, the important home, and the last station, on the South Platte.[27]

In emigrant days the Platte was almost devoid of trees--the travelers had cut them down for firewood. Today the trees, mostly cottonwoods, are plentiful.

In 1863 George A. Bruffey, an emigrant traveling on the South Platte road, tells of a fellow traveler with a drove of 500 turkeys, bought in Iowa and Missouri, that were being herded across country by two boys. His 6 horse and mule team pulled the wagon that was loaded with shelled corn for turkey feed when needed. Along this stretch the turkeys foraged on grasshoppers and at night they roosted all over the wagon and some flat on the ground. At early dawn the turkeys were up chasing grasshoppers again. Herding was easy when the wind was favorable, but if it was blowing from the west the boys really had their hands full. Their destination was apparently Denver City. It was learned later that the turkeys got along well and losses were few.

A log cabin on the trail
courtesy Colorado State Historical Society

Emigrants were able to buy food and supplies and get blacksmith service all along this South Platte road because of well stocked trading posts and stations, unless of course they had been raided by Indians. If these entrepreneurs kept a cow and chickens and grew a garden they could offer fresh milk, eggs and produce. Then there was always the inevitable whiskey merchant. They usually had their cabin back off the main road but plenty handy for anybody wanting their repulsive tasting drink.

The stage and mail stations and the military installations did not allow liquor on the premises.

In 1863 the Postal Department made a study of the entire Overland line to determine what improvements could be made in dispatching the tremendous amount of mail going both east and west. Mail going into Denver averaged from 350 to 500 pounds daily and 150 pounds coming out. Frank A. Root, who had two years experience in dispatching overland mail pouches from the Atchison post office and as express messenger accompanying the daily overland mail stages from there to Denver, was consulted. His suggestions were accepted. At this time Mr. Root was feeling the strain of the great responsibilities and hardships of riding six successive days and nights, along side the driver of the coach, without rest or opportunity to even change clothes. The mail had to go through in spite of blizzards, Indian attacks, floods and the ever increasing plunders by stage robbers with the advent of gold being shipped from the mines. Root was offered, and he accepted, on Dec. 8, 1863 the position of local agent of the Post Office Department at Latham.

1865 Overland Stage Line way-bill
Courtesy Colorado State Historical Society

LATHAM, at the mouth of the Cache la Poudre River on the South Platte, was the most important and probably the busiest home station on the trail. The stage station was the only house there. It was a one and one-half story log building facing south. On the north side was a large one story, rough board addition, fronting both east and west, which contained a large dining room, kitchen, bedroom, storehouse and telegraph.

This being a junction point, Mr. Root stated that stages to and from Denver and those going east and west on the main trail made close connections. Mail pouches, at this point, had to be taken off the stages, resorted and reloaded for their destination. It being a junction, there were often stages from all three directions at the station at the same time with as many as 40 passengers.

At this point, the South Platte River makes a big bend in its course. After heading near Hoosier Pass in the mountains above Fairplay, Colorado, the Platte courses southeast for several miles until it sharply turns northeast flowing through Denver and on north to Latham-Greeley where it turns east and north-east where it joins the North Platte River in Nebraska.

At Latham station, travelers going to Denver would go south along the east side of the South Platte River, but those going either west or east on the Overland Trail had to cross the river, which was stated to be one mile wide. When the water was low, the wagons could ford, but quick sand was a hazard to fear. Occasionally a wagon would mire so badly it had to be unloaded and left in its place. The wagon beds were raised above the running gear by blocks or poles, to keep the water out. A ferry was available for $1.00 per wagon. However, most of the wagons had to be dismantled to get them onto the boat, then reassembled on the opposite side.

Hundreds of wagons crossed this river every day from 1862-1865, going west, because new placer gold deposits were being found in Bannock, Idaho and in Montana.

On May 20, 1864 the great flood roaring down Cherry Creek and consequently into the Platte River, struck Denver resulting in a great amount of property damage and loss of life. By the next day the water had reached Latham and the river was out of its banks. By the 27th it was still flooding - ten to fifteen feet high and taking houses, barns, animals, bridges and debris with it. The stages could not cross so Mr. Root had to ferry the mail bags across in a skiff. They were deposited on the highest dry piece of ground near the bank, but while waiting for the east bound stage, he realized, to his horror, that the water had surrounded him. On his small island many anxious minutes passed and when the stage did arrive, it could not get close. Mr. Root had to pack each individual mail bag on his shoulders and wade waist deep to the coach. None of the mail got wet.[28]

Stage drivers have been portrayed as drunken, eccentrics but Mr. Root found the great majority to be courteous, level-headed dependable men. Veteran drivers gathered mail from, and delivered mail to the stations, and was kind enough to collect mail along the road from the emigrants.[29] They tried hard to keep schedule, and year around travel was the goal for mail delivery, but deep snows, floods and Indian attacks caused delays for many days and up to months until travel could begin again. Mail would stack up into such a volume that Holladay's specially designed freight wagons were needed to transport the load.

Mr. Root recounts one of the pleasures of the stage drivers:

> "Occasionally a wild Mexican broncho team would be harnessed up and hitched to the stage-coach for the first time; then for a little while there would be a feast of genuine amusement for all hands. No one appeared to enjoy the sport better than the driver handling the lines. He would be in the height of his glory. For a few minutes the show would be a sort of "Wild West," equal to if not better than an ordinary circus. Each team would have to be held by the bit until all the passengers had taken their seats inside the coach and the driver his place on the box; this done, the performance would almost instantly begin. Usually the animals would at once go off jumping and plunging on a lively run, while the driver would keep on throwing the lash among them. After running a mile or two at pretty fair railroad speed, the animals would finally get cooled down; then, for the balance of the trip, they would go along at the accustomed gait of a stage team.
>
> "Now and then the wild, unbroken steeds would cut up some extremely ludicrous antics. I never saw so much sport in so short a time as I once did in the spring of 1864 at Latham station, on the South Platte. A team of six wild bronchos were for the first time hitched up, late one afternoon, to the east-bound California stage destined for Atchison. When the passengers were seated and the driver said "Let go," the off leader immediately jumped over the near one, while the near wheeler jumped over the off one, and soon every animal was down. All were plunging and kicking and I never before saw such a mixed-up and

tangled lot of stage animals. Every mustang was down and not one of them could get up. To me it appeared that the mixed-up steeds could not be untangled and get out alive. For several minutes it required the services of a half-dozen drivers and several stock tenders, the stage and mail agents and some others at the station to get their harness righted, and everything again in proper shape to make another start.

"But the drivers, as much as any one else, invariably enjoyed the highly exciting sport. They thought it a genuine stage picnic. In such a mixup they were always equal to any emergency; but to a number of anxious, timid passengers inside the coach the situation was not quite so interesting. Where such wild, spirited teams were used, the roads were usually level as a floor, and there was little if any danger of an accident from a runaway."

Monument at Latham Location
Courtesy Colorado State Historical Society

Latham station operated until Oct. 1864 when the junction point to Denver was changed to Bijou station.

After this change Latham maintained a post office, store and school until 1870. Nothing remains of any of the stations along the South Platte River trail, there being only a monument at the Latham location, 3 miles east and 1 mile south of present day Greeley.

For years afterwards relics of all kinds were picked up at all these places. Mr. Jack French of Ft. Collins showed us his extensive collection of bottles -- wine, beer, bitters and medicine -- that were made in many different colors and shapes and sizes.

Millard Johnson, historian and collector, of Laramie, Wyoming states that, "In 1851 the "Maine Law" was enacted prohibiting liquor selling on a state wide basis. In 1862 the Internal Revenue Act was passed which heavily taxed alcohol beverages. At this time many enterprising people took advantage of this and went into the Bitters business. The 100 proof alcohol had a few herbs added to it and was sold as a tonic and medicine making this a legal and non taxable item."

The popular "medicine" was supposed to cure almost everything and tee-totalers especially swore by bitters because they made them "feel so good".

Bitters bottles have been found prolifically all along the trails and if found unbroken, they are a cherished addition to anyone's collection.

LaPorte was 35 miles up-stream on the Cache la Poudre River from Latham. Holladay's list gives no mention of one of his stations in between these places, probably because his mail coaches all went to Denver first. The Overland Emigrant Trial, from Latham, paralleled this river on the north side. There was no station between Latham and Laporte all the while the Trail was being actively used. In 1872 or 1873 a rooming and boarding house, called "Halfway House" was built just west of the present town of Windsor. Windsor's downtown Main Street was built on top of the old Overland Trail.

In this vicinity was a very large Cottonwood tree under which the Arapahoe and Cheyenne Indians held important tribal councils. It was reported that in 1862 Robert Strauss, an early settler, saw the Indians hang a red-skin enemy from one of its branches. This victim was probably a Pawnee or Ute whom they had captured. This tree was named the "Council" and "Hanging" Tree.

In the year 1858, a small group of trappers and mountain men, namely Antoine Janis and his brother Nicholas, Elbridge Gerry, Todd Randall, Raymond Goodwin, John B. Provost, Oliver Morisette, A. Le Bon, Ravofiere and others surveyed, mapped and laid out the settlement of Colona, 35 miles up the Cache la Poudre River from its confluence with the Platte.[30] This location is where this river emerges from the mountains. These men knew that placer mining was not very lucrative but the miners did have to eat, so established the area as farm land, The name was later change to Laporte, meaning the gateway. The Cache la Poudre River received its name from the cache of gunpowder and lead, hidden in the bank of the river by the Wm. H. Ashley party in 1825.

At this time Indian attacks became more frequent and strikes were made all along the South Platte, with the red men stealing rifles, ammunition and livestock, in preparation for an all-out war.

Stage traffic was heavy going in and out of Denver City. Gold mining was at a fever pitch. Coaches and military going on west from Denver took the road directly north along the front range to **LAPORTE** to again meet the Overland Trail.

From Latham the mail stations going into Denver were **BIG BEND, FORT LUPTON,** and **PIERSON'S**. The Holladay Overland Mail office was located in the heart of Denver City. On the road out of Denver north, Holladay had his first stop at **CHILD'S**. Child's stage Station, or apparently more well known as **CHURCH'S** and **TWELVE MILE HOUSE** was located about three miles south of the site of Broomfield. Churchs was a large twenty room house.

BOONE'S Stage Station was located on Boulder Creek which was intermediate

Stations from Latham to Denver

between Church's and the next station called **SAINT VRAIN,** which stood on the bank of the river of the same name. This is in the vicinity of todays city of Longmont.

The next station along the front range was **LITTLE THOMPSON** which was located near the present town of Berthoud.

About 13 miles beyond was the station of **BIG THOMPSON** which is near the present city of Loveland. This settlement was started, before Holladay's Mail run in 1862, by a squatter named Mariana Modeno. He had named his place "Namaqua". The meaning of this name was not known but it was thought to be a Pawnee proper noun as Pawnee proper nouns generally ended in "qua".

About 13 more miles was the small station of **SPRING CREEK.** This stood in the southwest part of the present city of Ft. Collins.

The next station was **LAPORTE,** on the north bank of the Cache la Poudre where traffic either forded or ferried the river. This was the Provost Ferry.

Some covered wagon emigrants went into Denver first then up the front range to meet the Overland Trail. This road was not just for Holladay's mail and the Military.

All travel, from Denver and on to the west necessitated crossing the swift Cache la Poudre river. June 6, 1859, the diary entry of E.H.N. Patterson, who was prospecting for gold in the hills around Colona, states that the Colona mountaineers, one being Provost who had a grocery store and a saloon in town, after much difficulty, devised a ferry and crossing cost 50 cents a man. On that same day several California bound wagons crossed. The ferry, called Provost Ferry, was small and two trips were required to bring over one wagon, it having been dismantled. The June 12th entry states that this same wagon train returned on their way back to get onto the Oregon-California trail going over South Pass. They had traveled as far as the North Platte River crossing, approximately 170 miles westward, and could not ford the river so had to turn back. These unfortunate travelers were to lose much time and possibly animals by not having any previous knowledge of what to expect. This may possibly have been the first emigrant train to try to cross on the Overland Trail.

There is a discrepancy in the recorded history of this. The above gold prospector, in his journal, tells of the ferry just being built in 1859. Another reference states that at first there was a bridge, privately owned, charging 3 to 8 dollars to cross. As many as 2,000 wagons crossed in a single day. This account continues with the bridge being washed out in the 1864 flood then Provost built the ferry. This last account is certainly to be questioned.

The site of the Overland Trail ford and ferry over the Cache la Poudre River can be seen at the bridge on Overland Drive a short distance south of Main Street in Laporte, Colorado. Nearby, on this same street, a sign is posted at the site of the stage station. Nothing remains of it. An old log cabin, built in 1858, still stands on Overland Drive directly south of Main Street in Laporte.

Laporte, a home station, is one of the few stations that has grown into a pleasant community.

The January 22, 1914 issue of the Ft. Collins Courier wrote on the John Robinson Circus that came to Laporte in the summer of 1867. The price was $2.00 per person and half price for children. By this date the Laporte and Ft. Collins vicinity had become quite heavily populated so a big crowd of people came from all over by wagon, horseback, ox cart or on foot. Mountainmen in their buckskins, farmers and ranchers, tradesmen, saloon keepers and their ilk, horse thieves and Indians with their squaws and children.

The circus had the usual trained horses, trick mules, clowns etc. Indians were afraid of insane persons and they thought the clowns were a little off balance so with the Indians reaction to them, and along with the rest of the colorful and bedazzled crowd, the audience response was half the show.

Laporte Stage Station
Courtesy Colorado State Historical Society

When the trail was moved to southern Wyoming the Indians followed - Sioux from the Powder River country in Wyoming joined the Cheyenne and Arapahoes of northern Colorado. With increased necessity for protection of emigrants and mail stages from these Indians, the military in 1862 established the post, **CAMP COLLINS,** named after Lt. Col. Wm. O. Collins, on the banks of the Cache la Poudre River at Laporte. It was garrisoned by the 9th Kansas Cavalry. Unfortunately, Camp Collins met its demise in the flood of June 9, 1864. On August 21, 1864, Col. Collins submitted an official order for a site for a new military reservation to be established. With the inevitable Governmental red tape, Camp Collins was not rebuilt and occupied until 5 months later. This new camp was located ten miles east and rechristened "Ft." Collins. At the new location Capt. Wm. H. Evans, commanding officer of Camp Collins, took it upon himself to promote it to "Fort". In the army records there is no official order for the change of designation, but it became common practice to call it **FT. COLLINS.**[31]

Troops were few in the west because soldiers were still fighting the Civil War. They were stationed at Ft. Kearney, Ft. Laramie, Ft. Collins, Ft. Halleck, Ft. La Clede and Ft. Bridger.

The Ft. Collins soldiers protected the trail from Denver and Laporte west to Ft. Halleck. When stages carrying notable persons were running, the military supplied relays of escorts consisting of one non-commissioned officer and six troopers. The escorts were changed at each home station, thus: Denver to Virginia Dale; Virginia Dale to Big Laramie; Big Laramie to Ft. Halleck; Ft. Halleck to Sulphur Springs;

Sulphur Springs to Ft. La Clede; Ft. La Clede to Green River; Green River to Ft. Bridger.

Along the trails they were needed to protect the mail and telegraph line, to do scouting duties, escorting emigrant trains and coaches, pursue Indians and stolen livestock and fight battles alongside the station attendants. They couldn't keep up with all the raids. So many horses and mules were stolen that daily runs were reduced to tri-weekly runs for lack of teams. Troops were shifted as the need arose. Even though troops tried to retrieve the stolen livestock their efforts were almost always futile.

Indians took advantage of this situation. They seemed to appear out of nowhere. John C. Cremony, as an officer of the California Volunteers, worked with the government and lived for ten years - in the 1850's and 1860's - among the Apache Indians in Arizona. His observations on their tribal life, traits, beliefs, and fighting tactics is unsurpassed. He notes that the nomadic tribes throughout the continent did not differ. Cremony states "...the Indian never attacks unless fully convinced of an easy victory. They will watch for days, scanning your movement, observing your every act; taking exact note of your party and all its belongings. Let no one suppose that these assults are made upon the spur of the moment by bands accidentally encountered. Far from it; they are almost invariably the results of long watching - patient waiting - careful and rigorous observation, and anxious counsel."[32] Charlie Russell, a noted western artist, painted a picture entitled, "Planning the Attack".

Smoke signals were used by the Indians in the areas now known as Rawlins and Red Desert, in Wyoming. On a high hill just west of Rawlins still stands the sandstone cairn used for their communications. The sides of this cairn are much higher than the center fire pot. This was to regulate the fire and smoke from the prevailing winds. Charlie Russell, a noted western artist, painted another entitled "Signal Fire".

Cremony had learned the smoke signal language: "Smokes are of various kinds, each one significant of a particular object. A sudden puff rising into a graceful column from the mountain heights, and almost as suddenly losing its identity by dissolving into the rarified atmosphere of those heights, simply indicates the presence of a strange party upon the plains below; but if those columns are rapidly multiplied and repeated, they serve as a warning to show that the travelers are well armed and numerous. If a steady smoke is maintained for some time, the object is to collect the scattered bands of savages at some designated point, with hostile intention, should it be practicable. These signals are made at night, in the same order, by the use of fires, which being kindled, are either alternately exposed and shrouded from view, or suffered to burn steadily, as occasion may require."[33]

In his life among the Apaches, Cremony learned "Their enmity toward mankind, and distrust of every word and act are ineradicable. As their whole system of life and training is to plunder, murder and deceive, they cannot comprehend opposite attributes in others. He whom we would denounce as the greatest scoundrel they regard with special esteem and honor. With no people are they on amicable terms, and never hesitate to rob from each other when it can be done with impunity. There is no sympathy among them; the quality is unknown. After a successful raid in which they have captured many animals, and having selected the best for riding, retire to some remote fastness to feed upon the remainder so long as they last, they will freely share to the very last bit with any and all comers of their race. This seeming hospitality is, however, not the result of kindliness, but the prompting of

Indian Smoke Signal
Tower near Rawlins Wyoming

a selfish policy, for they are aware it assists to unite them in one common band of plundering brotherhood, and to preserve those relations toward each other without which they cannot operate advantageously.

"The savage, after having killed his foe will leave the body to be desecrated and mutilated by some other member of the party. He seldom takes part in it himself, unless influenced by unwonted excitement; but when he does, he proves himself the master spirit, and his treatment is carried to the extent of savage excess. Precisely as the cat or terrier dog teaches its young how to catch and torment their prey, does the Apache instruct his disciples. In their heathenism, and barbarous ignorance, the dead bodies of their enemies are mutilated, and left in localities where they are sure to be found, to convey a sense of dread rather than from any innate disposition to deface that which they know to be insensible to their acts. Their philosophy and treatment of the captive is entirely different. In such a case their savage and bloodthirsty natures experience a real pleasure in tormenting their victim. Every expression of pain or agony is hailed with delight, and the one whose inventive genius can devise the most excruciating kind of death is deemed worthy of honor." Cremony came upon the scene, of a grisly attack in a canyon in Arizona, shortly after it had been perpetrated by the Apaches. The men of some traveling Mexican families "..had been seized by the Indians, bound to the wheel of a wagon, head down about eighteen inches from the ground, a fire made under them and their brains roasted from their heads. The women and children of this group were carried off. The bursted heads, the agonized contortions of the facial muscles among the dead, and the terrible destiny certain to attend the living of that ill-fated party, were horribly depicted on my mind." Later in this book you will read that a soldier, on the Overland Trail in Wyoming, suffered a similar fate.

It is safe to assume that Indian trails criss-crossed this entire part of the west. They were thoroughly familiar with their own hunting grounds and no doubt the

Camp Collins/Ft. Collins

territory of their enemies. Like game trails, they chose the easiest and most logical routes. Again it would be logical for the trappers and explorers to take these trails and eventually the emigrants would follow.

Laporte was the gateway to the mountains. Travelers were to experience the steepest hills they had yet encountered.

The covered wagon trail, and the old Cherokee Trail headed directly north from the present area of "Ted's Place," the little wayside stop, at the entrance to Poudre Canyon, on highway 287 out of Laporte. It went up thru the swale between the hills over the ridge west of the present highway which parallels the location of old railroad track. From the highway trail ruts can be seen in this swale. Ted's Place was torn down in September 1989.

Ten miles from Laporte was the **BONNER SPRINGS STAGE STATION,** located south of Owl Canyon. Very little is known about this station tucked in a beautiful part of the Rocky Mountains. In this vicinity is the grave of little Eddie Hale, age 19 months who died on the trail April 17, 1864. This land now is all a privately owned housing complex with locked gates.

From Bonner the emigrant trail, following the Cherokee Trail, lies a short distance west of the present day highway 287 and Owl Canyon then angles northwest to present Livermore. Trail ruts can be seen here. Sarah Raymond, an 1865 emigrant, wrote in her diary that she placed her name, along with many others, high up a hillside on a sandstone rock somewhere in this vicinity. Neither the rock nor the names have been found.

Aerial Photo by Les Erb, August 1989
Present Highway 287 traversing the cut through the long, high ridge.
Trail ruts can be seen, in the center picture,
crossing the grassy flat by Flattop Hill, and going to "Double Team" hill.

About a mile beyond, the trails deviated for a few miles. The Cherokee Trail kept the northwest direction and the Overland Trail, after making a big swing west, then east, around a high, long sandstone bluff,(through which a cut has been excavated for the present highway 287 and an irrigation canal) turned north again traversing the edge of the next hill, called Flattop, to skirt the eroded washes. After about a half mile of easy going the wagons went up an incredibly steep, rocky incline. The emigrants built this road by moving the large rocks to the outer edge and forming a dugway. The emigrants had to double team their wagons to get up this hill. (We refer to this as the Double Team Hill later.) The road went across the top of this hill for about a half mile then down hill on the other side onto the east bank of Stonewall Creek and **STONEWALL** or **CHEROKEE** or **10 MILE STATION.** All three names apply. Flattop is readily discernable by unsightly rubble that was dumped over the top from a limestone mining operation. The eroded trail ruts can be seen on this hill from the present highway. Stonewall Creek was aptly named from the high, vertical, rugged rock cliff formations along its bank.

Somewhere along this way was reported to be the graves of two men killed by Indians. There was much Indian and Military activity along this stretch of the trail. Troops moved back and forth from Ft. Collins to Ft. Halleck.

An interesting emigrant, Ruth Shackelford, a housewife from Clark County, Missouri wrote in her diary of July 8, 1865, "While I was getting supper a group of soldiers came tearing down out of the mountains on their way to Ft. Halleck." Two days before the Shackelford's had caught fish out of "Castor Pool" (Cache la Poudre).

Cherokee was 10 miles from Bonner and is located on the east side of the present highway 287. It is privately owned land. There are only a few foundation rocks remaining.

North and a little east out of Laporte, (see map), Ben Holladay, in 1862, established a freight and stage road that, one fork terminated in Cheyenne, and the other met the Overland Trail again at the Cherokee Station after winding through the hills. A freighter named Dobson scouted out this trail in 1862. This served as an alternate route to the Overland Trail, with apparently a saving of mileage in mind. About ten miles from Laporte, Holladay built the Park Creek, or Overland Park stage station located on the bank of Park Creek. This first station, built of logs, had a tunnel, or more likely a covered trench, dug from the cabin to the barn for use during Indian raids. This first station was destroyed by Indians, and a second Park Creek station was built but the year is unknown. This station had accomodations for overnight travelers. All that remains now of the Park Creek station are many nails, much broken glass and a few pieces of logs, some of which show evidence of having been burned. It is not known what the fate of the second Park Creek station was, but from this evidence it may also have been burned. Today this is a privately owned cattle ranch.

Just a short way north of Park Creek Station, and across the creek, is a large level piece of ground where the freighters camped. At this point the stages and freight wagons, whose destinations were Virginia Dale or on into Wyoming via the Overland Trail, left the Cheyenne road and traveled northwest up through hills. The valley, at the beginning part of this road was marshy in places, especially in the spring, necessitating a detour farther to the west near the edge of the hills. As the trail progressed the hills became steeper and more difficult to travel. On one little flat bench, at an unlikely place among the hills, was a blacksmith shop. However, this shop was about one half mile off the main road and the wagons

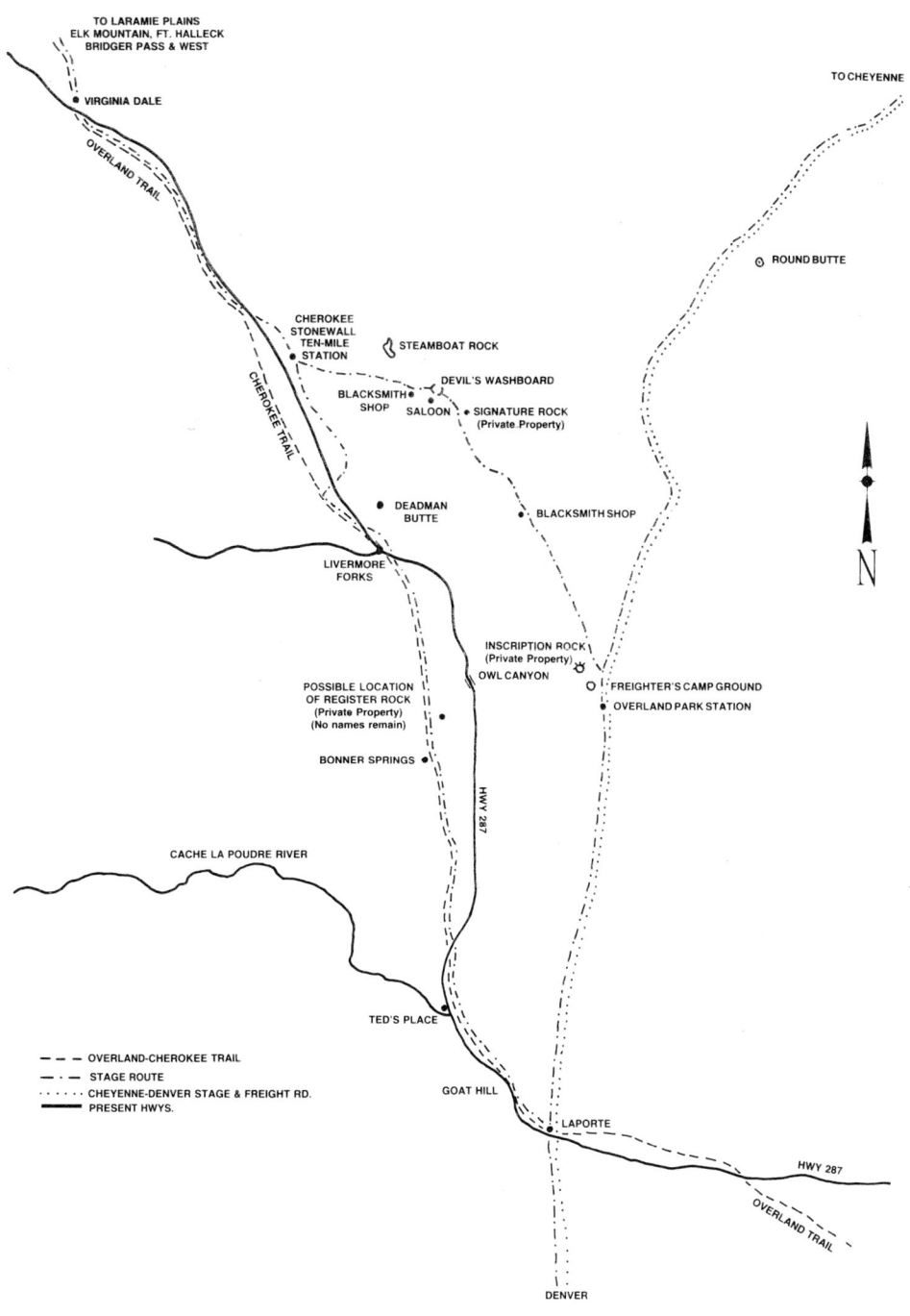

had to drive into it and then out the same way. This was certainly a needed service for stages and wagons that might break down on the road or to care for animals that needed to be reshod. A ways farther west the travelers left their names on Signature Rock then came to another incredible high, steep, rocky cliff, called the Devil's Washboard, over which one wonders how those coaches and big wagons and teams ever made it — in either direction! At the bottom of Devil's Washboard, on the west bank of a tributary of Stonewall Creek, are the foundation rocks of an old saloon. Needless to say this was needed to steady the nerves no matter in which direction the travelers were going.

This brought up the suggestion, among a group of historians recently, that this road was one way going west and the Overland Trail was one way going east down the Double Team Hill, in order to negotiate these steep hills. Doubtful perhaps.

Photo by Les Erb
The "Devils Washboard" road from the top looking down into the valley

In the next draw to the north of the saloon is the outline of the foundation of another blacksmith shop. Trail ruts are still visible here. A ways further on, the trail passed the beautiful sandstone formation called Steamboat Rock then on down into the valley to Stonewall, or 10 Mile where the two trails met again. All of this is a private ranch now, but Steamboat Rock can easily be seen from the highway.

For the map, "Cherokee — Overland and Trails Ft. Collins North", we are greatly indebted to Mr. Richard Baker and Mr. M. H. Schloo, both western history enthusiasts, of Ft. Collins, Colorado. And especially we are indebted to Mr. and Mrs. Evan Roberts who filled us in on so many interesting trail details of the portion of the Overland Trail from Ft. Collins to Virginia Dale.

This part of the Overland Trail had the most beautiful scenery the travelers would view. Emigrants traveled over green rolling hills and large parks of buffalo grass. To the south and west the snow topped Rocky Mountains rose to their

Photo by Louise B. Erb
"Steamboat" and "Tug" Rock Formations site of Cherokee
or also known as Stonewall and 10 Mile Stage Station in the foreground

14,000 foot majesty. The soft blues and greys of the afternoon light defined each of the smaller ranges into a misty paradise. They passed by rock outcrops where the wind and weather had sculpted the red and yellow sandstone into unusual shapes. One being Steamboat Rock that was a landmark seen for many miles. Today as you pass this way pause to enjoy this land. And note the northern-most rock on top of Steamboat looks like an elephant! The big rock formation just to the south of Steamboat is called the Tug. Steamboat Rock is directly east of the Cherokee — Stonewall — 10 Mile Station site.

The Cheyenne branch of the stage road out of Laporte experienced heavy freight traffic for three years after the transcontinental railroad was completed through Cheyenne in 1867 and to Oct. 3, 1870 when the Kansas Pacific Railroad, associated with the Denver Pacific Railroad, a rival of the Union Pacific Railroad ran their rails through Greeley and on into Denver from the main Union Pacific line in Cheyenne.[34]

Twelve miles from Cherokee Station, travelers reached **VIRGINIA DALE,** the last station in Colorado Territory. Virginia Dale, located among beautiful rock formations and rolling hills covered with rich buffalo grass, was a well stocked home station and center of Holladay's stage Division which extended from Denver to the North Platte. A variety of food, supplies and feed for the animals was kept in the warehouse and as the need arose, provisions were freighted out to the other stations. A number of trail officials, as well as the station workers lived there full time. Home stations also employed a full time hunter to keep them supplied with game. The first superintendent was the notorious Jack Slade and the station was named for his beautiful wife. Slade had built Virginia Dale station and several of the other stations along the line. He was an extremely competent man and when he was appointed Division Agent from Denver to North Platte, he executed his duties with great efficiency.

Virginia Dale Station - Colorado Territory
Courtesy Colorado State Historical Society

As time went on and liquor controlled him, it was learned that he was involved in the stage robberies and raids on the stations. He had a quick temper and when someone crossed him his reactions were dramatic. He was discharged from his duties because of drunkenness, shooting sprees and his association with desperados. Slade and Old Jules Beni had a hatred for each other and after unsuccessful attempts at taking each other's lives, Slade caught Jules off guard. Jules was wounded and Slade tied him to a corral post cut off his ears, nailed them to the post, then ended his life with more bullets. One of the ears was worn by Slade as a watch-charm, and the other remained on the post. As to where this event took place is certainly a matter of conjecture. Guesses have been placed at Latham, Cheyenne, Torrington and probably all places in between. Slade's continued depredations, highway robberies and murders took him into Montana where he was hanged in Virginia City.

R. J. Spotswood replaced him as Division Agent on the 4th Division of the Overland Stage Line.

On the morning of June 29, 1865, Indians raided Virginia Dale and ambushed the station hunter, Jim Enos. Enos managed to crawl back to the station with an arrow through his chest, where he died in a short while. He was buried in the little station cemetary. The station lay beseiged for several more days. The Leavenworth Times newspaper reported "...the hills are swarming with Indians. The Indians are undoubtedly preparing for a desolating war. They are gathering from every direction."

The station keepers at that date were Mr. and Mrs. William S. Taylor.

Virginia Dale is in the National Register of Historic Places. It is the only stage station still standing in Colorado and in good repair. The station building stands away from the highway out of sight of passersby and is about six miles from the Wyoming border.

The station is currently owned by the Community of Virginia Dale.

Here at Virginia Dale, at an altitude of 6977 feet, the trail had almost reached its highest point, and after that it made a fairly easy descent onto the wide Laramie Plains in Dakota Territory.

Wagon Trail Ruts Across a Prairie
Courtesy Wyoming State Archives,
Museums and Historical Department

Emigrant trains often deviated from the established road. Short-cuts, whether real or imagined, were tried. As a simple example, on the flat open plains, if there was no imminent danger of Indians, the wagons would spread out and pick their own way along. A few miles on either side of a regular stream crossing, fording was done when water height allowed. One of these was May 26, 1858, when Capt. Loring of the Loring-Marcy party wrote in his diary: "...left (Lt.) Bryan's road 4 or 5 miles before reaching the (North) Platte, making a road to "Baker's Ferry" at this time the only one in the vicinity fordable; the water being high, found this one difficult and dangerous." This same party took off from apparently the Pine Grove area, and "struck for the head of Bitter Creek", passing over the Continental divide at about Jepp's Canyon. This by-passed Bridger Pass to the north. This is also one of the reported Evans-Cherokee routes. Trails went both north and south around Medicine Bow Butte, or Elk Mountain as we know it today. Another trail was the Walbach cut-off which followed Lodgepole Creek from its confluence with the South Platte, near Julesburg, to its origin in the "Black Hills" or Laramie Range. This trail over Cheyenne Pass, avoided the swing down through northern Colorado and back up again. In the late 1850's, Camp Walbach, a military post, was established at the location where this trail entered the Laramie Mountains about 30 miles northwest of the place where the town of Cheyenne was to be founded 9 years later. The camp was abandoned in 1858. This cut-off route was approximately the route that highway 30 and the Union Pacific Railroad used to build, later, into Laramie. It then crossed the Laramie Plains and joined the Overland Trail at the Little Laramie station. This cut-off was heavily traveled by emigrants in the 1850's, but little is recorded on it. The diary of Silas L. Hopper of Blandinville, Illinois, from April 27, 1863 to July 21, 1863 called this road "awful" and declared it a "humbug".[35]

The observation of this trail site in the 1970's by the Wyoming State Historical Preservation Office, found a few places where ruts were still visible and at the Warren Pole Creek Ranch was a grave marker of an emigrant.

Actually, the whole Overland Trail was a cut-off, as compared to the Oregon-California Trail. But more-so, it was a relocated Holladay Overland Stage and Mail route, as existed on the other trail.

HOLLADAY'S LOSSES FROM JULY 1864 TO FEBRUARY 1865
Of the Colorado Station on the Trail According to Testimony Before the Committee on Claims, 1880

American Ranch or Kelley's	58 oxen at $100.00	$5800.00
	Barn destroyed	1500.00
	30 tons hay at .50¢	1300.00
	227 sacks corn (25,424 lbs. at .22¢)	5593.28
	2 horses at $250.00	500.00
	2 sets four-horse harness at $110.00	220.00
	8 stage horses at $250.00	2000.00
Antelope	House, barn, and corral burned	5000.00
	25 tons hay at $50.00	1250.00
	125 sacks corn (14,000 lbs. at .20¢	2800.00
Beaver Creek	75 sacks corn (8400 lbs. at .22¢)	1848.00
	1 stage horse	250.00
Bijou	48 sacks corn (5376 lbs. at .22¢)	1182.72
	7 tons hay at $50.00	350.00
Dennison's	Barn and corral burned	2500.00
	25 tons hay at $50.00	1250.00
	200 sacks corn (22,400 lbs. at .22¢)	4928.00
Julesburg	1 mule	100.00
	1 set 4-horse harness	120.00
	2 bales clothing	1500.00
	Barns, sheds, warehouses, telegraph office, blacksmith shop, houses burned	35,000.00
	Damage to coach	500.00
	30 tons hay at $50.00	1500.00
	3500 sacks corn (392,000 lbs. at .20¢)	78,400.00
	Provisions and stores	2000.00
	1 horse	200.00
Spring Hill	House, barns, furniture destroyed	6000.00
	20 tons hay at $50.00	1000.00
	90 sacks corn (10,080 lbs. at .22¢)	2217.60
Lost on road	2 stage horses and harness	450.00
Valley	20 tons hay at $50.00	1000.00
Virginia Dale July, August 1865	2 mules at $200.00	400.00
	1 mare and colt	250.00
	8 cows at $50.00	400.00
	1 mule killed	200.00
	1 bull killed	75.00
Stonewall or Cherokee	2 yoke oxen at $100.00	200.00
		$169,784.60

Fredericks, J.V.; *Ben Holladay The Stagecoach King*, Appendix G.

Virginia Dale

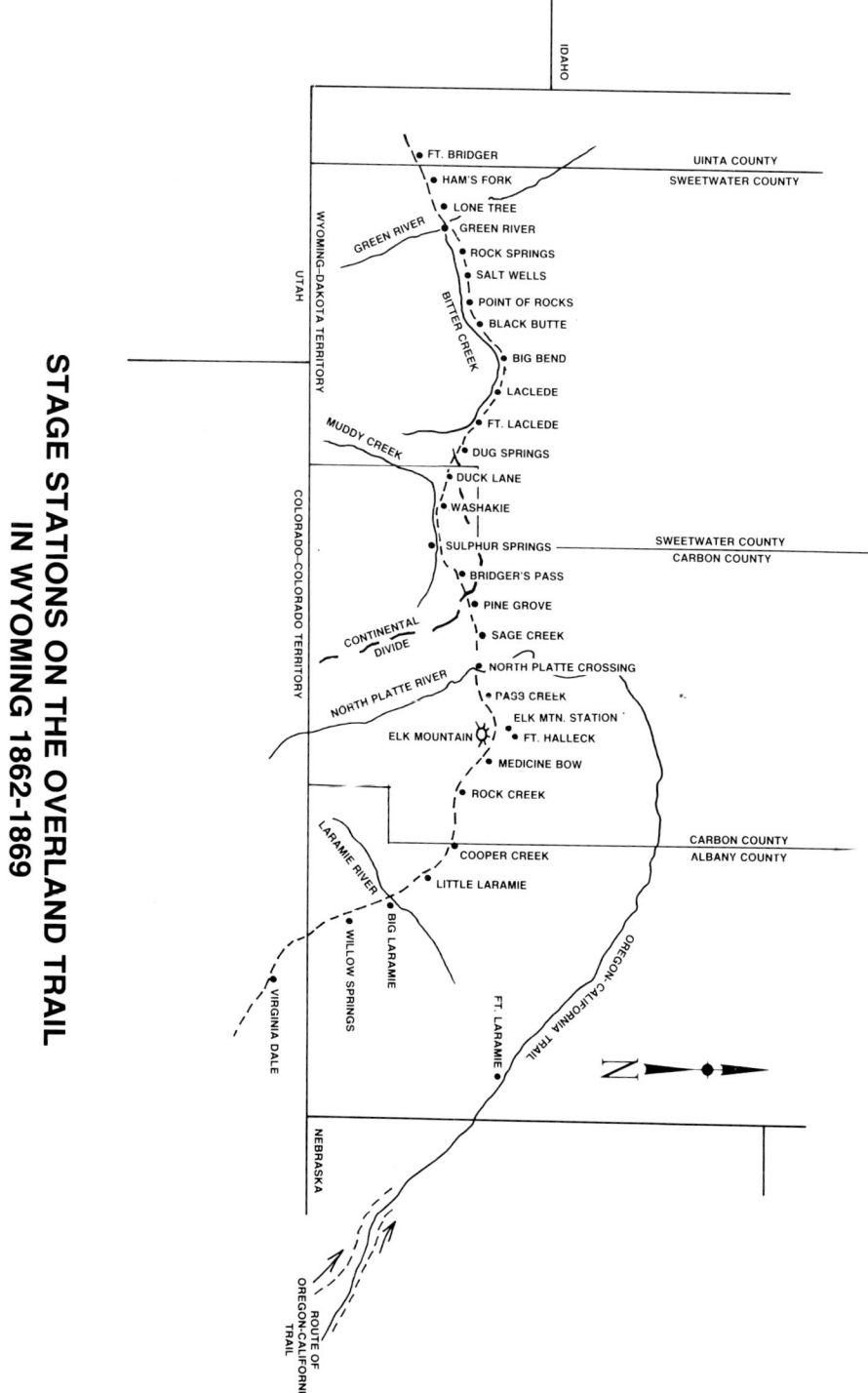

Virginia Dale

STAGE STATIONS THROUGH WYOMING

The first station in the Dakota Territory was the small swing station, **WILLOW SPRINGS,** 15 miles from Virginia Dale. A 1955 reference of Robert H. Burns of Laramie, WY. states that this station was out on the prairie, west of the present highway and about midway to the point of Boulder Ridge and about 2 miles west from the Tie Siding on the RR. It was at a grove of willow trees and a good spring. This was a small log structure and corral that, during its course of existence, had been raided several times and burned. No visible evidence of this station remains, however archeological finds, by the Albany County Historical Board, headed by Russel L. Tanner, indicates it's possible location. This site, in Albany County, Wyoming is owned by Kinnard Windham.

In early 1865 travel and mail service all along the trail was stopped. Stations, mail coaches and wagons were vandalized, burned, scattered and lost. Holladay asked for more military protection for the mail. In Washington, Senator John Conness denounced the mail contractor's claims, saying that Holladay hired Indians to create a stir every time he wanted a new mail contract. As more depredations occurred, Speaker Schuyler Colfax came to personally evaluate the situation. In May and June he and his party traveled by stage over the length of the Overland Trail. They were fortunate not to be attacked, but from graphic evidence seen, realized the gravity of the situation. Thirty minutes after his coach had left Willow Springs, the station was raided.[36] Arms and ammunition as well as horses were stolen.

Fifteen miles further on, **BIG LARAMIE,** a home station, was located on the Laramie River, in beautiful ranch land, approximately eight miles upstream, southwest, from the present city of Laramie, Wyoming.[37] This station consisted of a barn and two log living quarter buildings connected with a narrow, covered "breeze-way" which was later completely enclosed. Near this was a privy which was a welcome relief from the embarrassment of the open trail![38] The blacksmith shop, was a good sized log building a short distance northeast of the living quarters and it had a fresh water spring under the floor. All these buildings still remain on the site of this cattle ranch owned by the Bath families since the early 1900's.

As time went on, the Big Laramie was a hub of increased activity. Troops from Ft. Collins and Ft. Halleck were on the move. Freight wagons brought more supplies and more stage passengers needed lodging. This necessitated additional space so more rooms were added to the bunkhouse in about 1864.

The Big Laramie Station was divided by the river. After the passengers had alighted from their coach at these buildings on the east side of the river, the horses were driven about another quarter mile to cross the river to Ben Holladay's stables which also had accomodations for the stable keepers, and feed and storage room. This was an "L" shaped structure.

Today, this "L" shaped, remodeled building with its original hewn log exterior, is the lovely ranch home of Margery Richardson who also operates the ranch. She and her late husband added the large sunporch.

The Richardson's
Overland Trail Ranch

Fording the Big Laramie at this crossing was easy. The banks were low and the river bed was covered with gravel. But on the west side, the ground was wet and marshy which necessitated a corduroy road bed being built. This was made of 8 to 10 foot long, 10 inch diameter logs stacked and layered side by side.[39]

Tom Alsop was station master at one time.

Between Big Laramie and Little Laramie the wagons traveled over a large open grassy depression in the terrain called Big Hollow. The early maps of this area called it "The Sinks" but in 1863 emigrants were calling it Big Hollow.

In 1865, two diarists from the same wagon train mention passing a large alkali pond where the water had evaporated and the alkali had built up to about a three inch layer. They both had seen animals die from drinking alkali water. The accepted immediate treatment for that was to get lard or some kind of grease down into the animals stomach.

20 miles northwest of the Big Laramie, at the confluence with Brown's Creek is the site of the **LITTLE LARAMIE STATION,** a little southeast of the present Amy Lawrence Ranch. Nothing remains of the old log station buildings. In 1865 the station and corral burned and it is possible the site was changed when rebuilt, but with time it has disintegrated. The old blacksmith shop was moved from the site to the Phillip Mandel ranch.[40] Mandel, who managed the station, bought and traded livestock from the emigrants and built up a good cattle herd for himself. This recorded practice was also carried on in 1861 by Mahlon Brown at a station on the South Platte River.[41]

Near-by was the small ranch operated by Rocky Thomas. He offered deer, antelope and elk meat for sale. He also sold all kinds of skins, including buffalo and beaver, that the Indians had tanned.

Photo by Les Erb
Overland Trail Crossing Highway 130 west of Laramie

At Seven Mile Creek, west of Little Laramie, a detail of nine men of the 1st Colorado Cavalry, under Sgt. Cooley, were escorting two government supply wagons when they were attacked by a band of Indians. Sgt. Cooley was shot in the head and the two teams, numbering twelve mules were run off. Pvt. Baker, a Michigan soldier was captured. After a bloody and desperate resistance his captors chained him to a wheel of the wagon, scalped him then piled bacon, with which the wagon was loaded, around him, and setting fire to the pile burned him to death. From Aug. 16, 1865 Rocky Mountain News interview of E.N. Lewis, Ft. Halleck hospital steward.

COOPER CREEK STATION, about 17 miles from Little Laramie, was located on the now Albany-Carbon County border. It was on a busy part of the trail and had its share of excitement. Dwight Fisk was station keeper. His wife was with him at the station and on August 30, 1864, Dr. J.H. Finfrock, the post surgeon at Ft. Halleck, after an all night coach ride from Ft. Halleck, delivered her premature baby girl. The baby lived only 2 hours.[42]

At this station, on May 13, 1865, Mrs. Fisk witnessed the killing of Hod Russell, the cook at Ft. Halleck, by Bob Jennings, a hunter, trapper, gambler, and confederate sympathizer. Jennings was not apprehended until May 20th when William Comstock, an Indian trader, disguised as an Indian and with a few of the friendly Arapahoes, by a devious trick, overpowered him and took him to Ft. Halleck.[43] His trial was set and Mrs. Fisk was subpoenaed as the only witness but before she could get there from Cooper Station he had been hung. The posthumous verdict was "guilty".[44]

Cooper Station did not escape the Indian raids. The station and contents were pillaged and stock driven off several times.

Mrs. Mildred M. Wood who now lives in Laramie, Wyoming has written a wonderful account of the Cooper Creek area where she spent fourteen of her early years. We want to share her letter with you.

"The trail (Overland) went over the hill, which our neighbors call Immigrant Hill, in just about the same location as I 80 does. The hill I am speaking of overlooks Cooper Cove Valley as you are headed west. Practically all of the Trail has been obliterated except for ruts which go down the hill diagonally between the east and west portions of I 80. Headed toward Laramie the ruts are still quite plain, probably 500 to 750 feet from the brim of the hill. The trail went diagonaly across Section 28, T.18, R77 (which was later homesteaded by Clement S. Bengough whose grave is just east of I 80). It exited at the NW corner and crossed a small corner of Section 29, then turned north and crossed a tributary of Cooper Creek into Sec. 20, which was our home section. It continued north and crossed Cooper Creek, thence a little NW across a very swampy area. Incidentally there were still a couple of telegraph pole stumps (which were put up in the 1860s) in that area when I was a small child; also remnants of corded poles (poles tied together with rope) which had been used in crossing the swampy area. In the spring and early summer that area was so difficult to cross that another route just east of Sec. 20 was used. I know where all of the crossings on Cooper Creek and it's tributaries are and could show you. After the Trail left Sec. 20 it went over the hill to the north in Sec. 17, and again, it has been obliterated by I 80. All of the ruts have been covered up, but when I was a child they were very deep--in fact, too deep to travel on with a team and wagon. After the trail leaves that area it goes into Carbon County and I'm not sure of it's route from there to Arlington.

"As a child I played in an area behind the old Stage Station which was located a little over one-half mile west of the location where the Overland Trail crosses Cooper Creek. I picked up many pieces of broken crockery; of course they are long gone. Now I would treasure them! There was also an old hand powered bellows there. At that time the foundation was very plain and at the present time it is still visible (if you know what you are looking for).

"I have quite a few oxen shoes which were picked up along the Overland Trail and also have a beer stein which was given to my mother by Bobby Neilson. It is heavy blue crockery with an Indian on it and was given as a premium with a certain brand of flour. I wish I had paid more attention to details, but it was either found at the stage station or at the location where I spent my early childhood. Anyway, it must have been used in that area during the time the Overland Trail was being used or shortly thereafter.

"The house I lived in for the first 14 years of my life was also used as a stopping place for the immigrants. It was about one fourth mile east of the stage station. It was a one story log house whose floor boards were worn through and the logs of the wall structure were getting pretty rotten by the time my parents built a new home just a little west of the stage station location.

"In the early 1870s a Dr. Latham, a U.P. Surgeon owned a portion of Section 20. After that E.L. Dixon filed on the property; then it was passed on to his daughter and her husband, Bobby Neilson. They left the ranch in 1908 and my great uncle, Flake Hall, took it over on a mortgage. My parents acquired the land in 1912. The old house was full of bed bugs and my parents lived in a tent all summer, while they fumigated it. They kept sulphur burning in the house all summer and even after they were able to move into the house they found several live bugs.

"My mother had a lady visit her in 1916 whose name was Cassidy. She said her family were squatters on Section 20. She told about her family seeing what appeared to be a bunch of horses traveling in single file. They came over the brow of Immigrant Hill where the Overland Trail was located. As they got closer the Cassidys could see Indians mounted on the horses. Their heads and upper torsos were bent over the backs of the horses to make it appear that the horses were riderless. Of course her family was terrified, thinking the Indians would surely kill them. They went on to Dutton Creek where they did kill John Luber who was herding sheep in the area. They scalped him and cut his back in strips. Mrs. Luber came to the Cassidys and told them about her husband's death and they went over and brought the body back to their place. It is buried just across Cooper Creek north of the old stage station.

"Bobby Neilson also visited my mother and told her about the grave of two small immigrant children (2 little girls) who died as a result of scarlet fever. The location of that grave was about one fourth mile west of where the Overland Trail topped the hill in Sec. 17. I tried to find it a few years ago, but it has been obliterated by a pipe line which went through the area in the early 1980s.

"Another tragedy occured on the ranch in 1887 when Mr. E.L. Dixon's hired man shot and killed a man named Embree, who had just been released from Joliet prison. Embree had been convicted of cattle rustling, through the testimony of E.L. Dixon and as soon as he was released from prison he landed in Laramie. After a few drinks too many at a local bar he boasted that he was going to kill Dixon. The latter was warned and whenever he and the hired man were in the fields they carried a gun. One day the hired man saw Embree dart from one tree to another on Cooper Creek and shot him. Embree's grave is in Sec. 21, still visible. I wish it could be marked. As far as I know I'm the only one left who knows where it is. Mr. Dixon and the hired man were acquitted, since the action was in self-defense.

"In the book, *Wyoming's Pioneer Ranches* by Burns, Gillespie and Richardson, is a picture on p. 401 of the E.L. Dixon Ranch house (my home until the age of 14). The caption under the picture states that the place was on Four Mile, but that is a mistake.

"There are a couple of graves located about a mile north of the Four Mile Overland Trail crossing and I wouldn't be surprised if they were immigrants. It would be nice if they could be marked also."

There is no visible evidence remaining of this station. The ranch is now owned by James and Martha Jankowsky.

Near Cooper Creek, "Dutch Fred" operated a small ranch. A few miles west of Rock Creek a ranch was owned by Robert Foote and Eckler. One of their small buildings displayed the word "STORE", in large letters, over the door. These

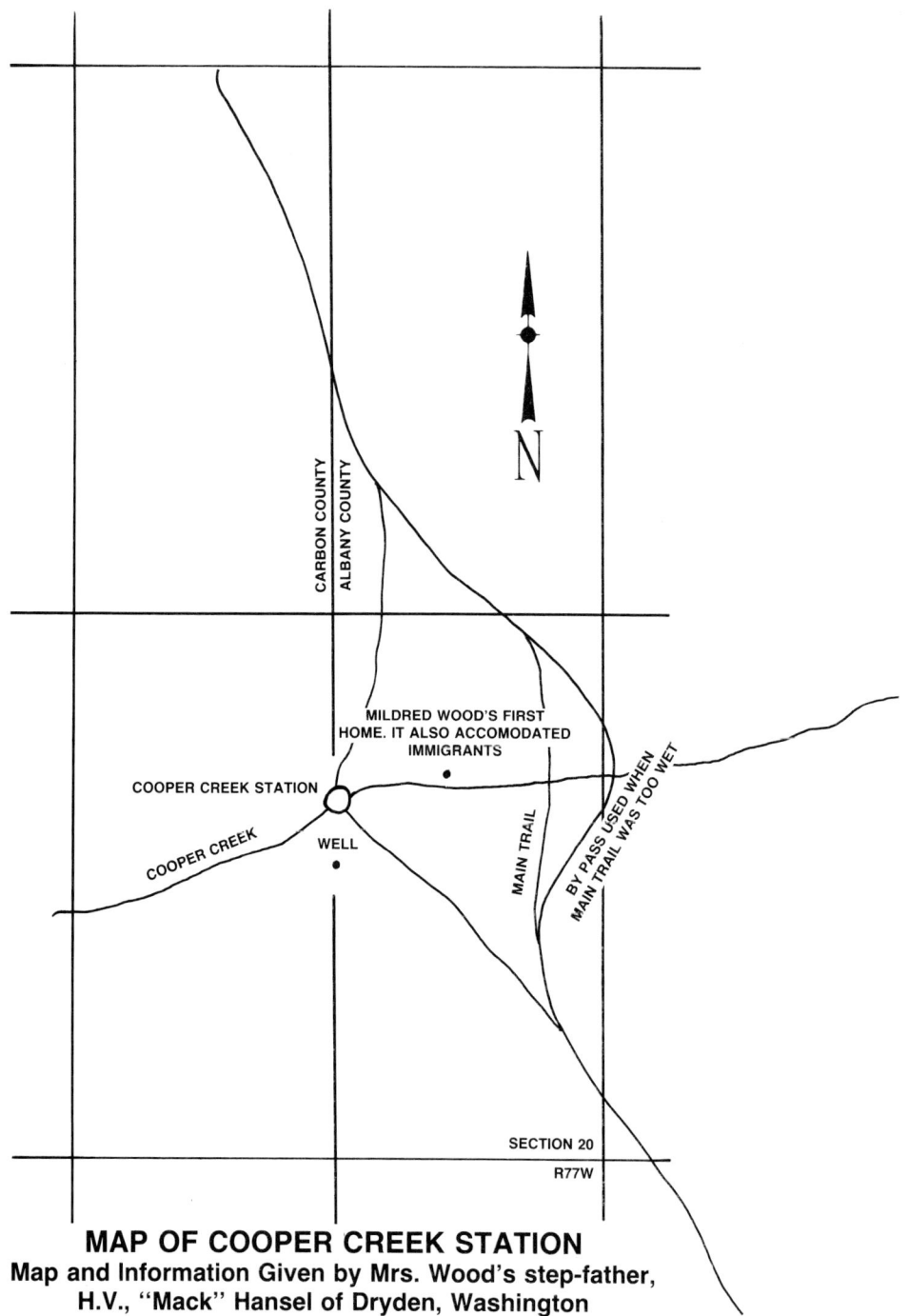

Map of Cooper Creek Station
and location of her early home until the age 14

"ranches" were not the livestock enterprises as of today but more of a trading post or general store. The stations or the Forts were not allowed to have whiskey but the men could readily get it at the ranches.

Eleven miles from Cooper Creek, the **ROCK CREEK STATION** was situated at the base of a high, heavily wooded mountain, where through a narrow gorge a noisy, impatient, icy cold stream pushes its way forward. The stream bed is covered with large round tumbled river rocks and the water was so high and swift that making a ford was impossible, so a sturdy log bridge spanned it. Emigrant wagons crossed for a toll of 75 cents each. A short way down stream fording was possible when the water was low.

Old Rock Creek Crossing

Mrs. Goldie Pitcher, who with her husband, Chet, owners of Rock Creek Ranch at Arlington, Wyoming, has kindly given us information on the site, In 1860, Joe Bush built the buildings, which included a sturdy log, two room, homestead cabin, on the west side of the road. Mr. and Mrs. Bill Williams took it as a squatter's claim and homestead in the very early 1880's. They operated it as a way station for several years and the government put in a post office called "Rock Dale". The year for this is unknown as well as when the name was changed to Arlington and why that name was chosen. Besides the inn and post there was a blacksmith shop, dance hall and saloon in the two-story building still standing. The structure also served as a bunkhouse and school. Mrs. Pitcher has now made the homestead cabin into a museum.

J. Zeamer, an immigrant in 1865, wrote of his experiences, *"Across the Plains by Immigrant Wagon"*

"..The place **ROCK CREEK** consisted of the station buildings, a small store and five or six houses and had the appearance and business activity of a small village. Some swarthy squaws were working near the buildings, scraping and dressing skins and so intent upon their occupation that they hardly looked up to take a glance at our wagons as we passed. These industrious squaws were likely the wives of white men for a lot of half-breed children were playing near them. The squaws were sullen and silent but the children romped and played with the dogs and prattled loud enough for us to hear them out at the road".

The Cheyenne and Arapahoe Indians, in this section of the country, were the only two tribes that were friendly toward each other, a friendship that had existed for many years. They both belonged to the same linguistic family but had to use sign language to converse. They often camped together and sometimes conducted ceremonies in each others presence but the tribes never intermarried.

The Cheyenne were more warlike and better horsemen, and unlike the Arapahoe, Cheyennes never ate dog nor gave up wives to other men.

The Arapahoes were the "friendly Indians" and were fed all winter at Ft. Halleck. The white men's Indian wives were Arapahoe.

June of 1865 was just issuing out a persistent cold and stormy winter which would suddenly become a dreadful sanguineous summer.

The heavy spring run-off swelled this creek to flood stage and washed out the bridge. Mail and emigration was stopped until the bridge was rebuilt.

In the Colorado "Pike's Peak" gold rush days, flakes of gold had been found in the tributaries of the Medicine Bow River. Someone at this time found a few flakes of gold in the Rock Creek vicinity and another minature rush was on. O.J. Goldrick, a journalist, whose accounting he did not question, reported in the *Daily Union Vedette* of Salt Lake City, "Before coming to Ft. Halleck, we passed through Rock Creek mines. There are in all about 100 people prospecting, developing and drinking whiskey, in and around Rock Creek "City". Gold and Silver abounds there, to hear the people talk, in "mass and position"; but as yet, there are few shafts sunk, and the placer claims are scarcely opened to the bed rock." Mr. Goldrick, a graduate of Dublin University, and called "The Professor" opened the first school in Denver in 1859. He then engaged in journalism where he took many liberties with his words. An editor once said, "Professor Goldrick, the Adonis of the Rocky Mountains, wears the best clothes, smokes the finest cigars, looks the most a millionaire on the street, and enjoys what there is in life. Stocks may go up; governors may go down, but Goldrick goes on forever."[45]

Mr. Zeamer, again reports in his July 27, 1865 entry. While the wagon train had stopped for lunch and rest at Rock Creek, a baby was born to a German couple, in an adjacent wagon. They traveled on and a few days after they had passed the Foote and Eckler ranch, with the "STORE" sign, Indians captured and burned the buildings and drove off 100 head of stock. The proprietors were able to escape.

Mr. Zeamer records his version of the Fletcher incident. From the date he had been in Rock Creek and the time he put on the happening, the story must have gone through several mouths. He states,

> "...in August, here they burned an entire train, killed eight men and captured three women. One of the women was subsequently killed but the other two were carried off and subjected to the indescribable horrors of Indian captivity. An infant child was also killed and its body stuck upon a pole and the pole stood up by the road side. The act is almost too revolting to relate or believe, but it tallies with many of the shocking and devilish mutilations which the Indians used to practice upon the bodies of their victims and is likely true. The locality of Rock Creek furnished contrasts in those days. For one train a child is born in a wagon by the road side and for another a child is murdered and its body fiendishly stuck up on a pole."

In battles, the Indian braves would lash themselves to their ponies with rawhide thongs so if they got injured or killed they would not fall off. Their comrades could easily catch their horse and take them away. The Indians always removed their own casualties from the battle field. Frederic Remington, the early western artist painted a picture, called "Indian Warfare", of Indians carrying off a dead companion.

In July, 1865 Demas Barnes, a stage coach passenger describes his experience, "We had whistled to keep our courage and tried not to believe in Indians for some time. But evidences accumulated very fast, and we were quite willing to keep our escort very near us. We were not allowed to travel nights any longer. We, thirteen of us, slept on the earth-floor of the station at Cooper Creek, soldiers guarding outside. We procured eight mules the next morning, and had proceeded six miles, when some horseman came riding down upon us like lightning, crying "Indians." Eleven rifles sprang to the windows (there were eleven passengers on this stage), and my hair sprang to my head; the coach wheeled about so quick as nearly to tip us over--and if we did not make a race, I am no judge. We ran our mules five miles, until we intercepted an emigrant train, and also a company of cavalry. A council of war was held; it was decided to proceed. We were forty-four military and twenty civilians strong--your humble servant the only person seen on the route not provided with a Spencer or a Henry's rifle; but I had a revolver, and thought at close quarters I could take a hand. The Indians, in turn, retreated but kept on our flanks, and killed one poor boy belonging to the military escort, who had followed them too far. We recovered his body. The diabolical wretches! ---they had stripped him entirely of his clothing, dug out his eyes, torn off his scalp, opened both his breasts, took out his heart and entrails--a tribute to his bravery--cut off both his feet, cut his head nearly off, and otherwise disfigured him--leaving one bullet in his head and eight arrows through his body. I have one arrow, which I shall carry home. They afterwards intercepted us at the crossing of a gulch and at the brow of a hill. We were in for a fight, and drew up in line. I felt my day had come, and wished myself home. My life is of too much importance to others, if not to myself, to throw it away ignobly, fighting Indians! I much prefer to be a living coward than a dead hero. But there was no return--no escape. We approached on a slow trot; got in firing range, the bullets flew from every gun. Their leader fell, and our force being large, they skedaddled as fast as they could run. They were very shrewd, and sent out small parties, endeavoring to beguile "the whites" into some place of ambush, when hundreds of their warriors would have sprung upon and hewed us to pieces. We did not follow. For me, the realizing sense of a whole scalp and a pull at my canteen was a great relief. This is only a sample of what is daily occuring. Two of our pilgram companions were killed the same day. The stage company is minus horses, the government without a tithe of a military force, and the people without sufficient to eat. There is not enough force here to guard the station, let alone hunting Indians. It will require sixty days to march from the river, and I do not believe things will be safe or in shape until one year from now. Ten thousand troops are needed in this country."

From a painting of Indians attacking a coach
Artist unknown
Picture courtesy of Colorado State Historical Society

An article in the July 7, 1865 Rocky Mountain News quotes:
   "It seems to be ascertained beyond a doubt that Indians that committed these outrages, and others on that line, recently, are the band of Arapahoes under Black Bear, who have been fed by the government during the winter as "friendly", only awaiting a favorable time to commence their work of murder..."

The trail was still besieged by Indians in 1867. On May 12th Col. Mizner reports in a letter to General Augur: "Indians have run off stock and burned Rock Creek Station".

Mrs. Pitcher adds:
   "The original homestead, preserved for posterity, stands in mute testimony to the hardships endured here a century ago, to the family that may have huddled around a wood stove, their feet scuffing on earthen floor as they prepared a simple meal in the light of a coal oil lamp. These relics are a monument to that family and others like it; to Alvy Dixon, homesteader, freighter, mail carrier by team and horseback and rancher, and all who passed this way on the Overland Trail."

This ranch is now owned by Chet and Goldie Pitcher of Arlington, Wyoming. The Rock Creek Station is in the National Register of Historic Places.

After leaving Rock Creek the Overland Trail starts on its 17 mile journey to **MEDICINE BOW STATION.** Our emigrant friend, Mr. J. Zeamer, again wrote in his journal:
   "The first stream we came to on this day was named Wagon Hound Creek, which ran through a deep ravine with high rugged hills on each side. The approach to it was down a long stony hill and the road was narrow and uneven. As we arrived at the top of the hill the stage was coming up and the road being narrow and sideling we waited at the top until it passed us. Near the foot of the hill a wrecked and abandoned

wagon was lying by the roadside, an object of misfortune that helped us to remember Wagon Hound Creek. The stream was spanned by a toll bridge. There was no one on hand to collect toll, but we learned that it was a sure enough toll bridge from a sign posted nearby, on which the name of the owner was given and the source from which he had authority to put a bridge there. The rates of ($2.50 a wagon) toll were also stated on the sign but as there was a fording just above the bridge and another just below it, the immigrants saved all toll charges with very little inconvenience to themselves.

"The country was uneven and streams were now more frequent. Before noon of this day we came to another, the Medicine Bow River, which flowed through a wide bottom and was bordered with large cottonwood trees. Where we crossed it it was split up into strips, or smaller streams, each of which was spanned by a toll bridge, but as the streams were all fordable toll bridges meant very little. The lowland on the banks of this stream - or several streams - was a beautiful and inviting place for immigrants to tarry in, and traces of encampments were scattered around on both sides of it. The buildings of the stage here are beautifully shaded by large trees and a strong detail of soldiers were quartered in them for their services were frequently needed on this section of the road."

The 1867 journal of Edward Ordway, *"Reminiscences of Edward Ordway"*, as printed in the July-October 1929 issue of *Annals of Wyoming*, describes:

"The stage company only had one building, a long log stable arranged in the usual way, stalls on each side for horses and spaces for hay and grain, with an alley running from front to back through the middle and a large room partitioned off in the southwest corner for the stocktenders to live in, with a trap door in the floor leading into a tunnel which ran under the road into a small fort opposite the alley way through the stable. There was a lot of timber and brush on both sides of the river which made it easy for the Indians to watch an opportunity to slip into the back end of the stable and get away with the horses. And not a summer passed without one or more attempts to enrich themselves, by what a white man would consider desperate chances." But more so just a cunning ability.

"The last attack was made in the summer before we were there, and, as they told, it happened at noon while the men were eating their dinner. They heard a disturbance among the horses and one man opened the door and catching sight of an Indian drew his head back just in time to miss a good chance to stop an arrow that the Indian had ready for whoever might step out. The boys lost no time in barring the door and getting into the fort. The first shot was from a shotgun that took off one Indian's arm and slightly wounded two more. It appeared that they were not wise about the fort. The Indian who made the noise that queered the game had jumped in alongside of a broncho that was, as the Spanish speak it, "Muy brave" and, resenting the intrusion upon his privacy by a heathen savage who smelled strongly of kinikinic and willow snake, pulled back, breaking his halter and immediately taking to the woods.

"The others had better luck in the stalls, but lost out when they came within range of the guns that raked the alley. Only one got away with a horse."

Occasionally the soldiers had a respite from their duties of chasing Indians and trying to recapture livestock on the trail, as the diary of Lewis Byrum Hull, of CO. K 11 Cav. indicated:

"On June 9 (1865) - Large trains passing up, and Mormon train going down. I get permission to take a ride and go down to Medicine Bow. Have a dance with the Mormon ladies, "Brighamites" and "Josephities".

"June 10 - Escort back from up the road, bringing the boys that were killed and Caldwell and Wilson. Boys look very bad; faces all bruised and black. Thirteen wounds in Bodine and eight in Stewart. We bury them in one grave, with honors of war; six rounds fired over the grave. The colonel shot the chief, as they suppose, when quite near them, as the pursuit was ended by his death. All the boys but three back. Indians seen on this side of the river".

This fight took place at Sage Creek Station and when we reach there the accounting will be given. The diary continues:

"June 11 - Got a pass and with Curtis and Maxwell go to Medicine Bow. Stop at Mormon train, then go down to station and across to emigrant camp. Get "home" about 11 PM.

"June 12 - No trains passing; all stops at Medicine Bow. Race up at stations between Balkin's pony and Behymer's. Behymer's won. - $25. Citizens stopping till the road is reopened.

"June 13 - Take a ride with Behymer; meet train. Beauvais train camps with Whitcomb. Buy seventeen beaver skins off a trapper for only $59.

The Medicine Bow Sage Station was located in the vicinity of the present day town of Elk Mountain, in Carbon County. The station got its name from Medicine Bow Mountain, at which base it lies on the north. The mountain is called Elk Mountain now. A Mr. Campbell was the station master in 1862. There is nothing left of the station now.

The Medicine Bow Station and the present town of Medicine Bow, Wyoming are not the same.

About 8 miles west of the Medicine Bow station was the site of **FORT HALLECK.**

On July 20, 1862 Major John O'Ferrell with Capt. Francis M. Shipley's Co. A, 6th Ohio Cavalry came down from the Oregon Trail on the Sweetwater and chose a site for new Ft. Halleck, officially placing it at the northern base of Elk Mountain at an elevation of about 7300 feet. The 6th Ohio Cav. under the command of Maj. O'Ferrell transferred the entire Ben Holladay installation. The historian C.G. Coutant writes:

"The change was made during the summer of 1862, and remarkable to relate, the transfer to the new line was so successfully accomplished that not a mail was missed or a coach delayed. The rolling stock, horses and other property of the company was gathered at the station just above Devil's Gate. Company A of the 6th Ohio Cav. with Major O'Ferrell in command, was the escort at the time the transfer was made. The first day the long train of coaches, wagons, horses and mules made eleven miles from the station where the property had been gathered. The route chosen was directly south from the Sweetwater. The camp selected was in a gap in the mountains where there was a fine spring and plenty of wood for cooking purposes. Shortly after going into camp, the Major discovered that quite a number of his soldiers were intoxicated and he at once sent for Lieutenant W.H. Brown, who was officer of the day, and informed him of the condition of many of the men and gave it as his opinion that someone was selling whiskey in the camp...Lt. Brown received orders to search all these wagons (wagons of emigrants accompanying) and if he discovered whiskey, to destroy it. Taking a corporal and three or four men, they commenced the search for the contraband article. They examined every wagon in the camp except one; when they came to this they discovered a barrel of whiskey. The officer at once ordered his men to roll the barrel out, knock in the head and empty the contents on the ground. This was done, but it chanced that the spot where the whiskey was emptied was just above the spring, and the fiery liquid went pouring down into the water supply for the camp. The soldiers saw what was going on and they rushed forward with cups, canteens and camp kettles to save what they could of the whiskey. Those who were without the wherewith to hold the liquor stamped their boot-heels in the ground and caught the whiskey in the hole and lying down drank it. A half hour later the intoxicant was showing its effect pretty generally around the camp and soon there were few sober men to be found...The gap in the mountains in which the camp was made had never been named up to that date, but the soldiers in referring to it afterwards called it Whiskey Gap, a name which it bears to the present day." Whiskey Gap is located just east of Muddy Gap about 40 miles north of Rawlins.

This fort was named after a Civil War Union General, Henry Wager Halleck.

The country in and around Elk Mountain was in the heart of the Indian tribes battlefield. Beautiful grass covered meadows and slopes were fed by several small streams, and near-by tree covered mountains -- all abounding in deer, elk, antelope, bear and mountain sheep. Perhaps the whites infringement on this sacred ground, just as the whites plowing up the Ute's race track at Meeker, Colorado, helped lead to the Meeker Massacre, led to the bloody raids on the Overland Trail.

The A and C Companies of the 6th Ohio Cav. first garrisoned the post. These boys who did much of the construction were doing extra duty for 25 cents and a jug of whiskey a day. It seems that the money probably never was paid but the whiskey was.

A letter by J.J. Hollingsworth to John C. Friend states, "By the 20th day of December (1862) these two companies had built and completed two sets of company quarters, two stables large enough each to hold 100 horses, quartermasters and commissary storehouses, post headquarters, hospital, officers quarters, bake house, sutler store and the "jug" (jail). "...The buildings, all of them, with the exception of the hospital and headquarters building were composed of rough pine logs, notched at the corners and put up in panels. The last two mentioned were of hewn logs. The lumber for the doors, window frames, etc. was brought from Denver by three six mule teams...sash, hardware, etc. from Laramie (Fort Laramie)."

The barracks were comfortable and warm in the winter. Wood was plentiful from the near-by hills. The soldiers diaries indicate the food was ample and quality excellent. Canned oysters were often on the menu. The hunter, employed by the stage company, kept the fort well supplied with game. He would be out for 2 or 3 days at a time and hunt within a range of 5 to 6 miles.

The first doctor at the post was a Dr. Holladay.

The storekeeper at all of the forts was called a sutler, and at first, Ft. Halleck had two, O.W. Jones and Mr. Mills. The sutlers were appointed by the military and paid a fee for serving the area. Prices for the goods were set by a board of officers four times a year and the commanding officer had to approve of them. The sutler used one of the fort buildings or built one of his own. If the troops were to be gone for a length of time, the sutler could accompany them and sell to the troops from his wagon. Mr. Mills left the fort in November 1864 to return to the states (known as anywhere east of the Mississippi River) and Mr. Goerge Wilson took his place.

The soldiers were paid with green backs and paper money was used in the sutler's store. Five, ten, twenty-five and fifty cent notes were heavily discounted because of the large wartime inflation.[46]

Thousands of big freight wagons, annually passed along supplying the forts and trading post ranches. They carried flour, sugar, ham, bacon, potatoes, dried fruit, hard tack, clothing, canned goods of milk, oysters, fruit etc., coffee, candy, grain, tobacco, hardware, tools, bolts of calico and sewing supplies - well in fact anything a general store on the frontier would carry. Freighting continued in the winter as well.

Emigrants write of having to sort through a pile of mail at the Fort post-office to find their own. They could also make purchases from the sutler's store - fifty cents for a can of peaches and eighty cents for a packet of writing paper.

C.G. Coutant, writes in his *"History of Wyoming"*, "...he (Jack Slade) on one occasion entered the sutler's store at Ft. Halleck and amused himself by shooting holes through the canned goods on the shelf. At another time he took possession of the sutler's quarters and terrorized everybody connected with the establishment. For this offense the commander of the fort had him arrested and refused a release unless the stage company would first dismiss him from their employ. This was done..." This happened in May or June of 1863.

At Ft. Halleck, outside of the fort itself, and on the grassy meadow, stood the Indian tepees in which squaw men, their Indian wives and half-breed children lived. The "friendlies" and "loafers", who were fed by the Fort in the winter, lived here also. An emigrant thought them to be lazy, dirty, obnoxious looking creatures.

The 6th Ohio was replaced by Co. B 9th Kansas Cav. under the command of Captain Asaph Allen.

Midwinter snowstorms are a devastating torment in this part of Wyoming; snows are deep, winds are violent and temperatures plunge. February 1863, a blinding, drifting snowstorm, with a 30 degrees below zero temperature came up catching a troop of soldiers in the field. This troop under the command of First Lt. Thomas D. Clarke and Second Lt. John G. Reeves, were coming from Ft. Laramie to hunt down raiding Ute Indians. Col. William Collins, with a small group of men followed the next day and caught up with Lt. Clarke. Most of the men pushed on to Ft. Halleck but a small group were so benumbed with cold that Col. Collins stopped with them to try to start a fire for warmth but the wind only blew it out. They began to move again but Frank Courtwright of Co. C fell from his horse, too numb to sit in a saddle. The rest successfully made the fort but Pvt. David Hancher of Co. C and Col. Collins remained with him and Pvt. Joseph Hudnell who was also in bad condition. Col. Collins went on to get help. Help came, but Courtright died just after getting to the fort. Hudnell recovered. Col. Collins was paralyzed from the

The only remaining Ft. Halleck building
at the Palm Livestock ranch

waist down by the cold. Dr. Holladay, at Ft. Halleck said that one half hour more in the blizzard would put him beyond help. Corp. John Griffiths of Co. C, who was in the first party, died shortly after he was brought in. Mr. Jones and Mr. Mills, the sutlers gave dedicated care to the men.

The rear guard wagons were snowed completely under and were abandoned.

Many others lost their lives from freezing before the trail was abandoned.

The Utes, or Utah, Indians were indigenous to the mountains of Utah and Colorado and as long as they stayed in the mountains they were not confronted by their enemies, the Sioux, Cheyenne or Arapahoe. The raids by Utes on Ft. Halleck at this time were supposedly directed toward these other Indians but the whites must have been in the way.

In the spring of 1863 the Utes increased their depredations. The latter part of June, a band of these Indians came into Ft. Halleck begging for food and provisions under the pretense of being friendly. A few days later, after getting what they wanted, they stole the mail company's horses and mules from the Elk Mountain station. Soldiers vainly tried to retrieve the stock. A few days later horses were stolen from the mail company at Cooper Creek. In a few hours 70 soldiers from Ft. Halleck rode in pursuit. After a hard thirty mile ride they came upon the Utes and a pitched battle ensued that lasted two hours. The Indians wounded five soldiers and killed one. It was estimated that over 60 Indians were killed or wounded. The Indians broke and scattered just as the troops were firing their last round of cartridges.[47]

This ended the Ute raids along the Overland Trail.

On Sept. 28, 1863 Co. B 9th Kansas Cav. was relieved by Co. C 11th Ohio Cav.

On Oct. 17, 1863 Dr. J.W. Finfrock, left Ft. Laramie to take over the physicians duties, from Dr. Holladay on Dec. 18, at Ft. Halleck. His diary states:

> Oct. 17 - Left for Halleck - Cold windy day - encamped on "Chug" 20 miles from Laramie.
>
> Oct. 18 - Camped on Medicine Bow Creek - Very cold - Lost four horses and three mules over freezing and hard driving.
>
> Oct. 19 - Reached Halleck at 12 midnite.
>
> Oct. 23, 1863 Co. F, 11th Ohio Cav. arrived and Capt. Thomas L.

Mackey was the new commanding officer.

Dr. Finfrock's birthday was Dec. 9th. He was 27 years old.

1864 began with a heavy snow storm, like the year before, and Dr. Finfrock stated that the one o'clock p.m. temperature was 35° below zero.

Continuing with excerpts from Dr. Finfrock's diary:

1864-March

4 - Daily mail commenced from Denver to Halleck.

27 - One of the worst storms

28 - Storm still continuing with unabated fury. Men coming from herd got lost--Boggs came near freezing.

29 - Serenade in the evening

30 - Had a "dance" at Co. C's quarters

31 - Sutlers train arrived--Had wine in the evening--Ten "Sioux" here from Laramie

1864-April

17 - Halston; Co. F died of scurvy

18 - (other) scurvy cases improving--Capt. Clark gone to Denver for vegetable. Serenade in evening.

20 - Many emigrants passing

21 - Boys had a dance at Co. C's quarters. Six ladies present-- 65 wagons and 118 pass

23 - Dance at nite 6 ladies--Wagons passed--Extracted tooth $1.00

27 - Left at 3 p.m. for Big Laramie to see Thompson. Stopped overnight at Rock Creek. Prescribed for a pilgrims wife $10.00

28 - Left Rock Creek at 9 a.m. took dinner at Coopers Creek--Two pilgrims sick and Hallis child--Bill $20 paid--Sick man at Little Laramie, sore foot.

29 - Thompsons wound deep--Gave Mrs. Thompson prescription.

1864 May

13 - Wrote wife telling her to start as soon as convenient sent for dental instruments

15 - Had picture taken - gave copy of group of Major (Mackey) (Lt.) Drake, (Lt.) Talpey (Lt.) Johns and myself to Mrs. Clarke.

16 - Gold found on Rock Creek a few days since. Had foot race - Hemman beat Games (?) 100 yards

28 - "Dutchman" Picture man left after borrowing money and c (?) from boys--supposed to have gone on "Mission to Utah".

1864 June

8 - Horace Russell and Miss Mary McNeil were married at "stage station" by Capt. Clarke. Had dance and supper.

From June 17 to August 3, Finfrock went to Julesburg via Ft. Laramie to meet his wife and bring her back to Ft. Halleck. They returned to Ft. Halleck August 3.

1864 - August

5 - Visited old man 4 miles east of Fort injured by team running away.

7 - Old man died of injuries of breast on Friday.

10 - Old man Wm. L. Gray of Zanesville, Ohio amputated arm-- died in 2 hours.

These August entries are care given to emigrants. Mr. Gray was one of the many emigrants who accidentally shot themselves with their own guns.

There appears to have been a lull in Indian activity at this time. Some of the soldiers are prospecting, some elk hunting.

On May 22, 1864, Lewis Byrum Hull accounts in his diary that a "Drove of

4,000 or 5,000 sheep go past, going from New Mexico to California."

In the fall of 1864, Company D of 7th Iowa Cavalry arrived at Ft. Halleck under command of Captain W.D. Fouts. It was apparently a quiet time at the fort and the Iowa soldiers built a stockade around the commissary and quartermaster's buildings.[48]

On the survey of Historical Sites by the Wyoming Recreation Commission in the summer and fall of 1967 they state, "there is no evidence, based upon present available sources, that the Fort ever had a stockade surrounding it."

Many diarists among the emigrants write of many of their party having a fever and general malaise. Doctors, who were fellow travelers, were kept busy treating them, quinine being the accepted treatment. Dr. Finfrock wrote to the Boston Medical and Surgical Journal on this condition.

> "Messrs. Editors, - Our command has enjoyed excellent health for the past two years, having lost but three men from disease, out of eight companies. A species of remittent fever, called by the citizens "mountain fever," is the prevailing disease. It is easily controlled by quinine. Pneumonia is unusually fatal, several citizens having died of it within the last year in this region. Does the altitude - 6070 above the Gulf of Mexico - and the consequent rarity of the atmosphere, have any influence? This is the general impression of the inhabitants. Our meteorlogical table for the present month stands - Daily mean, about 18 degrees above zero. Coldest day last month, 13 degrees below zero. Have had no rain for ten months - but have had awful snow storms. The soil is sandy and unfit for agriculture. The country is rich in minerals; gold, iron and coal in abundance.
>
> Respectfully, & C.,
> John H. Finfrock Asst. Surg. 11th O. V. C.

This may also have been tick fever although ticks are not mentioned. Cap. Jacob L. Humfreville of Co. K 11th Ohio Cav. writes in his book, *"Twenty Years Among Our Hostile Indians"* on the upstanding character of the soldiers fighting in Indian country.

> "Of all the services required of the trooper in the military service of the United States, there was none that could compare with, or even approach, that which was required of him in fighting hostile Indians. It was a service so unlike any other that history fails to furnish a comparison.
>
> "It was necessary that the soldiers should fight these wily savages after their own peculiar mode of warfare, on their own ground, and at their own time. Preparations could not be made in advance for these fights, and the troops had to be in readiness to act on the agressive or defensive at a moments notice. They had to be ready to accept defeat, and to protect themselves instantly under all circumstances; otherwise massacre and annihilation, which so often occurred, were sure to follow...
>
> "To be good Indian fighters the troops had not only to act independently, and fight after Indian fashion, as well as secure every advantage possible, but had also to preserve their military cohesion, and obey the commands of their officers according to military tactics. Each trooper was expected to act at once as an individual, as well as a part of the whole command. When fighting Indians he should be a mixture of white

man and Indian together; he must have the courage of the Indian, and the coolness and judgement of the white man. It was absolutely necessary that he never be out generaled by the wily red men, and under no circumstances must he permit his ammunition and strength to be wasted without effect. Should it be necessary at any time for him to engage in hand to hand conflict with one or more of the savages, he must do so without hesitation or command. It was also of vital importance that he be a good shot; for his entire supply of ammunition was generally on his person, and he was supposed to make every shot tell. He should also possess great endurance and ability to go for a long time without food, water, or sleep. It was essential that he be an experienced horseman, and know just when to use the bit and spur, as every move made in battle against the warriors was the result of some maneuver on their part and had to be met instantly by the trooper.

"In fighting Indians it was often necessary for the troops to pursue and overtake them in order to give then battle; and when the Indians allowed themselves to be overtaken they were generally ready for the fight, and in such strong position that the troops were at a great disadvantage.

"After traveling a long distance, and undergoing great hardships, the troops generally arrived at the battleground in exhausted condition, both men and animals being much reduced to strength from lack of sufficient rest and food. Hence they were necessarily at a great disadvantage and were handicapped from the start. Again, the red man had two or three fresh horses with which to fight, whereas the trooper had but one, which was often jaded or worn out when the time and place to fight were at hand. Should his horse become disabled or be killed; the trooper must keep with the remainder of the command, fighting on foot, and under no circumstances permit himself to become separated from it; if he did, there was but one thing left for him, namely, to blow out his brains, for it was tacitly understood by all troopers that they must never allow themselves to be captured alive by Indians.

"To see the American trooper on the plains in a hostile Indian country, after interminable marches, wearied and reduced by exposure, protracted work, and insufficient food, with his worn-out rusty uniform, one would at first glance write him down as a slouchy kind of soldier. And this judgement would be correct if one compared him to the gayly bedizened and dashing French hussar, the prim and strait-laced British cavalryman, or the precise and machine-like German Ulhan, when on field review. But wait, and you will see in the American trooper something that can never be seen in any other. The bugle sounds; and these apparently ungraceful troopers, after long marches, and a few hours of sleep, perhaps on the wet prairie or on the snow-covered ground, will swing into their saddles with a motion that dazzles the eye by its mechanical precision.

"There they sit motionless; and scanning their faces one will observe that unmistakable look of intelligence which is not the result of discipline, but of education, and which is noticeably absent in the automatic soldiers of the Old World. When the bugle sounds again mark the soldierly ease and elegant grace with which these troopers dash off, though they have been weeks on the march, half-starved meanwhile, fighting Indians day by day, passing sleepless nights, enduring every kind of weather and privations, undaunted by pitiless frosts and snows, the dust of the great plains, or the terrible thirst of the desolate alkali deserts, and one must say, in view of their great endurance, their ever cheerful readiness and easy but perfect discipline, that American soldiers are the best in the world. It is owing to these qualifications that we had in them such excellant Indian fighters. And I venture to say that nowhere in the armies of the Old World could a body of troops be selected, of equal numbers, who would compare at all favorably with them in Indian campaigns."

Aside from Indian problems the soldiers were needed to manage civil matters. By order of Maj. Mackey, Commanding Post John H. Boalt - Lieut. 11th OVC Past Adjt. issued the order:

"Sergt. Creed Co. D 11th Ohio Vol. Cav. will proceed at once with one Corporal and nine (9) men of Co. D, OVC fully armed and equipped to North Platte Station and arrest the wagonmasters or proprietors of such trains as have in disobedience of Special Order No. 42 impressed the hay belonging to the keeper of North Platte Station. Lt. Sergt. Creed will bring the persons above mentioned to this post without delay unless they shall make immediate and satisfactory remuneration for the property destroyed."

Dr. Finfrock continues:

October - 1864

Oct. 20 - Went to North Platte to see Drago's boy - Kicked by a mule - piece of left side frontal bone size of half dollar broken in - 2 oz. brain escaped - enlarged wound in scalp and elevated the bone. No signs of compression - doing well - boy will only ? die.

Oct. 21 - Boy restless - inflamation setting in. Drago's bill $40.00 to pay it when called on.

Oct. 24 - Drago's boy getting along all right.

November - 1864

Nov. 2 - Went to Platte to see Drago's boy - is better

Nov. 6 - Terrible snow storm.

Nov. 7 - Storm continues unabated.

Nov. 17 - Snow three inches deep.

Nov. 29 - Rec'd 22 chickens from Footes.

Nov. 30 - Had dance at Russels (Hod)

December - 1864

Dec. 5 - "Muss" at Riffenbergers - Co. D 7th Iowa Cav. engaged in it - attempt to steal my chickens.

Dec. 8 - Platte Boy (Drago) getting along fine.

Dec. 10 - Storm still raging very cold.

Dec. 13 - Gave Hod Russell $45 to get fruit at Denver for me.

The last entry of Finfrock's 1864 diary:

"Number emigration passing Halleck in 1864

Wagons	4,274
Stock	50,000
Men & c	17,584

From record -- kept at Halleck"

Ft. Halleck

The beginning of 1865 again experienced bitter cold and snow. Two men froze to death in February. Lewis Byrum Hull, Co. K 11th Ohio Cav. writes in his diary:

March - 1865

Mar. 9 - Very stormy, the worst since we came to Halleck. Snow blowing all day; no wood yet; have to tear down old shop for fuel to keep from freezing. Too cold to work, so go to bed to keep warm.

Mar. 11 - Getting up wood. Mail long looked for arrives.

Mar. 12 - Snowing considerably, but pleasant. Indians killing all the stock. Capt. Rinehart killed by them.

Mar. 21 - Coach came up, but mail lost in Cache la Poudre river.

Mar. 24 - Mail up at noon, part of it wet.

In April 1865 when the Civil War was ended desertions among the soldiers were frequent as they felt that there was no longer a reason to serve even though their term of enlistment may not be up. Guards had to be placed at the stables so the horses would not be taken. Indians knew the line would be low on men.

Indians were making simultaneous attacks on stage stations and isolated farms and ranches, along the South Platte, all along the North Platte road since some emigrant trains still went that way, and on emigrant trains on the Overland Trail. And they were succeeding very well from their side of the controversy. All the trails to the west were infested with fighting Indians. Passages were blocked; the wagon trains could not carry their freight. Mail was accumulating at some places without hope of moving it on. It was no rare occasion for the stage to run through the dangerous division of Ft. Halleck, Bridger Pass and Sulphur Springs at night, the soldiers being so few in number and the distances so great; the maximum at any station being ten men.[49]

In 1865, Col. Preston B. Plumb was in command of the Fort, with five companies of cavalry. Groups of soldiers from this garrison were distributed among the stations from Ft. Collins to Green River. The section of road, immediately east of the Fort and as far west as Sulphur Springs, was considered the most dangerous part, and Col. Plumb's period of command was by far the most turbulent. All Indians during these years were conscientiously working together to stop the white man's invasion of their country.[50]

Mail destined for Salt Lake, the gold mines of Montana, Nevada and California accumulated at Ft. Halleck, where as many as half a dozen large Government wagons were needed to transport it west as far as Green River, under an escort of cavalry.[51]

In 1865, Dr. and Mrs. Finfrock became the parents of a son, William Edmund Finfrock, born at Ft. Halleck. Dr. Finfrock's tour of duty at Ft. Halleck ended in 1865.

In the spring of 1866 inspection trips were made by Army officers to locate a new army post that would be easier to supply and also to be nearer the proposed route of the coming transcontinental railroad. Ft. Halleck and Ft. Collins would be eliminated. The new location was on the Big Laramie River near where the present city of Laramie, Wyoming lies. It was first called Ft. Buford but later changed to Ft. Sanders. July 4, 1866 Ft. Halleck was abandoned and Sept. 7, 1866 Ft. Collins was abandoned.

The city of Fort Collins grew around the abandoned fort and has successfully survived. It is the home of Colorado State University.

In 1867, travelers noted thirty graves in the small Ft. Halleck cemetary. Many of them were whites killed by Indians.

Today there is one old building, possibly of the Ft. Halleck complex, still standing along with the Palm Livestock Company's ranch buildings, that occupy the original Fort grounds. This ranch is owned by Mr. and Mrs. Norman Palm.

A stone marker is located in the abandoned Fort Halleck cemetary, now a hay meadow. The inscription on the marker reads, "Fort Halleck, U.S. Military Post, July 20, 1862 - July 4, 1866. This monument was erected by the State of Wyoming and the Jacques LaRamie Chapter of the D.A.R. in 1914. Ft. Halleck, in Carbon County, is in the National Register of Historic Places.

The pleasant and prosperous city of Laramie, Wyoming, in Albany County grew up around **FORT SANDERS**. Laramie is the home of the University of Wyoming.

Of all the Fort's buildings, only one crumbling guardhouse building remains, protected from vandals by a fence. The red sandstone of which the building was made, and the white lime for morter was obtained from the near-by hills. The guardhouse originally contained two major rooms, one for guards and a slightly larger one for prisoners. Within the prison room were two small cells located in adjacent corners, and between them a wood burning stove. Four high and small windows, three still fitted with iron bars, gave the prisoners a view of Wyoming's big sky. The single exterior doorway led to the guardroom. That room had three large and low windows, without iron bars. An 1875 drawing shows the guardhouse had short stone chimneys topping each gable end, but these have since disappeared as well as the roof. The guardhouse was completed in 1869 and it was usually full! Ft. Sanders operated until 1882 then abandoned and sold.[52] The Fort Sanders Guardhouse is in the National Register of Historic Places.

Fort Sanders

Ft. Sanders

ELK MOUNTAIN STATION was a small log building, similar in design to all the other swing stations, and located a mile west of Ft. Halleck. It had its share of Indian raids and stolen stock. Elk mountain had its light side also. Pvt. Frank Tubbs, Co. K 11th Ohio Cav. wrote in his diary on Dec. 4, 1864, that the boys (from Ft. Halleck) came to a dance and had a good supper at the station. Nothing remains of this small Carbon County, station today.

14 miles beyond Elk Mountain and through Rattlesnake Canyon the small station of **PASS CREEK** was reached. In the year 1863, Indian trouble started early in the season. In an official report, dated Feb. 27, 1863, Capt. Aspah Allen states:

> "Sir: On the 19th, a report came to me that the Ute Indians had broken up the station at Pass Creek, driven off the mail stock, cut up the harness, and committed other depredations. I started Lieutenant Brandley, with all the available force here (not having but 20 horses at the post), after them. He overtook and killed some of them, and was badly wounded by a ball through the left arm. He shot the Indian through the head. I brought my herd of horses in and went out myself, and hunted the hounds three days."

Lewis Byrum Hull, Co. K 11th Ohio Cav. writes in his journal in 1865:

June - 1865

June 14 - Behymer saw two Indians this side of Pass Creek. We move into commissary and fortify.

June 15 - Was on mounted patrol all night; did not go to bed at all. No alarm. Trains camping on Pass Creek

June 16 - Cold and disagreeable; snowing nearly all day. Went up to Pass Creek. Saw that the train was organized; over a hundred wagons altogether.

June 18 - Evacuate our fortifications and return to quarters again. Don't fear any attack now.

June 19 - Have regular guard mount again. F boys fire on Arapahoes.

June 21 - Train attacked at Pass Creek. Arapahoes up for rations.

June 22 - Alarm early in morning. Stage stock run off from Elk Mountain by Indians. Our boys ran after them but could not catch them. Train fired on four miles below the fort. Issue rations to Indians. Arapahoes come up and say that Cheyennes will be here in morning.

June 23 - Alarm at midnight. All move to corral. Beashaw's herd stolen. Indians seen on buffs during evening. Squad out.

June 24 - Slept in commissary last night; no alarm of any kind. Move back to quarters.

At about this very same time, the emigrant, J. Zeamer continues with his journal:

> "Beyond Ft. Halleck our course lay due westward. For two miles or so our road was up hill and after that for a distance of about twelve miles it was down hill. The descent was gradual with no steep pitches, such as frequently occur in mountain roads. During most of the afternoon our road followed a stream whose banks were thickly lined with bushes and whose current in many places was interrupted with beaver dams."

(This was Rattlesnake Canyon and a perfect place for Indians to hide in ambush.) To continue:

> "High hills shut us completely in on both sides making our way a narrow pass. That evening we reached Pass Creek Station which was located

on the edge of a large and level plain and where the outlook gave us the idea that there was easier traveling ahead. We went into camp a short distance north from the station and because of the news which had that day reached us, took careful precautions against Indian attack and stampede. The corral was securely closed and a strong force put on guard. I was on the detail for the fore part of the night and in capping my gun just before going upon my beat accidentally discharged it. As it was already dark the report caused so much uneasiness among the nervous persons in the camp that it required several explanations to allay it."

Nothing remains of this station. The Pass Creek Ranch, in Carbon County, is owned by Mr. and Mrs. Dan Wallis.

On Wyoming highway #130, about half way between Walcott Junction and Saratoga, a monument has been erected to the Overland Trail at the site where the road crosses the trail. Trail ruts can be seen on both sides of the road.

The emigrants had left the beautiful grassy and tree covered Elk Mountain area with its abundant clear, sparkling cold water to come out onto the dry, sandy sage brush flats. Artemisia tridantata, as Fremont and many of the early travelers called this pungent, gnarled, tencious little bush. The generally smooth, fairly comfortable riding they had so far experienced, turned into a slow, bumpy, jolty, dusty struggle until the trail ruts were established.

16 miles west of Pass Creek is the **NORTH PLATTE RIVER CROSSING,** an oasis in the desert country, but a dreaded experience to face in crossing.

Aerial Photo by Les Erb, August 1989
North Platte River Crossing - Johnson's Island

Emigrant Fitzhugh Ludlow, in June 1863, crossed on the Overland Trail and his diary indicates he found the ferry very interesting and he understood the mechanism.

"We crossed the North Platte by an ingenious contrivance which I here saw for the first time, though I cannot but think that some time or other it must have been employed upon many of our narrow Eastern streams at places too deep and rapid for fording. This is a ferry-boat whose motive power was the current it had to cross. I venture to believe many of my readers as ignorant as I found myself, and endeavor to give some idea of this ingenious contrivance."

"A stout post, square-hewn from an entire trunk, about eighteen inches in diameter, is driven firmly into each of the opposite bluffs, and between the two, tautened by a windlass, extends a heavy hempen cable, roven through a pair of lignum-vitae double-blocks, of sufficient breadth of eye and depth of groove to run without friction and quite independent of each other, from post to post. The lowest sag of the cable, just over midstream, brings it within eight or ten feet of water level. So much for the locomotive apparatus."

"The ferry-boat is a rough, strongly built scow, with standing room for (one wagon) or for a four-in-hand team and as many passengers as choose to wedge themselves in between horses and piles of baggage, -- a craft apparently of ten or twelve tons burden. At each of its square ends an iron ring-bolt is securely screwed into the keelson, and to each ring a double pulley-block is attached by a hook. Through each of these blocks a stout line runs to the lower wheel of the corresponding block on the cable which spans the stream, reeves through it, and, returning inboard, passes around the second pulley of the block hooked to the ring bolt to the hand of the ferryman, or a convenient cleat, where he fastens it with a half-hitch. By substituting the cable for a boom, a sloop's main-sheet may be made to give a correct idea of this apparatus and its modus operandi. When the two sheets are of equal length, the current strikes the side of the scow at right angles and it remains stationary. To set it in motion, it is only necessary to close-haul the sheet at that end of the scow which is intended for the bow pro tempore, and slacken the one at the other end. The current now performs the function discharged by a wind a-beam in the case of sailing vessels, and takes the ferry-boat across very cleverly."

"The ferryman was a fine looking solitary, who spent months at a time camped out under the cottonwoods of the margin without seeing a face except that of the emigrant or the traveler, yet lived in great comfort and contentedness in what might be called the most out-of-the-way spot on the northern continent. His calling was certainly of the most valuable character to his fellow-men, and equally so to himself; amounting to a monopoly of the entire transit business on the most important trail between the Missouri and California. He could not fail to make a fine income, charging, I believe, $5.00 a wagon".

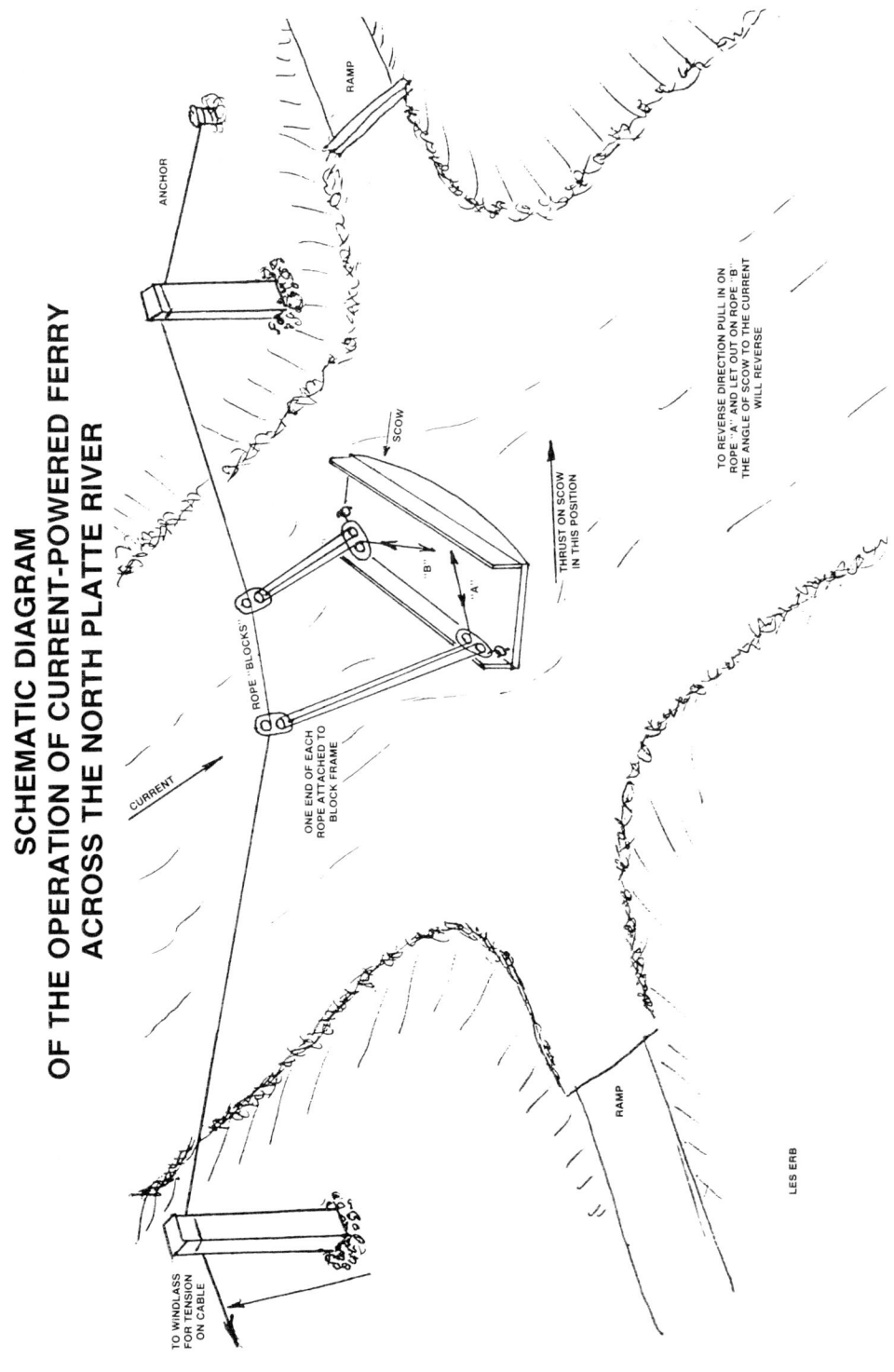

North Platte River Crossing

An interpretation of the North Platte River Ferry

J. Zeamer, the emigrant who gives an excellent description of the country in July 1865, continues in his diary,

"AT THE NORTH PLATTE RIVER. On the afternoon of the first of July, when the sun was at its hottest, we came to a point in that shadeless and utterly destitute country from which we caught glimpses of the North Platte River. Its banks were lined with large leafy cottonwood trees which formed a contrast with the country outside that was most fascinating and inviting. We hurried up our jaded animals and early that evening arrived on the banks of the stream. As its waters were deep and swift it was crossed at this point by a ferry that had a great deal to do. The river here came from the south and flowed off in a north easterly direction. A little ways to the south of the station buildings it came through a line of hills which ended abruptly, the end on the east in high rocky cliffs, (150 to 200 feet high). Several men of our train rode up the stream past these cliffs in search of a place at which it could be forded and the heavy toll rates of the ferry be avoided, but they returned without finding a fording. The large ox train which we overtook near Rock Creek, had reached the ferry before us and as the rest of the day would be required to cross it we were compelled to wait until the next morning for our turn. We drove up the stream a short distance and corralled our wagons on a piece of level ground near the base of the high rocky bluffs. In the river directly opposite these bluffs was a large island which was found to contain fairly good pasture. It also contained considerable timber and would have made an admirable camping place had it been accessible by wagon, but as that was not the case we could only make the next best use of it and put our stock upon it for the night. The channel, the island and our shore was deep and swift and in fording it many of our horses were swept down stream to the great amusement of the crowds that stood upon the bank. Driftwood being abundant the men detailed as guards that night built fires at suitable places on the island and kept them burning nearly all night, affording both light and warmth. Timorous persons in the train were fearful that the Indians might roll rocks from the tops of the bluffs, but the night passed without incident except that some of the horses becoming dissatisfied on the island waded and swam back to the shore. These were secured as soon as they came into camp and taken back to the island. The next day was Sunday, July 2nd. Sunday is a day of rest the world over but this particular Sunday proved anything but a day of rest for us. We were up with the dawn, broke camp early and hurried to the ferry in order to get ahead of the government train, which was also on hand clamoring for the right of way and claiming it by reason of being in government employ. It was a crossing experience much like that which we had at the Missouri and also at the South Platte, but the immigrants out numbered the government train and got the preference. The river was narrow and the ferry hauls only short but the ferry authorities charged four dollars for crossing a wagon not including the team. This was a heavy expense but could not easily be avoided. What expense could be saved was saved, and nearly all of our stock crossed above our camping place where the river was shallow enough to be fordable but where the nature of the banks made it inaccessible to wagons. I forded the river early with my team and was set to work hauling wagons from the ferry landing to the top of the hill. The ferry men worked hard and crossed wagon after wagon rapidly."

The good sized island in the Platte, is called Johnson Island. Some of the emigrants in another July 1865 train forded their wagons across to the island then across the water on the other side to get out on the west bank. They had some difficulty doing this because the banks were much steeper.

The ferrymen were Ed. Bennett and Frank Ernest. The 1863 emigrant mentioned only one ferryman operating this unusual ferry boat. A 1933 issue of the Cheyenne Tribune records a ferry operator whose name was Ed Ferguson. It is not known who built the boat. Bennett and Ernest took over in 1864.

For the emigrants to find so modern a ferry out in the western wilderness, 768 miles from their jumping-off place of St. Joseph, Missouri, must have given them a mental lift. However, some had misgivings about trusting their worldly possessions to the boat but it seems that very few mishaps occurred.

Albert D. Richardson, the diarist for the Schuyler Colfax party, writes in his 1865 journal:

"On a June day, cold as November, at the crossing of the North Platte River, we stood gazing at a party of recusant Mormans returning to the States, when running horses, reports of guns and loud yells announced an Indian attack. The wagons of the emigrants, with the women and children, were at waters edge. Beyond them in a little valley, were grazing their weary horses and mules, well guarded by the men. The Indians came over a hill, in a sharp dash upon the animals, hoping to stampede and secure them. The soldiers of our escort rushed to the ferry-boat to participate in the fray: but I reconciled myself to the decrees of Providence, content to smell the battle afar off--indeed with a secret wish that I were too far off to smell it at all. The river was a safe barrier between the savages and ourselves; for the waters were high, and a coach, horses, mail and all, which had gone to the bottom a week before, was still buried in its depths."

In late June 1866, a diarist for the Lewis-Burt command writes:

"...June twenty second we reached the North Platte River at the crossing....Now the rushing torrent was too swift and deep to be crossed, except by a ferry boat worked by cables and pulleys.

"For so large a command to be carried over there was a great danger to be apprehended. After waiting a few days, hoping for a fall in the river, the perilous trip began....

"It was not long before a crash came. In a second we saw the boat overturned in the stream; the white wagon top was carried down; mules quickly disappeared and alas, also the three men who were with the wagon. All vanished like a flash. The wagon proved to be one belonging to Company F, and with it was Sergeant St. John and two other good men of the company." Another reference said the rope broke.

The crossing of the North Platte offered a challenge, and struck fear into the emigrants. Their diaries concentrated on this and overlooked other details of interest to historians. Nothing is known of the exact location of the stage station nor of activities there except one traveler said they "ate dinner at the ferry station" after arriving from the east. However it is known that the station was on the east bank. There is a paucity of references to graves and names and dates carved into the sheer sandstone cliff by the river's edge. Debbie Chastain of Saratoga tells us that the dark colored names and dates, looking like desert patina, were painted on with wagon grease. And did no one know of the steep hidden "stairway" in the crevice in this vertical cliff?

On August 27, 1933 was held a dedication ceremony, under the auspices of the Rawlins and Saratoga Lions Clubs, in cooperation with the Wyoming State Landmarks Commission, making the North Platte River Crossing a State Historical Park. The eight acres of land at this site was a deeded gift to the State of Wyoming by Mr. and Mrs. Isadore Bolten. The featured speaker at the ceremony was a Wyoming pioneer, W.O. Owen of Los Angeles and Laramie, telling of the time he, as a 9 year old boy, on June 9, 1886, with his family crossed the river. He recounted the stop of the wagon train at the Platte, told of the ferry and of driving the cattle and horses across the river, and said, "You can imagine when cattle and horses and mules and wagons and people attempted to ford that pandemonium really existed." This was 1886 and must have been some of the last trains on the Overland Trail. The site was a gift to the State of Wyoming by Mrs. Ella Mary Davis and her son Roblin H. Davis in memory of husband and father, John C. Davis, a Carbon County pioneer banker, stockman, and merchant.[53]

On top of the bluff is the fenced cemetery. The stones of the graves have been realigned and headstones put back in place. There are eight known graves and historian, L.C. Bishop, in 1929 recorded the legible names and dates: (1) "LeRoy W. Morrison, Died, May ---", (2) "J.S. White, Died ---18th, 1863", (3) "George Layne" (4) "William M. Donald, Killed by Indians, June 1864", (5) "John Hunter", Aged 17 years, Died August 10, 1865", (6) stone in place, marks gone; (7) headstone broken off, marks gone, (8) "In memory of Mary E. Stockton, Died August 10, 1865."

Just to the north of the cemetery is the large granite monument, with the large round bronze covered wagon plaque and the inscription, "Overland Trail Platte River Crossing Erected in Memory of Those Brave Pioneers Who Passed This Way to Win and Hold The West. This Site a Gift to Wyoming From Ella Mary Davis and Family in Memory of Her Husband a Pioneer Banker Merchant and Stockman of Carbon County."

The North Platte River Crossing in Carbon County is in the National Register of Historic Places. The ranchland surrounding this Park is owned by Burton Tuttle of Saratoga, WY.

Today the Platte Crossing is again a lovely, quiet, tree lined river bottom. The names and dates on the cliffs speak to us from the past and the graves on the bluff keep their eternal vigil. Some of the stones that once supported the posts and cables on the ferry are the only things left, but these have been moved from the actual site of the ferry.

On November 24, 1892, the *Saratoga Sun* (Saratoga, Wyoming) printed a story, related by Joe J. Hurt, of a thrilling encounter with Indians in which he participated in 1865 on the Overland Trail between the Platte River crossing and Sulphur Springs stage station, about 30 miles south of Rawlins.
Mr. Hurt relates:

> "Overland stage station which occupied ground on the North Platte River several miles below Saratoga, and which is now on what is known as the "Pick" ranch, was in 1865 known as "North Platte".
>
> "I was there in June 1865, and the station then had been cut off

from communications with Sulphur Springs, west of us, for three weeks by Indians.

"Mail after mail came in for the west until a great pile of it accumulated. One day our superintendent decided to make a night run and get the mail through. That night three big coaches and two big cages were piled full of mailsacks, and six horses were attached to each. There was a lady in camp, on her way to join her husband in San Francisco, and when all was ready she begged so hard to be allowed to go that the superintendent finally permitted her to crawl in on top of the mail in one of the coaches.

"It was 11 o'clock at night when we started out and we were off like the wind. The night was a beautiful one with a full moon.
(Indians usually did not attack at night, however, moonlight nights were favorable for their depredations.)

"Our nerves were wrought up to a high pitch as we bowled along over the hard roads.

"I was a youngster at the time, but was one of a party of eight detailed to accompany the expedition as a guard. I had never had much experience as yet with Indians but I was wide awake and ready. I could see shadowy forms moving parallel with us on either side, and I well knew what it was traveling so stealthily along out there, but no one said anything. It was too exciting a time to talk. Most of us were probably speculating on our chances of being murdered--perhaps burned at the stake.

"About 3 o'clock in the morning we passed Pine Grove station, where the man in charge had been killed, the station burned, and the stock stolen sometime previous. It was a suggestive remnant of what might soon be our fate.

"Nothing had yet happened to us as day began to break, and we began to be hopeful that we would yet make it without trouble. Vain hope!

"We had as a driver of one of the coaches a young man whose name I have forgotton, if I ever knew it, but who went by the name of "Heenan" on account of his great strength and courage. There wasn't a man in the camp could handle him, and he was a superb driver.

"Our road went up through a narrow canyon several miles long; the walls of which rose gently upward on either side to about 100 yards from the roadway. As we were driving through this, just after day break, the Indians opened fire on us from either side. At the first volley two or three of our men were killed and it was a running fight from there to the top of the canyon. At one time it looked as though Heenan's outfit was gone. I saw an Indian with a colts revolver in his hands, lying prone on the bank of the canyon, his elbows resting on the ground taking deliberate aim at Heenan. He fired five shots in quick succession, all of which struck the box just behind Heenan. The Indian saw he had not made enough allowance for the motion of the stage, and mended his aim sufficiently that the sixth bullet broke Heenan's right arm above the elbow.

"It fell helpless at his side but nothing daunted, he caught all the lines in his left hand and never even slacked his pace. Just then the man by his side was struck by a bullet and toppled over into the stage boot. He would have fallen out to the ground, but Heenan caught him with one foot and held him in. A few moments later three of the horses in his lead teams were shot down. Heenan jumped to the ground, cut the four horses loose and drove to the top of the canyon with two horses, and with but one useful arm.

"The sun was just rising as we gained the head of the canyon and drove out on the level prairies. In hardly more time than it takes to tell it, we formed a corral of our coaches, placed the horses inside it, piled the mail sacks into a circular breastwork, and prepared to sell our lives as dearly as possible. The lady passenger had her handkerchief about Heenan's fractured arm, which was all the attention his injury received for more than 12 hours.

"Heenan seemed equal to any emergency. It was he who gave orders what to do and how to do it. The man in charge of the guards gave way and all looked to the young Hercules for inspiration and order.

"What a horrible day that was! A hot, broiling sun, not water or shelter, and our little party surrounded by approximately 500 hooting, yelling, murderous savages, who all day long, without intermission, rode around and around us, raining arrows and bullets on us like hail. When any of our men were killed, their bodies were piled on top of the mail sacks to help keep out the bullets. It was hard, but it was necessary.

"I have forgotten the lady's name, but she had nerve, I can tell you. She was busy all day long, loading guns and carrying ammunition. When she attemped to go to the cages for new supply, we begged and implored her to keep out of danger. "No" she said "I am only a woman and if I am killed I will not be missed, but if one of you men are killed that means just one less fighting man!" Back and forth, in a shower of arrows and bullets, that woman went fearlessly for ammunition and she was tireless and brave through it all. Before night the men worshipped her for her courage and invaluable assistance.

"About sundown the red devils pulled off, and seemed to be inclined to give up the fight. They had been kept at bay all day and we had sent a lot of their braves to the happy hunting ground. They had got some of us too, and the rest of us, thought there would be no hope--that when night came they would come down on us and we would be overpowered and annihilated.

"But when they withdrew at sundown, Heenan said "Up now and let's get out of this. Hitch up the horses, throw in the mail and we'll make another try at getting to Sulphur Springs." We flew at it and were soon ready to travel. How we drove! And how our nerves tingled! We were all nerves, hopes and fears in this attempt to escape the jaws of death.

"It was another silent drive without a redskin in sight, until it grew dark, when there were again those stealthy, shadowy forms keeping pace with us on either side, and we drove like the wind. However the Indians did not attack again until we were about a mile and a half from Sulphur Springs Station, when they opened another bombardment.

"It was down hill to the station and we kept going as fast we could. Meanwhile the men at the station heard the fighting going on, and when they rode out to take part the Indians again retreated. We drove the last mile to the station as fast as our horses could run and strange to say, we did not suffer even a scratch from their last bombardment.

"And our brave lady did not suffer the least injury in all the fighting, and lived to join her husband safely in San Francisco.

"The Indians must have decided we were too tough a crowd to pursue farther, for we were not molested again on that trip."

14 miles west from the North Platte crossing, the **SAGE CREEK** stage station was located, not on Sage Creek, but actually on the northeast bank of Miller Creek. This small log - pine and aspen - building, 25 x 60 feet, with a dirt and pole roof and an adobe fireplace in the northeast corner, was completed May 2, 1861[54] (?). On a half acre plot, out in the middle of a large, dry, open desert flat. Adjoining the building, on the north and east, was a pole or log corral, large enough to hold ten to twenty horses and mules. A well, completely gone now, was dug in the north bank of the creek, upstream, from the corral. The stream is dry part of the year.

At this little station, the visibility in all directions was very good and in return, Indians could watch every move that was made. About 3 miles to the north is the long, high Sheep Mountain rim with an interesting slide on the south side, almost directly in line with the station location. This slide is an area where a large chunk of the cap rock, with the accompanying dirt, has dropped down, in place, leaving a large notch in the rim. To the southwest is Miller Hill and about 18 miles to the west, the Continental Divide crosses the Atlantic Rim.

Photo by Les Erb

Sage Creek Stage Station site

This part of the trail was desolate with almost no forage and very little water for the traveler's animals.

A reference was made to the burning of this station by Ute Indians shortly after it was built. The attendants were reportedly killed.[55]

In 1863, the Sage Creek station and a wagon train were attacked, killing the station keepers and several emigrants and wounding others. The station was burned.

In 1865, for a 55 mile stretch of the road west of Ft. Halleck, Indians were concentrating their attacks.

The 2nd of June, 1865, two emigrants, traveling in the vicinity of Sage Creek, were shot full of arrows, one was scalped, and their horses stolen.

At daylight on the morning or June 8 of this same year, Lt. Brown of the Ft. Halleck command, reported,

> "At daylight the morning of the 8th instant the detachment at Sage Creek station was attacked by about 100 Indians. After one hour's severe fighting they were compelled to evacuate in consequence of a deficiency in ammunition. The men were all well mounted and accompanied by two citizens, names unknown. The moment they left the station they were completely surrounded. There ensued a desperate fight; the detachment retreated toward Pine Grove Station. The Indians followed them for eight miles, killing George Bodine and Perry Stewart, wounding and capturing Orlando Ducket, wounding Corp. W.H. Caldwell and Private William Wilson, all of Company K, Eleventh Ohio Volunteer Cavalry. The two citizens were also missing. Corporal Caldwell and Private Wilson escaped to Pine Grove Station. They and the detachment then retreated to Sulphur Spring Station, taking the detachment at Bridger's Pass with them. Next morning they started back, commanded by Sergeant McFaddin, who was up the road on escort duty (for the Colfax party) with ten men of Company K, Eleventh Ohio Volunteer Cavalry. They found the bodies of Perry Stewart and George Bodine lying in the road, horribly mutilated, the latter scalped. They also found one citizen. The other citizen and Private Ducket of Company K could not be found. My opinion is that they were buried in Sage Creek Station, which was found burnt by the command on their return. Ten of the men have returned to this post; the balance are doing all they can to keep open the road, but the force is inadequate to cope with the number of Indians..."

Ducket returned later, unharmed, having managed to escape. The station was rebuilt each time it burned.

In the 1865 list of Holladay's losses to the government (see page 103 of this book), he listed on September 4, 1865, the burned station and 2 men killed. This may have been the June 8th event.[56]

J. Zeamer again recounts his travels,

> "Early in the day we overtook and passed the large ox train. Passing it was considered a stroke of policy as it gave us first chance to the eligible camping places, but it was not without cost for the hurry necessary to accomplish it wearied our stock and make it less valuable for the after part of day. By mid afternoon we reached Sage Creek. Sage Creek wasn't a stream but the dried-up course of a stream which here crossed our road and gave the place its name. There had been a stage

station here until about a month before we passed when the Indians wiped it off the earth, killing two men and burning the buildings. It was a very warm day and we halted for a little while and from a water hole, which was by courtesy called a spring, we gave them water to drink mixed with flour. The country was now one vast wilderness of sage brush. In every direction, and as far as we could see, this dusty gray shrub covered the landscape and scented the air. We had been meeting it for several weeks but never before in such great abundance and never before was its scent so strong and disagreeable. Our train became stretched out along the road for miles, the cattle teams falling far behind the horse teams. No particular effort was made to keep the teams in a compact line as it was believed that better progress could be made by traveling in a sort of go-as-you-please style. It was probably more of a go-as-you-can style. While we were not entirely out of danger but had no reason to fear attack during the day time and concerned ourselves chiefly about reaching the next favorable camping ground. The hot sun, hard driving and lack of feed was too much for the team of which Asbury Wanless had charge and they gave out. They were attached to the heaviest wagon in the outfit. Not withstanding the fact that my team had hauled quite a number of wagons from the ferry in the morning, they stood the drive well and seemed vigorous. To facilitate our progress Cotterill ordered that Wanless and I exchange wagons which we did and got along better".

No doubt there are several graves in the vicinity of this station. One that is known was that of Carl Oscároose. All locations unknown.

This station site is on public land and can be reached by taking the Bolten-Saratoga road that exits east from the Sage Creek road, south from Rawlins, just past the Teton Reservoir. Travel about three and one-half miles and the site is about one-half mile south of the road. Today nothing remains, except possibly the faint indication of a foundation and the very smallest bits of midden-charred wood, glass etc. In the center of the area, the Carbon County Historical Society has placed an upright piece of 3 inch diameter, 3 feet tall pipe, painted yellow and on which the words **SAGE CREEK** are painted. Trail ruts can be seen in places.

Photo by Les Erb
Overland Trail Ruts and Marker
from the Sage Creek Road

One and one-quarter miles south of this exit, on the Sage Creek Road, at a stream bed a concrete post with the **OVERLAND TRAIL** imprint can be seen on the west side. This marks the trail and ruts are visible.

The Sage Creek Station, in Carbon County, is in the National Register of Historic Places.

From Sage Creek across 10 miles of dry, dusty, sagebrush, greasewood and rabbit brush country **PINE GROVE** was reached. The station was located at the foot of Miller Hill, out in a grassy meadow on the bank of Pine Grove Creek, near a beautiful grove of evergreen and quaking aspen trees. At times water and green grass greeted the travelers. In mid-summer it was dry. The cabin, made of logs from trees on the nearby mountain, was of the traditional size and shape.

In May of 1867, A.K. McClure wrote in his account, *3000 Miles Through the Rocky Mountains*, that there were less than 300 troops between Denver and Salt Lake, a distance of 600 miles and of that number less than one-third were mounted.

On June 5 of this same year George Ingman, a Holladay Division Agent, sent a communique to James Stewart, also a Division Agent, that, "I was attacked yesterday by a party of about seventeen Indians, between here (Sulphur Springs) and Pine Grove. Fought all day from nine until dark. Nichols was killed. Another man in the employ of Mr. Wilson was killed. Myself wounded in the right arm. They took fourteen head of stock. We must have a larger escort from here to the Platte. The country is full of them. The boys at Bridger's Pass fought all day. Five Indians killed."

He mentions nothing about Pine Grove being burned but McClure's account states, "...When we neared (Pine Grove) it was in ruins, and the remains still burning." He also told of the Indian atrocities done to the keeper's pet dog. This shows up Cremony's evaluation of the Indians.

The station was rebuilt.

Many years ago graves with headstones were seen on a small ridge about 100 yards north of the station. Now these headstones are gone and the graves are not discernable.

Photo by Les Erb
Site of Pine Grove Stage Station

On June 15, 1867, a letter written by Mormon Elder Zebulon Jacobs described an incident, "At the next place we came to were the charred remains of a ranch; here the proprietor had taken the precaution to make an underground fort, with port holes just above the surface of the ground. He informed me that here four Indians were killed, but the keeper escaped. Everything was burned. Pine Grove Station was still smoking, though burned to the ground."

Today the station site is marked with a yellow **PINE GROVE** pipe. A few small pieces of logs remain. To the east of the pipe there is evidence of an excavated area about 8 feet square and now only about 18 inches deep.

The Pine Grove site in Carbon County is on the private ranch of Mr. and Mrs. Bruce Thayer. The station is in the National Register of Historic Places.

Photo by Les Erb
From the top of the Continental Divide looking east
to Elk Mountain. Road shown is not the Overland Trail.

After leaving Pine Grove station a steep ridge of hills was crossed then the travelers went down into a beautiful, wide sage covered valley where the **CONTINENTAL DIVIDE** was crossed. This is a gradual rise that is barely discernable except for knowing that the water courses run to the east and to the west. On the east, Sage Creek flows to the North Platte River thence to the Mississippi and Gulf of Mexico. On the west the Muddy Creek flows into the Little Snake River thence to the Colorado River and on to the Pacific Ocean. Towering on the west side of this valley is the Atlantic Rim and on the south and east is Miller Hill in the Sierra Madre Range.

This country was and still is the home of antelope, deer, some elk and sage chickens. For many years the American Bison, or Buffalo as they are commonly called, had roamed this part of the country but by the time the Overland Trail was established in Wyoming they had almost all been killed. The authors often found bison horns and all or parts of skulls.

Photo by Les Erb
Remains of Log Cabin at site of Bridger's Pass Stage Station

Photo by Les Erb
Yellow Pipe Trail Marker at Bridger Pass Station

About one and one-half miles south-west from the summit of the Divide and nine miles from Pine Grove the small log **BRIDGER PASS STATION** was reached. It was built a half mile west of the main trail in a site that provided good grass and plenty of water from springs and a small stream. Bunch grass between the sage offered good grazing for the animals. The stage coaches left the trail on the access road to go into and out from the station.

In the winter of 1864 Lee Humfreville, in *Twenty Years Among Our Hostile Indians* tells us,

> "In the winter when snows were deep the teams frequently became exhausted, or the driver lost his way. Then the stage was abandoned, and the driver and as many of the passengers as could mount the animals did so, going to the nearest station; but when lost they could, by following the trail, return to the nearest station whence they came. When the snow was very blinding those on foot were instructed by the driver to take hold of an animal's tail and hold on until the nearest station was reached. On one occasion, during a blinding snow storm, when going through Bridger's Pass, the horses arrived at the foot of a hill in an exhausted condition. The driver requested the passengers to get out of the stage and walk to the top of the hill. This they refused to do. Before they realized what had happened, the driver left the box, un-hitched the team, and mounting one horse and leading the others was on his way back to the last station, leaving the coach and passengers in the snow. When they realized the situation there was consternation among them. The driver on arriving at the station reported what had occured, whereupon the men hitched up twelve fresh animals and brought the passengers in. The latter could not have returned alone as the blizzard was blinding...It sometimes happened that stages became lost in a blizzard, remaining out twenty-four or thirty-six hours before they were able to proceed."

On July 2, 1865, the interesting emigrant J. Zeamer wrote of a sad incident. In his train was a good natured, well liked fellow emigrant who was a deaf mute by the name of Calvin Wall. His wife was also a deaf mute. They had four small children. Wall drove a team of mules and he also had an oxen team driven by another deaf mute whom he employed. His mules being faster, he was quite a distance ahead of the ox team. It was late afternoon when he came to a camping place near Pine Grove. He took care of the mules then decided to walk back to meet his driver and to hurry the ox team along. He came over a hill just as another emigrant, named Jo Watts, was coming up. In the dusk of the evening Watts and his wife mistook Wall for an Indian. Watts called out but of course Wall could not hear nor call back and since Watts got no response he fired two shots. Wall was seriously wounded and was placed in his wagon. He lived through the night and the next day the train started on. About sundown of the second day Calvin Wall died. The next day was the 4th of July but there was no celebration, only mourning for their friend as his body was carried over the Continental Divide.

When they reached Bridger Pass Station they paused to water their teams in the stream and J. Zeamer wrote of seeing some small water wheels that were made by the station hands or soldiers. "These under the current of the stream were turning rapidly and attracted attention and elicited comments from immigrants as they passed."

The funeral train started on and Mr. Zeamer again writes:

"...soon afterwards we came to Bridger's Pass of which we had heard much. It consisted of a narrow defile which wound through a range of barren mountains that seemed flat upon the top. Its general course was a little west of north, and our road through it was down hill all the way with frequent steep pitches. A crooked stream flowed through it Up on a high point on the left of the Pass the edge of a large bank of sand was visible from the road below. This had been drifted there by the winds in the same manner as the winds drift snow banks in winter time. On the day following we got out beyond the Pass and looked back over these hills and then a large area of shifting sand dunes was revealed to us."

At the west end of Muddy Creek Canyon they arrived at Sulphur Springs Station. Mr. Zeamer continues:

"A short distance beyond the station, on the left hand side (south-west) of the road, was a small hill with a rounded top on which were a number of graves. Here our train halted and to the graves already there added another --that of Calvin Wall. Several days before, the Powell train with which we had traveled, buried a child in this same little cemetery in the wilderness."

In the fall of 1866, a visitng English author, William Hepworth Dixon, writes of travling across the Overland Trail in a light wagon. He states:

"...Paddy Blake, an Irishman, from Virginia City, keeps a ranch near the summit of Bridger's Pass, in a field which is the very model of desolation. He lives at Fort Laramie; by trade he is a sutler, but he finds it pays better to sell bad spirits to the teamsters at three dollars a bottle, and cake-tobacco for chewing at six dollars a pound, than to deal in decent stores among soldiers and civilians at the fort. A small log-hut contains his stock of poisons, which he vends to the passserby, including Utes and Cheyennes, about four months in the year, while the roads are open and the snow is off the ground; taking buffalo and beaver skins from the red man, dollars and kind (the kinds too often stolen) from the whites."

In early June 1867, A.K. McClure who with his wife was traveling by coach, in the Continental Divide area, had come upon fresh evidence of a party of raiding Indians who were not far ahead. As the McClure party got within sight of Bridger's Pass Station they saw it in flames. The Indians had not seen them and had gone down through the Pass. As the coach reached the head of the Muddy Canyon they saw a light in a deserted ranch, or cabin, across the Muddy Creek. By this time the Indians, upon hearing the coach, were caught by surprise but knowing they could not attack, withdrew and in so doing set fire to the cabin.

Edward Tierney of Rawlins states that a cabin was built at this location on the Muddy Creek by a trapper and trader, named Satiel, but there are no records of it in the Land Office. It is a possibility that this is the cabin mentioned in the above last two accounts, however, it does not seem likely that the liquor merchant would have a cabin across the creek from the main road when there was no bridge.

Apparently, in the authors' young days in that country all physical evidence and any remembrance of a cabin at the head of the Muddy Canyon had long disappeared. Old timers never mentioned the site.

The Indian depredations early in 1867 were virtually a continuation of the Sioux difficulties in the Powder River country of the year before. It was apparently at this time when Bridger's Pass was burned that 2 men were also killed and stock driven off. Citizens far and wide were reacting to the wide spread Indian wars. Central City, Colorado raised $5000 to be paid for Indian scalps, at the rate of $25 a scalp, with ears attached![57]

Today at the Bridger's Pass Station site in Carbon County, a small two room log cabin still stands but in a dilapidated state. A short distance to the northeast of this cabin are some logs and a dug-out place that looks as if it may have been a cellar. It was always known to us as Black Gus's Cabin. The yellow pipe trail marker placed in front of the cabin was erected by the Carbon County Historical Society.

There are early graves but exact locations are not known and sage brush has overgrown the area.

Bridger's Pass Station is in the National Register of Historic Places.

The ranch land is owned by Burton Tuttle of Saratoga, WY.

Photo by Les Erb
Concrete Trail Marker on the south side of the pass

Just west of the Pass about half way to the head of the Muddy Canyon a concrete **OVERLAND TRAIL** post has been installed by the side of the road. This type of trail marker was also erected by the Carbon County Historical Society.

Head of Muddy Canyon. Site of Muddy Creek Massacre.

The head of the Muddy Creek Canyon is a large open area on the north side of Muddy Creek. On a beautiful clear day in August 1863 a large covered wagon train, under military escort, had come through the Pass and stopped here to fill their water barrels, but certainly with no thought of the impeding tragedy. The day book of the Commanding Officer of Sulphur Springs Station, Major R.A. Morse, records that Indians had been seen all around but scouts had reported no war parties so travel seemed safe. Suddenly Cheyenne and Sioux Indians appeared on the bluffs and sent arrows and bullets flying into the train. Part of the escort took after the attacking redskins. As they got over the rim they were immediately surrounded by more Indians but instead of a full ambush developing they were just trapped from returning to the fight.

With the escort split and disorganization reigning among the wagons, Indians attacked from all directions causing many casualties. The soldiers and emigrants were able to get into a defensive position against the steep rocky rim on the north of the canyon and held back the Indians with steady and accurate fire for a time. Soon the Indians, by sheer force and manpower, forced themselves into the line and it then came to hand to hand combat.

The sound of gunfire was heard at Sulphur Springs and Major Morse and his troops of A, C and D Companies of the First Kansas Volunteer Cavalry went to the assistance of the train. The Indians withdrew when the troops arrived.

The day book accounts that 29 white men, women and children were killed, 17 severely wounded and 10 slightly hurt. 90 Indians were reported killed or wounded but accurate numbers were difficult to determine since Indians never left their own casualties on the battlefield.

The whites were probably all buried there but it has always been wondered if some have been buried in the little cemetary at Sulphur. The site of the **MUDDY CREEK MASSACRE** is so thickly covered with sagebrush and rock which has washed down from the canyon walls that grave sites are obliterated.

Sketch by M.D. Houghton
Sulphur Springs Station looking east up the Muddy

Photo by Les Erb

Sulphur Springs Ranch today

The authors of this book wish to clarify a misidentified picture of an original sketch by M.D. Houghton, entitled "Bridger Pass Station on the Overland Stage Route" issued by Courtesy of University of Wyoming Library. This picture has appeared in several western history publications under this title but, as you can see in this book it is properly identified as the **SULPHUR SPRINGS STAGE STATION** on the Overland Stage Route. We had the privilege of growing up on this ranch, which our grandparents owned, and we know this country well.

Photo by Les Erb
The Muddy Creek Canyon looking east from Sulphur Springs

THE SPIRIT OF SULPHUR SPRINGS STATION
Original poem by Jean Stewart Tallman

I am the Spirit of Sulphur Springs Station,
A stop on the "Overland Trail."
I sit at the mouth of my canyon
And review the past in detail.

My life has been an adventure,
Like unto the struggles of man
Wild, boistrous, ambitious, contentious,
Mild, gentle, unselfish or kind.

I've seen all the history in making,
That surged and swelled round my door
And now in the quiet of the evening,
I dream of the days of yore.

The Red Man loved my canyon
With its stillness and its shade
Where wild life hid and made its home
In every grassy glade.

The White Man came down my canyon,
And blazed his "Overland Trail,"
To the gold of the far Pacific,
And an Empire in travail.

He came with his scouts and his caravans,
His pony and his stage,
He sat him down beside me
To rest on his "Overland Trail."

His soldiers came to guard him,
And made their homes with me,
And their old dug-outs and their tunnels,
Are still quite plain to see.

These pioneers struggled westward.
They fought and bled and died,
To attain what was all around them-
But hidden from their eyes.

They carved their names on my balanced rocks.
They buried their dead on my hills.
Their wheels cut deep in my valleys,
And these records remain with me still.

They passed away with their strivings,
And a gentler time set in-
*A sweet soul came to dwell with me
Who spoke ever of Peace and Good-will.

And brave men still stood by me,
Who looked Life square in the eye,
And gamely matched her dealings,
And did not cringe or cry.

So I sit beside my canyon,
At the end of an Autumn day,
And dream of the life of struggle
That one time passed my way.

The stars came out in their glory
And the moon beams clear as day,
The poor-will calls in the valley,
So sleepy and far away.

So I dream my dreams by Jim Bridger's Pass
And a new age surges nigh,
I smile and nod by my canyon.
It too will soon pass by.

JST - A daughter of the Ranch Jean Stewart Tillman *"The sweet soul," my mother

Sulphur Springs Station

Balanced Rock
still stands but the wind, rain and
snow have erased the names

Rifle Pit
from which the tunnel went
to the spring of water below

Photo by Les Erb

Sulphur Springs Station

Our Aunt Jean Tallman wrote of the Sulphur Springs Ranch in 1935, "From perhaps 1849 the Bridger Pass Trail was in constant use by the white man.

"Proof of this are the names and dates found all along the Trail but especially on a large sandstone monolith we called, "Balanced Rock". This is located, close to the Overland Trail ruts, about two miles west of Sulphur Springs ranch, high up on a bank of the Muddy Creek near a fording place. Thirty-five years ago this large rock was well covered with names and dates but time and erosion have done their work of obliteration till now only a few of them remain. The earliest date that was seen on the rock a quarter of a century ago was that of "1849" showing the use of the Trail that summer. This name and date (now lost) may, without much stretch of the immagination, have been put there by a member of Captain Evan's Party. (Doubtful. The Cherokee Trail was further south than that. I have seen it often. J.S.T.)

The following is a list of the names and dates still on the rock in the summer of 1929, the time I recorded the names.

"July 4, 1851"	"From Mo. to California, June 12, 1854"
"John Bacon, July 7, 1859"	"P.M. Johnson, July 14, 1859"
"M.G. (?) S. Aingen (?)	June 21, 1860"
"M.B. (?) Sutting	June 21, 1860"
"L. Walker	June 4, 1860"
"J.B. Moffat	June 21, 1860"
"M.S., July 24, 1864"	"Isaac Eton 1865"
"W.R. Inn, June 4, 1868"	From Mo."
"W.R. Sutting, June 1868"	J.M. Turner
"L.T. 1868 Mo."	June 29, 1868"

The coming of Holladay's Mail Service in 1862 heralded the time the Sulphur Springs Ranch, as a human habitation, came into use.

The Sulphur Springs Stage Station had been built for use by the military, and as a Home station for Holladay's Mail Route, about July 11, 1862. The 1st Kansas Volunteers, commanded by Major R.S. Morse, was headquartered there. Its position at the western end of the Muddy Creek Canyon made it a very strategic point from which to guard the travel through the canyon and as far northeast as Bridger's Pass and down the creek to the west. There were many springs located at Sulphur, one a deep clear spring for drinking water and farther away in the banks were many fast flowing Sulphur Springs which fact gave the place its name. There were also level bottom lands covered with blue stem grass among the sage brush, that would provide abundant and nutritious horse and oxen feed.

So it came to pass that this "Home" station was established. In order to guard the mail properly from the extremely hostile and awakened Indians, soliers were distributed along the Trail at different stations and Sulphur Springs, being one of the most important points to be guarded because of the deep canyon through which the road had to pass, had a rather large contingent. The remains of the soldiers' camp at Sulphur is still traceable.

On top of the knoll, just above the station buildings are the remains of three lookout depressions. There is also the remains of the tunnel, from the spring of good water at the base of the hill, up to the top at the eastern-most pit. This tunnel was actually a trench covered with boards and brush. At one time part of a support post for the boards could still be seen on the side of the trench.

There were some eight or ten dugout depressions with stone masonry breastwork. the location of some of these was up on the side of the north canyon

Sulphur Springs Station

wall just east of the mouth. With these and the rifle pits on the south of the station, the soldiers could see both sides of the canyon for quite a distance east. Two miles west of the Station, at the Muddy Creek ford near the Balanced Rock was another rifle pit, with the stone breastwork, up on the side of the hill. This gave a good view of the Trail toward Washakie station and back toward Sulphur.

Just north of the above mentioned spring was a level meadow which was used for the "Elephant Corral" so-called, for covered wagons, and the ever needed blacksmith shop. There was a toll bridge on the creek at the eastern end of the "Elephant Corral" which cost 50 cents per team to cross. The road down the canyon was wide enough for two wagons to travel abreast, an old timer said. This may have been in certain parts but not all the way. Later, when the land where the "Elephant Corral" had been located, was plowed, it proved to be a perfect mine of relics, many of which have been donated to the Rawlins Historical Museum. Among them were sword hilts, broken swords, army pistols, oxen shoes, ox bows, innumerable mule and horse shoes.

The Muddy Creek has made many changes in its course in the more than a century since covered wagon days so that the present road down the canyon does not follow the emigrant trail at all points. However, east and west of the canyon the old trail can be followed in many places. Most of the old trail does not follow any present day road in Wyoming. Old trails can often be traced by the tall variety of brush which grows on them.

Some of all this can be seen today — 120 years after their use.

The emigrant, Ruth Schackelford, writes that their large train of 200 wagons passed through Sulphur Springs on July 24, 1865. She describes the station as having "a two room cabin built of round poles and a blacksmith shop and stage". This was probably the telegraph and mail building. The station, run by a Mr. Niel, was very busy with "five hacks" being worked on. The round pole bridge over the Muddy Creek cost 50 cents to cross.

Sulphur Springs had the acid battery type repeater on the telegraph line. Some of the telegraph poles that were left standing after the trail was abandoned were used in the building at the Willow Stage Station south of Sulphur on the Rawlins-Baggs Stage Line. Pieces of blue-green glass telegraph insulators were found in abundance, and also one broken, Hemingray insulator, but still screwed on the wooden support and with the piece of galvanized iron attaching wire. Shot off by an Indian bullet? Ah, the excitement of the Old West! The threaded insulator with the matching threaded wooden peg was patented in 1865.

Photo by Louise B. Erb
Insulator from the telegraph line at Sulphur Spings Station

Buildings at Sulphur Springs Stage Station. Now gone.
Top dug out - Arsenal and later a root cellar.
L to R - ice house, food and other storage.
Building on right was always used as a blacksmith shop.

Hay Shed built about 1865 at the Sulphur Springs Stage Station on the Overland Trail. It was torn down in 1945. This shed held hay for stage and freight teams on the Rawlins-Meeker line also.

The buildings at Sulphur Station were built of logs. Indians ran off the stock many times but the station was never burned. The two stone buildings shown in some of the Sulphur Springs pictures were built after 1900 by the Robertsons. They were not part of the old Station. Probably some of the rocks used in these buildings were taken from the breastworks on the rifle pits.

About 3 miles up the Muddy Creek from Sulphur Springs Ranch, about the middle of Bridger's Canyon (or Muddy Creek Canyon), there is a grave with the following inscription on the headstone: "G.A. Lovesey, Drowned July 4, 1860," and on a little hill immediately west of the Sulphur Springs Ranch house is a small graveyard (now enclosed with a sturdy wire fence.). There are five graves to a certainty and it is not difficult to imagine a trace of two more beside them. One of these graves bears the following inscription on its headstone and the name again carved deeply on another stone on the grave: "P. Briley, Aged 13 (or 18) years" and the date as nearly as can be deciphered is "1865." Two of these graves are large and three are medium sized. They are all covered with heavy flat stones. No one ever knew who was buried in these other graves but in our present research we know that in one of these large graves is Calvin Wall the well liked deaf mute emigrant who was killed in 1865. And one of the small ones is a child who died the same year.

One of the few marked graves left. G.A. Lovesey drowned July 4, 1860 and was buried in the Muddy Creek Canyon not far from the water's edge.

This grave is just west of the Sulphur ranch house. Robertsons built a wire fence around this site to protect it.

Stage barns built about 1862
Rock building at end built in early 1900s

Cal Briggs was in overall command of troops from Denver to Sulphur Springs. Major Daniel Darling from Medicine Bow to Sulphur. On Sept. 24, 1865, Cal Briggs gave Major Otis and his 'New Yorkers' a real taste of remoteness by sending them out on the line to Sulphur Springs." From *Cavalry & Coaches*. Author, Dr. John S. Gray; Fort Collins Westerners, publishers. CR 1978.

Daniel Y. Meschter, a mining engineer living in Wenatchee, Washington has been a stamp collector since boyhood. He is also a featured columnist in the Rawlins, Wyoming *Daily Times* and has contributed major articles to the Annals of Wyoming publication. Meschter has contributed the following condensed information for our use here.

"There is something spooky about reading the private letters of someone you don't know, especially more than 100 years later.

The envelope shown here was bid in at a recent mail auction on the strength of a 'lot' description of an August 1868 Wells Fargo cover docketed 1868, 'Sulphur Springs Dacotah Territory.' Wells Fargo & Co. had purchased the mail contract and stage service from Ben Holladay Overland Stage Co. in 1866. This letter mailed from Sulphur in 1868 has the Wells Fargo stamp on it as well as a date mark by Union Pacific Railroad.

Sulphur Springs Station

"Many covers can be shown by their markings to have been carried over the Overland Trail. This cover has unusual interest because the research confirms it was posted at a remote Wells Fargo way station on the trail only weeks before that part of the trail was abandoned."

There were four enclosures. They were letters written by P.C. Brink to his wife and daughters in Camden, N.J. Reproduced here is the letter with the envelope written at the Sulphur Springs Station by P.C. Brink.

> Sulphur Spring,
> Dacotah Ter.
>
> Friday, 6 p.m., August 28/68
>
> Here I am, having been staging all day. If you hear anything about Indians give yourself no concern, as we are 250 miles away from their whereabouts. I am very well & so far as staging is concerned, I am enjoying myself. This rocky mountain region is rough & many scenes magnificent.
>
> The sunset last evening was grand. I have today been almost always in sight of snow on the mountains within 6 miles of me part of the time. The air is clear and bracing. I trust you are all well.
>
> Affy,
> P.C. Brink
>
> p.s. I write this as I am waiting for supper.
> p.s. No. 2 Have just had supper of antelope & potatoes from Salt Lake City.

(The Meeker Massacre took place 10 years later. It's good he didn't know how close the Indians were.) -The authors

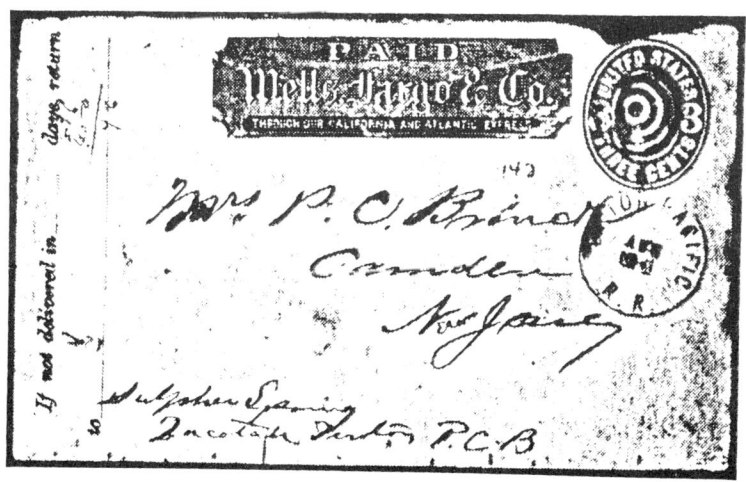

Dacotah Territory cover - using the contents to interpret postal history

The Sulphur Springs Ranch is now owned by the Jack Creek Land and Cattle Company of Saratoga, Wy. and all gates are locked.

Eleven miles west of Sulphur Springs is **WASHAKIE** station located on the north side of Muddy Creek. The trail generally followed the Muddy but the travelers had to pick their way around the treacherous eroded ravines. This is the beginning of the most arid part of the Red Desert.

Washakie, as well as all the next stations west were built of stacked slabs of native sandstone rock as there were no trees. These rocks were mortared together with a mixture of sand and clay from the site. The roofs were dirt and pole (brought in) and the floors were dirt.

Washakie was named for the honored Chief of the Shoshone Indian tribe in northern Wyoming. Occasionally it was spelled and pronounced Waskie or Washie by those who lived and traveled along the Overland Trail but that was probably a colloquial dialect.

Indians were constantly stealing Holladay's stage stock. In 1865 Col. C.H. Potter ordered that, "the mails be transmitted without fail. In case of necessity you can use cavalry horses and quartermaster's mules to haul the stages through until such time as the Overland Mail Company can replace their stolen stock."

However, even though some attacks took place here and farther west, Washakie was on the fringe for serious Indian attacks.

Photo by Les Erb
Washakie Stage Station Ruins

Division Agent Robert Spotswood once stated that from Virginia Dale to Bitter Creek, "a man's life was in constant danger, for an Indian was likely to jump up from behind a bush at any point and shoot him down."

On June 12, 1867, A.K. McClure noted in his narrative that the Washakie station keeper had improvised a fake cannon, as had Virginia Dale and some of the emigrant trains, and displayed it for the Indians to see. The redmen knew and feared this weapon.

Washakie, in Carbon County, on public land, is under the jurisdiction of the Bureau of Land Management. In 1987, Alice Bronsdon, a B.L.M. archeologist directed a group of Rawlins Boy Scouts in Troop 253 in erecting a barbed-wire fence around the remaining ruins. There are graves on the hill behind the station but the exact location is not known. Along side the trail at this station has been erected a concrete **OVERLAND TRAIL** post but it has been broken off by cattle rubbing against it.

Washakie is in the National Register of Historic Places.

Approximately eighteen miles south of I-80 on the Baggs-Creston Highway No. 789, where it crosses the Overland Trail, a monument has been erected. Trail ruts can be seen on both sides. Washakie Station ruins are located about three and one-half miles east of this highway.

Photo by Les Erb
Trail Ruts and Overland Trail Monument on Creston-Baggs Road

After the trail departed from Washakie it still followed the Muddy Creek for about two more miles then the creek coursed south and the trail went west.

Thirteen miles from Washakie was the small station of **DUCK LAKE.** In stage coach and covered wagon days this station stood in an area of a lake and springs and "the grass was two feet tall". No doubt it was a home and nesting place for many ducks.

The emigrants liked this little oasis. A pleasure that brought a smile were the lovely sweet smelling wild roses that grow in the arid west.

Very little history was recorded about this station. The *Deseret News* of Salt Lake City, on June 26, 1867, published some letters from Elder Zebulon Jacobs on his trip across the west. In one letter Elder Jacobs remarks, "...we rolled on to Duck Lake and camped. This station has also shared its stock with the Indians."

Today Duck Lake is a fenced, wide, sparsely vegetated flat. Spring-time may show a little water but otherwise is dry. There is no visible evidence of the station. This is privately owned ranch land.

Duck Lake, in Carbon County, is in the National Register of Historic Places.

After the Overland Trail left the flats of Duck Lake, in about five miles, the road entered a long draw called Barrel Springs Draw. At the beginning of this draw and about 200 yards north of the trail is a large singular red sandstone rock, called simply **RED ROCK.** This was a popular place for the emigrants to pause and scratch their names and dates into the surface.

Red Rock is on private ranch land in Sweetwater County, Wyoming. It is in the National Register of Historic Places.

Photo by Les Erb

Red Rock

Photo by Les Erb
Pioneer names on Red Rock

Traveling through here was dreaded because of the deep sand and dirt and not much water or grass. The billowing clouds of dust heavily laden with alkali was breathed into travelers lungs, no doubt making the ill members of all the trains more miserable.

After traveling about seven more miles **DUG SPRINGS** or **BARREL SPRINGS** Station was reached. This place was eagerly anticipated because of the good fresh water spring. At an early date someone had dug out a small spring to increase the flow and later placed a barrel in it to collect the water. One emigrant wrote that their train watered 200 head of stock out of buckets then had to travel six more miles for grass.

Traveling into this station was a laborious pull up a slope and through deep sand. The oxen would be breathing heavily when they reached the station, thus it earned another name of Puffing or Puffin' Bull. Often they had to double team to pull through.

Dug Springs endured many raids by Indians to steal their stock. In July 1867 the telegraph line was cut near this station, two poles torn down and six or seven hundred feet of wire carried off. Often the Indians would cut the wire then lie in ambush nearby waiting for repairmen to come and fall prey to them.

Some of the rock walls of the buildings and the rock corral has been stabilized to some extent. A substantial wire fence encloses the whole station area. The site of the spring still seeps a little water.

Dug Springs Station, in Sweetwater County, is in the National Register of Historic Places.

Photo by Les Erb
Dug Springs Station Restored

Fort LaClede, Wyoming Ruins
Courtesy Wyoming State Archives,
Museums and Historical Department

Dug Springs/Barrel Springs

About 13 miles from Dug Springs and out on an open flat was **FORT LACLEDE**. Situated on the south side of Bitter Creek, this fortified stage station was a large, native rock complex consisting of two main buildings and a large corral. One of the buildings was quarters that could house a sizable number of soldiers. The other building was a high gun and lookout tower that had a cellar in which the powder was stored. Loop-holes were in the sides of the walls and rifle pits were around the fort and on a bluff called Signal Hill, located about 200 yards northeast of the buildings.

Edward Teirney of Rawlins, grew up in this southern part of Wyoming and as a young man began an interst in the history of the Overland Trail. Long after the trail was abandoned he states that he was privilaged to have seen this gun tower intact before the complex began to deteriorate.

Ft. LaClede had an official military designation as a Fort. In 1863 it was garrisoned by four companies of the 11th Ohio Cav. Volunteers. Troops were on scout and escort duty at all times patrolling from Ft. LaClede east to Sulphur Springs and west to Green River. In 1865 these men were relieved by the 11th Kansas Cav. under the command of Col. P.B. Plumb and were involved in a great deal of Indian activity during the life of the trail.

Today a few partial walls still stand but evidence of the rifle pits and the twenty eight graves in the station's cemetery has disappeared.

Photo by Les Erb
LaClede Station Ruins

Approximately a mile and a half down Bitter Creek is the small station called **LACLEDE**. There is some question as to whether this was a station or a ranch because of the shape of the building. More archeological examination would be needed to determine this.[58]

The type of stone used in this building was a sandstone and limestone that is solidly packed with fossilized fresh water snail shells as evidence of an ancient lake bed that existed in the Eocene-Tertiary geologic period fifty-five million years ago.

This station was known to have a nice, cold water spring. The emigrant, Sarah Raymond, took a drink of it and cringed from the "horrid stuff". Bitter Creek certainly earned its name from the taste.

The walls have deteriorated badly but a good fence protects them from the cattle rubbing. This site is in the National Register of Historic Places.
Both LaCledes are on state land in Sweetwater County, Wyoming.

The stage drivers considered the Bitter Creek area
"the most despised part of the whole route".

Photo by Louise B. Erb
Big Pond Station on the Banks of Bitter Creek

Ft. LaClede/LaClede

Twelve miles west of LaClede the swing station, **BIG POND**, was located on the bank of Bitter Creek. The flat vegitated area adjoining the station on the north indicates that it had been a large shallow pond at one time. The buildings were made of flat slabs of the fossilized snail shell sandstone-limestone that was obtained in substantial amounts in the surrounding hills. The partial walls that still stand indicate that the station buildings were spread out. One building, the standard size of Holladay's Station, was on the bank of Bitter Creek. Another building that appears to have had a fire place is located about 200 yards to the west on a little rise. Adjoining this there appears to have been a corral. For this site appearing so large our curiosity is aroused as to why the buildings were so far apart.

Photo by Louise B. Erb
Big Pond building on hill above station

Very little is known of this station, however, it probably had its share of Indian raids. On July 20, 1867 a party of 150 Indians who had been unsuccessful at raiding LaClede swept down onto Big Pond station and burned it.[59] If graves are there they are not evident now. The walls have badly deteriorated.

Big Pond is owned by the Union Pacific Railroad and the Sweetwater Livestock Company.

Fourteen miles beyond, was the swing station **BLACK BUTTE,** named for a large dark colored butte five miles to the west.

Adrian Reynolds, in the October 1961 issue of *Annals of Wyoming* states that he visited the station site, on the south bank of Bitter Creek, in 1932 and found the two front rooms with partial roof timbers, intact. Across the road to the south was remnants of possibly a powder house. Today these two places have deteriorated considerably.

At this area along Bitter Creek a large outcrop of good coal was noted before emigrant days and the pioneers found it would burn well in their camp fires. With the coming of the trains in 1868 the Railroad developed this coal bed extensively for its use in their steam locomotives. Today the coal mining is done by the Black Butte Coal Co. The Overland Trail station ruins, located in the center of the Coal Co. property, are technically on Bureau of Land Management land, however, they are protected by fences put up by the Coal Co. Permission must be obtained from the Black Butte Coal Co. to visit and a person from the Coal Company gives a guided tour.

Photo by Les Erb
Black Butte Stage Station Ruins

Mr. Adrian Reynolds again noted, "Black Butte was the first place on the route where stage station and iron horse met."

Very, very little is recorded in the emigrants diaries of Black Butte and stations on west. No doubt their having to endure the choking dust, alkali, scant water and animal feed and the unrelenting wind, and sun left them no desire or effort to write.

Point of Rocks Stage Station
Courtesy Wyoming State Archives,
Museums and Historical Department

Big Pond/Black Butte

The next stage station, 14 miles west of Black Butte, was **POINT OF ROCKS.** It was often called **ROCK POINT** or **ALMOND STATION.** The site of this station is in the Bitter Creek valley at the base of a high cliff of jagged sandstone outcroppings. The buildings, made from blocks of these rocks, were located on both sides of the trail on the south bank of Bitter Creek. Adrian Reynolds, in the October 1961 issue of *Annals of Wyoming*, states that after the trail was abandoned the buildings were lived in by two consecutive families. The station was then deeded to the state at which time all the walls were intact and there was a huge bellows in the northeast corner of the middle wing. This was stolen a few years afterwards. In the 1930's names carved into the sandstone walls could still be seen. Graves with wooden markers were a short ways west of the station. After this time the station deteriorated. Today the main station, and L shaped building, has been reconstructed but it is not a true reproduction. Behind this building and across the trail are the crumbling walls of another building.

During its existence in stage coach and emigrant days, Point of Rocks supposedly was burned, at least once, in Indian raids.

In 1868 when the railroad extended west this ceased to be a station on the Overland Trail and became a junction point for the Union Pacific Railroad. It also became a starting terminal for stage and freight going north to South Pass City and the Sweetwater mines.[60]

Today Point of Rocks is a pleasant little village located on the north side of Bitter Creek across the creek from the old station. In addition to the Union Pacific Railroad skirting the town, Interstate 80 highway traverses it.

Point of Rocks Stage Station, in Sweetwater County, is the property of the State of Wyoming and it is in the National Register of Historic Places.

About 14 miles west of Rock Point was the small way station of **SALT WELLS** located on Bitter Creek. Holladay's men found that the water was salty and brackish so they dug three wells a ways from the bank of the creek before they got better water. The station keepers offered well water for a fee which emigrants protested but when they could find none better they were glad to pay.

Salt Wells was burned sometime between 1866 to 1868 but was never rebuilt. This site is on grazing association land.

Fourteen miles beyond was the station of **ROCK SPRINGS,** still on Bitter Creek and at its confluence with Killpecker Creek. The station was named for the little spring of excellent fresh running water that had been known since early trappers days. Before emigrants departed on their journey across the country they read numerous travelogs, one being Allen's Guide 1858, about the trail and were aware of many of these places. They looked forward to any place with good water and grass.

John Dickson, in the Oct. 1962 issue of *Annals of Wyoming*, stated that, "In addition to the customary buildings (at Rock Springs) the stage company built a very primitive rock hotel to serve as a resting place for the passengers.

"It is believed that Rock Springs was never burned. It may have been used for a livery stable or ranch," after the trail was abandoned. There is no visible evidence of any of the buildings today.

Now the site is surrounded by the city of Rock Springs in Sweetwater County, Wyoming. Close to where Springs Drive street crosses under the I 80 overpass, is a location marker.

Fifteen miles farther on where Bitter Creek flows into the Green River was the station of **GREEN RIVER.** This was on the west bank at a site about 30 or 35 miles upstream from the present city of Green River. The city of Green River has changed location four times since the Overland Trail station was built in 1862.[61]

At this station was the famous crossing of the Green. When the water was low wagons were able to ford on the gravel river bottom but a ferry was in operation in high water. Very early dates have been recorded for ferries being in use here. From 1842 to 1852 mountainmen operated one. The Mormons operated a ferry from 1853-1858. A post-office was established at this site in 1856. George Crofutts in his book, *Crofutts Overland Tours*, stated that before 1869 a ferry was operated by Bill Hickman who charged $5 to $20 for ferry transportation.

There is record of ferry service until 1896 when the first wagon bridge was built over the Green River. This bridge later served the original Lincoln Highway which closely followed the Overland Trail.

There was a great deal of travel both going west to Utah and California and after gold was discovered at South Pass, Wyoming people and wagons came from Utah and crossed to the east bank of the Green to take the Oregon Trail northeast.[62]

The Green River Game and Fish Department is now located on the site of the old stage station.

The Green River flows directly through the center of the 4th and present city of Green River.

Ruth Shackleford again writes in her 1865 diary that her husband, Frank, made a coffin for a young, popular member of the train, Neelie Kerfoot, who had died after many days of illness on the road. She was buried on the banks of Green River close to the Green River Station.

Frank Shackleford made another coffin and lined it, for a fellow traveler, Mary Gatewood, who died near Fort Bridger.

She was buried at Bear River.

The whole trail was lined with graves. In the future, if the ground penetrating electronic radar instruments prove sucessful for locating graves, all the ones along the trail can be documented.

About 14 miles west of the Green River station, and on the north side of Blacks Fork, was the small swing station of **LONE TREE** that got its name from a singular majestic pine tree that was a landmark for pioneers.

Nothing remains of the station buildings. Graves are in the area but time and vandals have destroyed the headstones.

The Lozier Ranch in Sweetwater County owns this site.[63]

Eighteen miles from Lone Tree was the home station of **HAM'S FORK** which had a telegraph office. These sandstone block buildings overlooked the confluence of Ham's Fork and Blacks Fork Rivers. It was also known as **SOUTH BEND STATION.**

There seems to be a difference of opinion between a 1972 National Park Service Study which was published by Aubrey L. Haines, an Oregon Trail Historian, in his book *Historic Sites Along the Oregon Trail*, 1981, and the 1974 Historic American Buildings Survey (HABS) on this station.

In Granger, Wyo., where the station building still stands, is a granite monument which reads:

The Old South Bend Stage Station Built in 1850
Gift of E.J. Brandly and Family
To the State of Wyoming
In Memory of Mrs. E.J. Brandly
On the Oregon Trail
And Pony Express

Russel L. Tanner, BLM archeologist (Rock Springs Division) and also a native of Granger, wrote an abstract in 1984 on *"The Controversy Surrounding the Granger Stage Station, Wyoming,"* to clarify errors in this inscription and doubt about the location and name of the station.

In summerization, the South Bend or Granger station (as shown in the accompanying photo) was built in 1862 by Holladay. Legal documents indicate that the site was deeded to the Wyoming Landmark Commission in 1932, not by E.J. Brandly, but by Clarence E. and Roy B. Adams and their wives. The Adams brothers were grandsons of Mrs. Mary Brandly, and step-grandsons of Mr. Brandly, and had inherited the land from Mrs. Brandly. (Office of the Sweetwater County Clerk, Green River, Wyoming).

Mrs. Brandly had the stucco overlay applied to the large building in 1920. As you can note in the picture, taken in 1940 by Agnes Wright Spring, that some of this had fallen off exposing the original rock structure. In 1978 the National Park Service awarded a contract for restoration work on the building. The remaining stucco was removed and the building was further stabilized for preservation.

Ham's Fork also known as South Bend and Granger Stage Station
Courtesy Wyoming State Archives,
Museums and Historical Department

Western Historian, Paul Henderson, stated that this building replaced a much earlier squalid station (on the Oregon Trail) in 1862. The HABS report states, "The name of the stop is known to have changed officially at that time from "Ham's Fork" to "Granger" (it appears thus on 1862 time-tables)" Tanner states the HABS report cites no documentation for this statement and it may be erroneous, since in 1867 a Wells Fargo time-table lists the "South Bend" stop, but neither "Ham's Fork" nor "Granger". He also states the name change to Granger may have occurred in 1868 with the arrival of the railroad, since the first post-master at Granger was a man named Lafayette Granger. This post-office was commissioned in February 1869. This still leaves a question in historian's minds.

The Granger Station in Sweetwater County is in the National Register of Historic

Places. In this vicinity the Overland Trail met and followed the Oregon Trail into Ft. Bridger.

Between Granger and Ft. Bridger were two small stations for changing stage teams. One, 12 miles from Granger was **CHURCH BUTTES** located at the confluence of the Muddy Creek and Blacks Fork. The name was given for one of the large, unique rock formations along the river where Mormons held church services. It is in Unita County and on private land.

The next, 8 miles from Church Buttes, was **MILLERSVILLE.** A small Mormon settlement grew up around this station but was abandoned for lack of water. This is on private land.

FT. BRIDGER was reached in another 13 miles. The trails separated here. The Mormon trail went on west to Utah and the California Trail headed on in a northwesterly direction. Ft. Bridger was a hub of activity for many eventful years. The Mormon uprising in 1857 took over Ft. Bridger and they built their own Ft. Supply. In this same year they burned both forts. The U.S. Army immediately took over the site and rebuilt Bridger in 1858.

Ft. Bridger, in Unita County, Wyoming, is in the National Register of Historic Places.

Fort Bridger, Wyoming
Courtesy Wyoming State Archives,
Museums and Historical Department

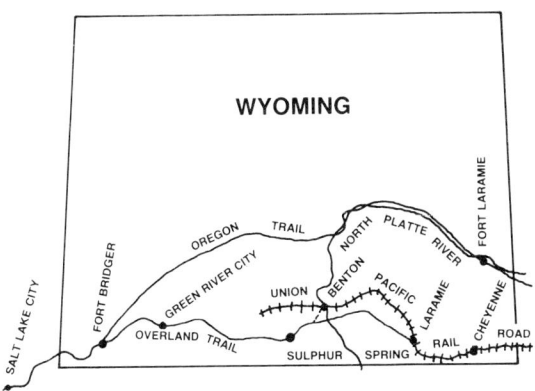

This map shows how far the Union Pacific Railroad had progressed in August, 1868 on its way to Promontory, Utah. The twon Benton was a tent town already in its decline then. According to the location on this map it was situated where Fort Steele is today on the North Platte River.

Stage Stations

The Union Pacific Railroad was rapidly pushing its way across the country. From the west and the east the rails would meet in Utah in 1869.

Ben Holladay had guessed the outcome of the trails and in 1866 sold all his stage and mail interests on this Overland Trail to Wells, Fargo & Co. The latter company continued operating the mail and stage route until on May 10, 1869 when the railroads offered faster and more comfortable service.

Indian depredations continued after Wells, Fargo & Co. took over. As the railroad progressed the Indians vented their anger on it. Rails were torn up, telegraph lines cut and railroad workers killed. One of the major losses to the railroad and the Chief Engineer, Major-General Grenville M. Dodge was the death of their finest engineer and surveyor, Percy T. Browne. Dodge wrote, "On July 23, 1867 Browne and his surveying party of eight, including escorts, were attacked by 300 Sioux on the warpath in the flat, waterless, sagebrushed Red Desert near Bitter Creek. After fighting from noon to dark, Browne was shot through the abdomen. His men had to give up their horses, whereupon the Indians fled. Browne begged his party to leave him and make their way to safety. They refused and carried him on a litter of carbines for 15 miles during the night to the LaClede stage station, where he soon died."

Emigrant trains were still being attacked. Sporadic Indian action continued thru 1869.

The West was now wide open. Wyoming had been in Dakota Territory until July 25, 1868 when it was officially declared Wyoming Territory. On July 10, 1890 Wyoming became the 44th state in the Union. In 1990 Wyoming celebrates its Centennial Year.

When the railroad was finished and the mail and express coaches were removed from the Overland Trail, most of the smaller stage stations gradually fell into decay. However, the trails were still used into the 1890s. Many emmigrants could not afford the price of railroad travel, or if they wanted to move all their animals and possessions, could travel alone without fear of Indian attack.

Some of the stations that had level land for meadows became ranches and prepared for the romance of the cattle days. Big Laramie, Rock Creek, and Sulphur Springs are the only ranches in Wyoming that still have the original buildings, or at least some.

HOLLADAY'S LOSSES DURING SPRING AND SUMMER OF 1865
Of the Wyoming Stations on the Trail According to Testimony Before the Committee on Claims, 1880

Station	Date	Item	Amount
Bridger's Pass	May 19	Flour and Sharp's rifle	$100.00
	May 26	9 horses at $200.00	1800.00
		8 sets single harness at $30.00	240.00
		Supplies	100.00
Cooper's Creek	July 1865	1 pony	50.00
		Corral, windows, doors, cooking and box stove destroyed	390.00
Elk Mountain	June 1865	22 mules at $200.00	4400.00
		4 horses at $225.00	900.00
		2 ponies at $50.00	100.00
Little Laramie	August 1865	Station and corral destroyed	3500.00
Medicine Bow	July 1865	2 ponies at $50.00	100.00
		Corral destroyed	1500.00
Pine Grove	June 9	2 sets harness and coal stove damaged	200.00
Rock Creek	July 1865	1 pony	50.00
		Corral destroyed	250.00
Sage Creek	May 22	9 horses at $200.00	1800.00
	June 8	5 horses at $200.00	1000.00
	Sept. 4	1 set four-horse harness cut to pieces	120.00
		Station and barn burned	2500.00
		2 men killed	
Sulphur Springs	June 1865	6 mules at $200.00	1200.00
		1 horse	225.00
		34 stage horses at $200.00	6800.00
		9 mules at $150.00	1350.00
Willow Springs	August 1865	6 mules at $200.00	1200.00
		2 horses at $225.00	450.00
		1 pony	50.00
		Corral destroyed	250.00
On the road	September 4	1 horse out of team	200.00
			$30,825.00

Stage Stations

WAGON TRAILS and FOLK TALES
1862-1979

RAWLINS
AND THE FREIGHTING BUSINESS

Carbon County Journal-March 4, 1899
"The Rawlins-Snake River Stage line is running very nearly on time, the only delay thus far being on account of waiting for the mails from the Union Pacific."

North section of Rawlins in the late 1800's. Penitentiary far left- Bruning house, barn and sheds marked with white star.

Rawlins Headlines-February 1, 1892-*Carbon County Journal*
"A Prosperous Year Ahead"
"Our cattle, our sheep, our gold, silver, coal, iron and copper and stone quarries, and an immense bed of red ochre 90 ft. wide found due south from the depot mixes readily with oil without a trace of sediment for a fine grade of paint!" (This paint was named "Rawlins Red" and our ranch gates and shed were painted with it, so was the Brooklyn Bridge in New York City.)
"Cashier Rumsey of the First National Bank confidently looks forward to a $20,000,000 business this year.
There are stage and freight lines running out of Rawlins in all directions to all of the camps doing a booming business."

Center of Rawlins- large stone buildings on the left- L to R- carbon County Court house 1882 and the Central School constructed in 1885.

South section of Rawlins along Union Pacific tracks.

Rawlins, Wyoming

CARBON COUNTY JOURNAL
Jan. 1, 1898
STAGE LINES

Rawlins-Dixon Stage leaves Rawlins every 2nd morning for Meeker and Craig, Colo. with passengers for Sulphur, Muddy Crossing, Baggs and Dixon, Wyo. and Hahns Peak, Colo. Carries mail.

Rawlins-Lander Stage leaves every morning at 8 for Miners' Delight, Atlantic City, Lewiston and Lander and Ft. Washakie. Carries mail.

Rawlins-Ferris Stage leaves for Ferris, Johnstown and intermediate points Mon., Wed., Fri. Carries mail.

Rawlins-Saratoga Stage leaves every day except Sun. for Rankin, Saratoga and the Upper Platte country. Carries mail.

What is left of a gypsy wagon
This is what was known as a light spring wagon.

Carbon County Journal-May 27, 1899
   "The gypsies who have been working our people during the week on the old 'fortune telling racket' pulled out for the west this morning."

Rawlins, Wyoming

The Murphy-Ready building at 5th and Front St. in early days - Rawlins

RAWLINS TO BAGGS STAGE LINE AND FREIGHT

In 1867, General John A. Rawlings discovered a spring of water in a draw near where the town of Rawlins is now. He called it "the most gracious and acceptable of anything" he'd found in the area. The town was named for him but the name Rawlins evolved.

The City of Rawlins is the county seat of Carbon County in south-central Wyoming and is situated at an elevation of 6755 feet. It is on the main line of the Union Pacific Railroad and where highways 287 north and U.S. Interstate 80 or old Lincoln Highway 30 intersect.

RAWLINS TO BAGGS STAGE-FREIGHT ROAD AND A FEW OFF THE ROAD RANCHES

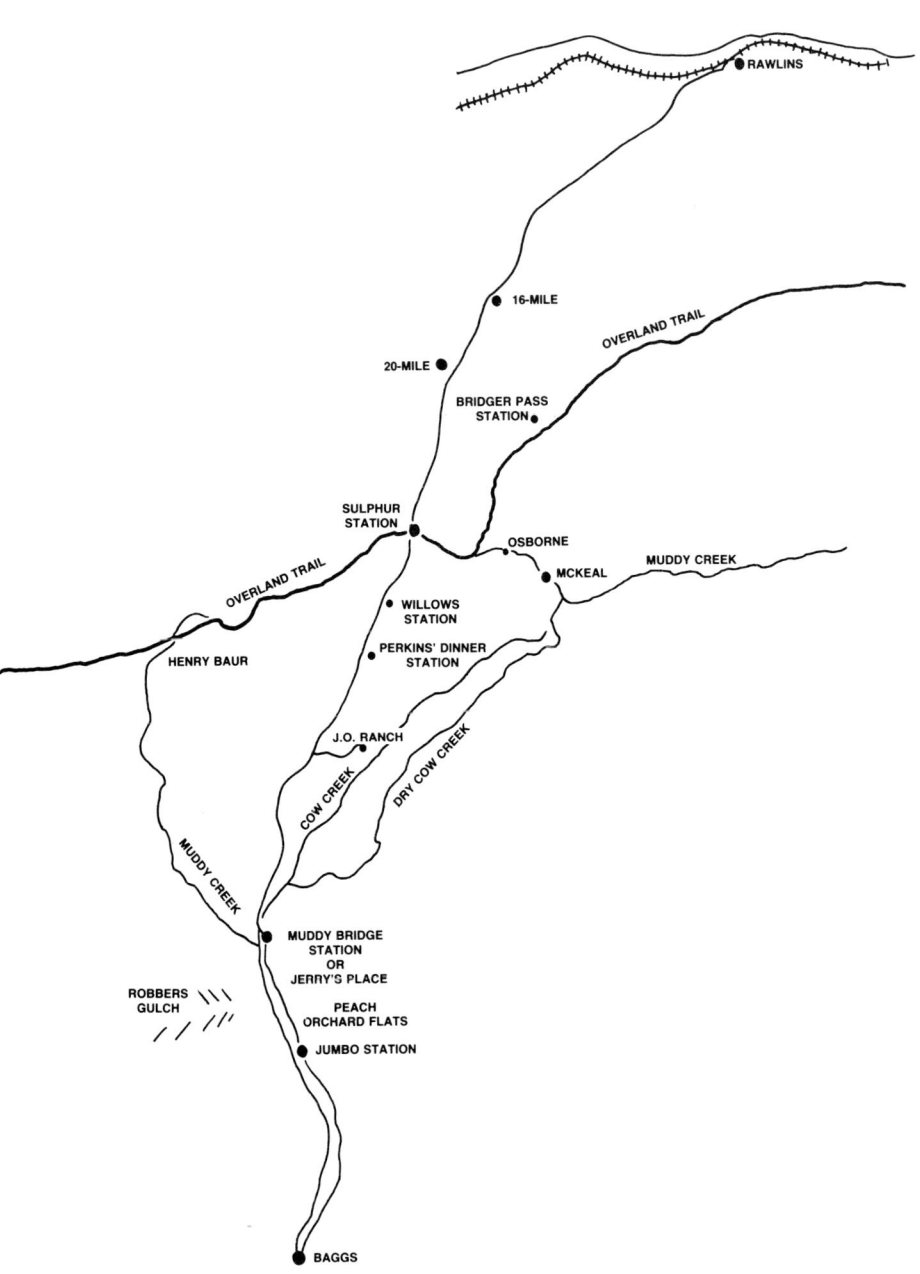

This town like most Wyoming towns teems with the romance of history. It is the secondary focal point of our account of our experiences growing up and being influenced by the intrigue of the stories told of days gone by.

Rawlins was the nearest supply center to our ranches on the Muddy Creek and Hay Gulch thirty miles to the southwest. The Sulphur Springs stage and freight station was a near half way location on the Rawlins-Milk River Route. This route was also referred to as Rawlins-Meeker or Rawlins-Baggs road depending on where one was going.

For our story and area of experience we are calling it the Rawlins-Baggs Road.

This was a very busy stage and especially freighting road from the time the railroad was completed through Rawlins until about 1912 (some reported as late as 1917). The whole Snake River Valley as well as northwestern Colorado and the Ute Indian Reservation were dependent upon supplies hauled over this road.

Stage stations were built all along the way. Smaller intermediate stations that supplied fresh changes of horses became known as "swing stations." Home stations differed somewhat, they were larger, having blacksmith shops, meals and lodging for overnight passengers. Sulphur Springs represented one of the more extensive stations. Concord coaches with from 4 to 6 horses were used to carry passengers, mail and express daily. The drivers received from $40.00 to $75.00 a month plus board.

The first station out from Rawlins was 16 Mile then 20 Mile. Sulphur Springs was already in existence. South of Sulphur was the Willows and three miles south of that Perkins' Dinner Station, next the Muddy Bridger Stop or Jerry's place, then the Jumbo Rest Stop and Baggs, Wyoming.

Previous to 1889, all goods had to be freighted by wagon from Rawlins, a distance of 155 miles, which made even the necessities of life very expensive but at the same time yielded a good profit. In the fall of this year the Rio Grande Railroad was completed to Newcastle, Colorado and it was closer to accommodate the needs of people of northern Colorado from Rifle, Colorado, the shipping point.

The stage wagon was an improvised model of a Concord Coach named after the town where it was built, Concord, New Hampshire. Portions were removed to allow room for freight in addition to passengers. This arrangement was to the discomfort of the passengers, but to the profit of the stage operators.

The average stage driver was above all Lord and master, the captain of his craft, the fear of timid passengers, the admiration of the stable boys and the trusted agent of his employer. That kind of man was hard to find.

A good driver had crossed the mountains and traveled the plains hundreds of times. He crossed when the roads were their worst; by day and by night, in storm and gloom and darkness; through snow and sleet and rain and mud and burning sun and alkali dust.

Back and forth he had gone with his life balanced on the temper of a horse or the strength of a coach and the attacks of Indians and outlaws.

The "Lander Clipper" (Wyoming), July 6, 1906, states "The last stage that will ever run on the old Rawlins-Lander (north) line ran today. It has been running for 20 years.

"Soon the snort of the iron horse will replace the crack of the driver's whip and the old stage line will fade into romance."

Perry Smith, postmaster in Rawlins, at this time wrote to postmaster Brown of Lander, "God bless the old stage line, she is doomed but it beat walking."

Three years later, the stage coach service from Rawlins through Sulphur to

A stage wagon carrying both freight and passengers.
Willow Springs Station, Wyoming Territory, 1880. Joe Dentz prop.

White River ended. Losing the mail deliveries was a major catastrophe for people who so desperately depended on it for contact with family and friends. Old frontier army posts and stage stations just faded away.

It is too late to hear the stories from the men and women freighters themselves, but we have found some interesting documentary material to include at this point.

There were three known lady freight drivers who drove 4 horse teams from Rawlins to Baggs and stayed at all of the stations along the way. Two were sisters, Maggie Humphreys and Marian Morgan and Madeline Adams, daughter of Jim Baker. Some owned their own outfits.

"Up to 1868, the freighting business east and west became very general and very profitable- prices for hauling freight depended on the bulk. Bulky freight as high as $1.50 to $2.50 per 100 pounds for 100 miles. Heavy freight as high as $2.50 to $4.50 per 100 pounds per 100 miles. Teams have been known to pay for themselves in one trip. It had to pay well for several tribes of Indians were very troublesome after 1864 until 1879.

I was attacked several times by Indians on the plains but only twice that they gave me anything of a contested battle."

The Freighting Business, A.W. Haygood[64]

"In the fall of '79, I was in Rawlins after freight when Joe Rankin made his famous ride from near White River, Colorado to Rawlins on the Rawlins-White River road to summon help for the government troops corralled there by the White River Utes.

"I was somewhat familiar with that country and have often talked with men who were in the country when it occured and was myself, for years, engaged in freighting there.

"On the 29th of September, 1879, the Ute Indians at the White River Agency, killed Indian Agent Nathan C. Meeker and the men employed at the Agency. They took Mrs. Meeker and daughter Josie prisoner and held them three weeks before they were rescued by General Merritt's troops.

"Major Thomas F. Thornburg, who was stationed at Fort Steele, had been sent to aid Indian Agent Meeker. He and his troops traveled from Fort Steele to Rawlins then south over the stage route. The Indians killed Thornburg and some of his men. The remainder of the troops dug pits in the ground and held off more attacks until help arrived.

"Two men volunteered to go for help. One was Joe Rankin, government scout and the other a private soldier whose name I've forgotten. Under cover of dark, Rankin started out and made it through to Rawlins, one hundred and sixty miles in 24 hours. Whenever he found a horse that he thought could carry him farther than the one he was riding, he took it and kept going. He got a fresh horse at every mail station from Timber Lake Station, Colorado south of Baggs to Rawlins.

"A private soldier was to try to get to a fort down on Grand River that was garrisoned by a company of colored troops. The colored troops were first to reach the beseiged soldiers.

"One of the boys, holed up in the rifle pits after Thornburg had been killed, later was telling the story. He said "I always hated 'niggers' but when those big black fellows came jumping into the pits with all the water and grub they could pack, I just loved those niggers!"

"The government, until about 1881, had contracted with independent freighters to haul supplies to the Indian reservations. After that time, arrangements were made for the Indians to haul their own freight.

"We freighters thought this was "the bunk" after observing the inefficient handling of freight by the Indians.

Owing to the increased amount of freight to be hauled to White River, the contractor could not get teams enough to move it and the government engaged 60 string teams paying them $25.00 a day and everything furnished in the way of feed and rations. These teams traveled in trains of about 12 teams to the train. Independent freighters also carried freight over the same route. They would usually let the government freighters break trail in bad weather.

"Bad roads, deep snow, bad bridges and weak horses caused many loads of damaged and delayed freight. One report says, "These men are 31 days behind time on their bill of lading and their freight is in terrible condition."

"A man named John Riley was on the road in a bad storm in winter of February 1881, loaded with government freight. He lost every hoof of stock he had and came in on foot.

"Some of my happiest days have been those spent with my old freighting partner, Dan Weller, talking over old times in the days when we were freighting pioneers fifty years ago." (1873)[65]

Some Recollections of an Old Freighter, T.S. Garrett

16 MILE STATION
**Interview with Lawrence Braig
and
Nellie Robertson, his sister**

Rawlins - August 1979

Wild horse trap

16 Mile Station about 1900

Lawrence Braig who lived with his family at 16 mile
This picture taken in Rawlins 1979

Nellie Braig Robertson
Lawrence's sister (1979)

Sixteen Mile is the first stage stop on the road from Rawlins to Baggs, Wyoming. This station stood on an open, flat piece of ground along the banks of 16 Mile Creek. All that now remains to show its location are a few foundation rocks, scattered pieces of rusted metal, twisted baling and barbed wire half-hidden under the sage brush.

Despite our many efforts to locate persons knowing anything about this station, 16 miles south of Rawlins, we came upon only two - Lawrence Braig and his sister Nellie Braig Robertson. These two had lived at 16 Mile about 1903 as children and we are indebted to them for the information which follows.

Rasmussen and Brodt, a Rawlins firm, had the contract for stage operations at that time. Their stages stopped at 16 Mile to change horses. Joseph Braig took care of the horses and other needs of the stage service. His wife, Dora, furnished meals and overnight lodging whenever it was required by the stage drivers and their passengers.

The stage ran once a day at that time - one going each way, Rawlins to Baggs, Baggs north to Rawlins.

Lawrence Braig remembers Bill Smith as one of the better known drivers. Another, "Tassel Pete" Jones was so nicknamed because of the tassels he decorated the horses' harnesses with. Frank Perry, a driver for MacIntoch Freight, put small American flags on the bridles of his horses.

Cal Lemons, another freighter, drove what is known as a "string team" consisting of 18 or 20 horses. Cal put a saddle on the wheel horse and handled the rest with a jerk line. Sometimes he would walk along beside the team. Occasionally Lemons pulled a small sheep wagon behind his freight wagon to serve as an overnight resting place.

In addition to passengers and mail service, much freight was hauled over this road after the Union Pacific railroad was completed and the population grew after the Civil War.

It was necessary to have good strong horses to haul freight. A couple of nearby ranchers, Jim Hansen and Jepp Peterson bred and raised especially fine Percherons. The freighters bought the horses from these ranchers.

Hansen and Peterson were both fond and proud of their horses. The story is told that during World War I, the army approached Jim Hansen to buy cavalry horses. Hansen rounded up about 1000 head and brought them to the stock yards at Rawlins for delivery. When the army representatives came for the horses Jim asked, "What is to be done with these horses? Will they go into the battle lines?" The answer was "yes." Then Hansen opened the corral gates and turned all of the horses out to go back to the open range on the Red Desert. The army had to go elsewhere for horses.

Lawrence Braig remembers as a young man, about 1913, helping put up hay at the JO Ranch about 25 or 30 miles to the south of 16 Mile Station. Herman H. Bruning, Jr. was the foreman there at the time. Braig also remembers Charles Bruning working at Cullen's store in Wamsutter, Wyoming.

Another memory Braig recalls is of the small store at 20 Mile Station down the road to the south four miles. This store was owned and operated by Jim Hansen. It was convenient for homesteaders, sheepmen, squatters, ranchers and others in the area to have a supply of non-perishable food and other goods available out there in the wide-open spaces. The young Braig boys used to go up to the store "to snitch Bull Durham tobacco."

At the time the Braig family lived at 16 Mile the Indians who had roamed the country at will a few years before had all been moved onto reservations. It was not at all uncommon for some of them to try to return to their old haunts on the Bear River in Colorado and they would come back heading south in the spring. In the fall the government would herd them all back north again up around Lander to the reservation.

The stage coaches ran this road until about 1909. Each coach was pulled with a four horse team. The best horses for this were thoroughbred, long-legged, fast-running horses. The stage coach could be seen coming a long way away in a cloud of alkali dust. They made the trip from Rawlins to Baggs in one day usually depending on the weather. The horses were changed at all stations. However, the winter took its toll. The snow was deep and often so crusted it would cut the horses' legs when they broke through the sharp crust. Often there was not sufficient travel to keep the roads open and it was no uncommon sight to see one of the drivers, or even the proprietors, start out with mail strapped to his back, using skiis or web (snow) shoes to negotiate the drifted snow. Sometimes the man would go 24 hours without sleep or rest.

In the spring the trails would begin to thaw out or "break up," teams could travel only after dark when the roads were frozen.

The farrier at each blacksmith shop was kept busy shoeing horses for the next run. The wagon and stage coach wheels had to be kept well greased or "doped" (the slang term). "Hot boxes" resulted in poorly greased wheels. Braig remembers the blacksmith, Harry Ford, from Rawlins, who came to shoe the stage horses at 16 Mile.

Sam Green ran a livery barn in Rawlins from where freight and stage lines came and departed. It was a popular meeting place. A lot of horse deals took place there, both legally and illegally. Many stories were told of wild horse roundups, weaner colts disappearing from their branded mothers, pastures and stone corrals high up on the ridges and hidden away in the hills where horses came away with altered brands.

Lawrence Braig remembers a man named Bill Biars (or Beyers). We remember him too. When we were small children at our ranch he was a popular and skillful cowboy who knew his way around the hidden pastures and stone corrals. Rustling was a common practice, and stories about rustlers always sounded thrilling, almost like the movies.

The high sheer bluff to the west of the 16 mile stage station was the scene of an early "buffalo jump". The famous western artist, Charlie Russell, painted a picture of a buffalo jump, called "Buffalo Drive".

The Indians, before they had rifles, in order to get their game easier would find a nearby herd and with banshee whoops and yells and many hides waving, stampede the bison over the cliff. The animals would either be killed outright or maimed to the extent the Indians could finish them.

In 1987, an archeological dig, headed by archeologist Jim Truesdale, and sponsored by the Wyoming Recreation Division, was held at this, the Espy-Cornwell site. Many strewn bison bones, as well as projectile points, were found. One point was found still sticking in a rib bone. Tucked back under the cliff in a little cave area were some grave sites. The remains of two Indian children were found along with some small beads and other culture midden.

TWENTY MILE and FILMORE RANCH

Interview with Mrs. Millicent Goffar, July 1979

The next stage stop was 20 miles from Rawlins, the 20 Mile Ranch. After an interesting visit with Millicent (Mrs. Michael P.) Goffar who has lived in Rawlins all of her life, we obtained the information recorded here. Millicent was born on July 11, 1900, her mother was Jim Hansen's sister, Karoline. Karoline had been married to Chris P. Miller on September 15, 1888.

Jim (Jens) Hansen had owned the 20 Mile Stage Station since the early 1900s. There isn't much left of what was then quite an extensive ranch and station. Old rock foundations stubbornly stand their ground. With a metal detector one comes up with old square nails, hinges, pieces of harness, horse shoes and other bits and pieces of metal identifying a stage station.

Mrs. Goffar, who spent the summers on her uncle's ranch, remembers a yellow three-bedroom house with a kitchen, large dining room and a storeroom. There was also the one room log cabin which served as the store. She fondly recalls that Uncle Jim loved children and knew they loved candy. He used to reach into the candy bins for a handful of hard candy to give to her.

Near the buildings was a large watering trough for livestock where water came from an active spring and was clear and cool.

The first record of ranching at 20 Mile is that of Robert Taylor who brought sheep from California to Carbon County about 1880. Taylor head-quartered at 20 Mile although he had sheep on the Red Desert and surrounding areas. Conditions at that time were ideal for sheep and Taylor was doing very well. He was referred to as "the Bitter Creek Mutton Monarch." A newspaper report says Taylor considered the outlook for sheep raising as "Immense." He felt assured of "a big crop of wool and lambs when the daisies bloomed." Taylor became the first president of the Carbon County Wool Growers Association in 1886.

In the fall of 1889 our grandfather, John Robertson, who was then raising sheep in Meeker, Colorado wrote to Mr. Taylor regarding the purchase of some rams. W.T. Hogg was manager at the 20 Mile Ranch at that date and reports "that Taylor had at the ranch some purebred French Merino bucks. Also some 800 of their own breeding to choose from. They are all well-wooled and square bodied. The price for the bucks of our own raising is $15.00 per head."

Jim Hansen was born January 25, 1864 in Naestbed, Denmark, and came to America with his sister, Karoline, in 1888. Within a few years he owned many sections of land, herds of horses, sheep and cattle. His was a swift success story. (He died in Rawlins November 1943.)

In addition to running sheep and cattle on his land holdings, Hansen upgraded the horse herds by importing a $3500.00 Percheron stallion from France. The horse was named "Mike". Horse herds grew in great numbers and were the beginning of the wild horse herds that now give the Bureau of Land Management many a headache.

Peggy O'Neil Gates, now living in Denver, Colorado, lived at the 20 Mile Ranch about 1915. Her parents, Flora and Tom O'Neil, were there as station attendants. Tom was station master. Peggy was a niece of Mary O'Neil and Tom Middlemass, a Scotsman. Tom Middlemass was a camp mover for Herman Bruning's sheep outfit in the 1930's.

Jim Hansen built the Filmore Ranch about 1912. This ranch was off the main stage road. About where Jepps Canyon touches the Rawlins-Baggs stage road, the road takes off to the west, and about seven miles across sagebrush country the traveler comes to the Filmore Ranch. This huge reservoir for conserving water was built by a crew of men - this kind of work being done in those days by a man and team of horses maneuvering a "fresno" earth mover.

Hansen loved music and had an accordian, a violin and a piano. One day a man came to the ranch, a violin hanging from his saddle horn. The man needed food and supplies, so he traded the violin to Hansen in exchange for the goods. A closer examination of the instrument revealed the name Stradivarias printed on it.

It was Hansen who was a prime mover in the starting of the Hansen-Ferguson Mercantile Store in Rawlins. The need was great as people were moving into the area at a rapid rate, along with their cattle and sheep, and there were few establishments which sold supplies. Shares of stock were sold to the neighboring sheepmen and the store was in business. Soren Frandsen was the manager and a friendly clerk named Skerner Rasmussen was remembered for years after he was gone. An additional store of supplies was put in the extra log cabin at 20 Mile Station, under the same management.

Jens (Jim) Hansen
a shy little man but mighty.

20 Mile Ranch and Stage Station.

Jim Hansen and his French imported Percheron stallion "Mike".

Jim Hansen was a surprisingly shy little man with great ambition and stamina. After building the large storage reservoir at Filmore he built another one on his land to the north on the Red Desert. (The accompanying photograph shows shocks of wheat from grain grown out there on the heat-shriveled soil of the desert. Wyoming could be fertile when it received water.)

After Jim's death, his nephew John Hansen (who had been working with his uncle for many years) and his wife, Jennie, took over the management of the Hansen ranch holdings and it is, at this writing, continuing to be a prosperous and well-run spread.

Jim Hansen's fresno teams at work on the dam at Filmore.
The Union Pacific road bed was also constructed in this manner.

Jim Hansen's wheat field on "The Red Desert".

To come out of the past into the glaring light of the present time, it is being reported that a proposed spur of the Union Pacific Railroad will be built south from Rawlins to 20 Mile to haul coal from future developments along this area — but, we read family letters dated in the early 1900s which say much the same.

John and Jennie Hansen
John - Jim Hansen's nephew

Millicent Goffar

SULPHUR SPRINGS STATION
1862-1979

The years between 1868, when the soldiers who had been stationed at Sulphur to protect the United States mail coaches left there and the time Leander Boner filed for a homestead at the location in 1892, not much is known about the place.

The military abandoned the buildings, the land belonged to the government so drifters and others occupied the buildings from time to time.

A survey map dated June 15, 1875 identifies Sulphur as "Iscos" Sulphur Springs Ranch."

Dan Healy and A.T. Corlett are names listed in 1890. Mr. and Mrs. Alex Via were there in 1885 and 1892. Leander Boner from 1892 to 1900. The John Robertsons from 1900 to 1940. Sanger Ranches of Saratoga bought it in 1940 and the Jack Creek Land and Cattle Co. of Saratoga, WY. are the present owners.

Mary Gideon (Mrs. George) of Baggs, Wyoming reported that the upper meadow at the Sulphur Ranch once was called Lamprey's Gulch. Lamprey's had a 4 room house up there years ago before Lee Boner bought Section 5 from the Union Pacific Railroad.

About 1901 W.R. Adams and his wife Effie lived at the Willows station 3 miles south of Sulphur Springs.

The interested and curious wanderer in Wyoming runs across quite frequently the remains of someone's hand-i-work of days gone by. There are squarish formations of rock once foundations for someone's cabin. A few rusty pots, pans, nails and pieces of wagons scattered here and there and sheep herder's monuments piled high with stones. No one will ever know who they were.

Sulphur Springs Stage and Freight station in the 1870's

Sulphur Springs Ranch

SULPHUR SPRINGS AT THE CROSSROADS

November 25, 1899 - *Carbon County Journal*

"Masked men in Route County, Colorado killed about 950 head of sheep belonging to the Geddes Sheep Company. The trouble grew out of the fact that a herder let his sheep cross the Colorado-Wyoming state line. The boundary between the sheep and cattle ranges was fixed by the Colorado cattlemen to conform with Colorado-Utah line on the west and the Colorado-Wyoming line on the north.

The masked men decended on the herder and his flock, tied the herder and kept him under guard while they demolished the camp and sheep wagon. The wagon wheel spokes were used to club the sheep to death."

John Robertson read the handwriting on the wall and on June 12, 1900 he traded ranches with Leander Boner. Mr. Boner's wife, Elizabeth, had died August 6, 1898 and he wanted to leave the place.

Mr. Boner owned the Sulphur Springs Stage Station in Wyoming which Mr. Robertson accepted in trade for his White River property near Meeker, Colorado.

There were a good many men going into the sheep business in southern Wyoming and there was less hostility toward them there.

John Robertson and Leander Boner Trade Ranches

STATEMENT OF CLAIM TO WATER RIGHT.—WYOMING TRIBUNE Print, Rawlins, Wyoming.

STATEMENT OF CLAIM TO WATER RIGHT by L. N. Boner owner of the "Sulphur Ranch" ditch.

TERRITORY OF WYOMING,
County of Carbon } ss.

I, L. N. Boner, being first duly sworn, according to law, do depose and say that I am the owner of the Boner Ranch Ditch located in Carbon County, Wyoming Territory, and I make this statement of claim to water right for the purpose of securing the right to the water of Muddy Creek in said county and territory, heretofore appropriated by me and for said purpose I do depose and say:

1. The name of said Ditch for which said appropriation is claimed is the Boner Ranch Ditch.
2. The name of the owner of said Ditch is L. N. Boner.
3. The Post Office address of the owner of said Ditch is Sulphur P.O. Carbon County, Wyo.
4. The head-gate of said Ditch is located in the South West Quarter of Section 33 Township No. 18 North, Range No. 90 West.
5. The general course of said Ditch is a Westerly course from the head-gate.
6. The name of the natural stream from which the said Ditch draws its supply of water is Muddy Creek.
7. The length of said Ditch is 1 mile.
8. Width of said Ditch is 3.0 on bottom, 5.0 on top.
9. The depth of said Ditch is 1.5 feet.
10. The grade of said Ditch is 4.0 feet to the mile.
11. The waters of said Ditch was appropriated by me for said Ditch by the original construction thereof on the 10 day of October A.D. 1886.
12. The amount of water claimed for said Ditch is 15.87 Cubic feet per second of time.
13. The present carrying capacity of said Ditch is 15.87.
14. The number of acres of land lying under said Ditch and being and proposed to be irrigated by water therefrom is 150 acres.

Sworn to and subscribed in my presence this 29th day of Nov 1886.

L. N. Boner

Recorded in Book L, Mis. Records Page 10. Carbon County, Wyo.

W. L. Evans, clerk

Sulphur Springs Ranch

The Sulphur Springs Station, so named because of the free-flowing spring water with high sulphur content which kept the stock tank full to overflowing. Livestock seemed to like the taste of this water and wild horses from the Sand Hills slipped in during the night to drink their fill. Most people, on the other hand, could not stand the strong taste, but we learned to like it well enough since it was cold and refreshing. Today the spring barely runs, possibly because of the other wells dug nearby which diverted the underground water.

The watering trough at Sulphur Springs.
Jean Robertson Tallman, Ann Robertson Leap,
Elizabeth Robertson Bruning - about 1935

Looking South
Stage-freight road ahead. Overland Trail turns east up
the Muddy to Bridger's Pass
and west through southern Wyoming

PLAT
OF THE
"SULPHUR" RANCH

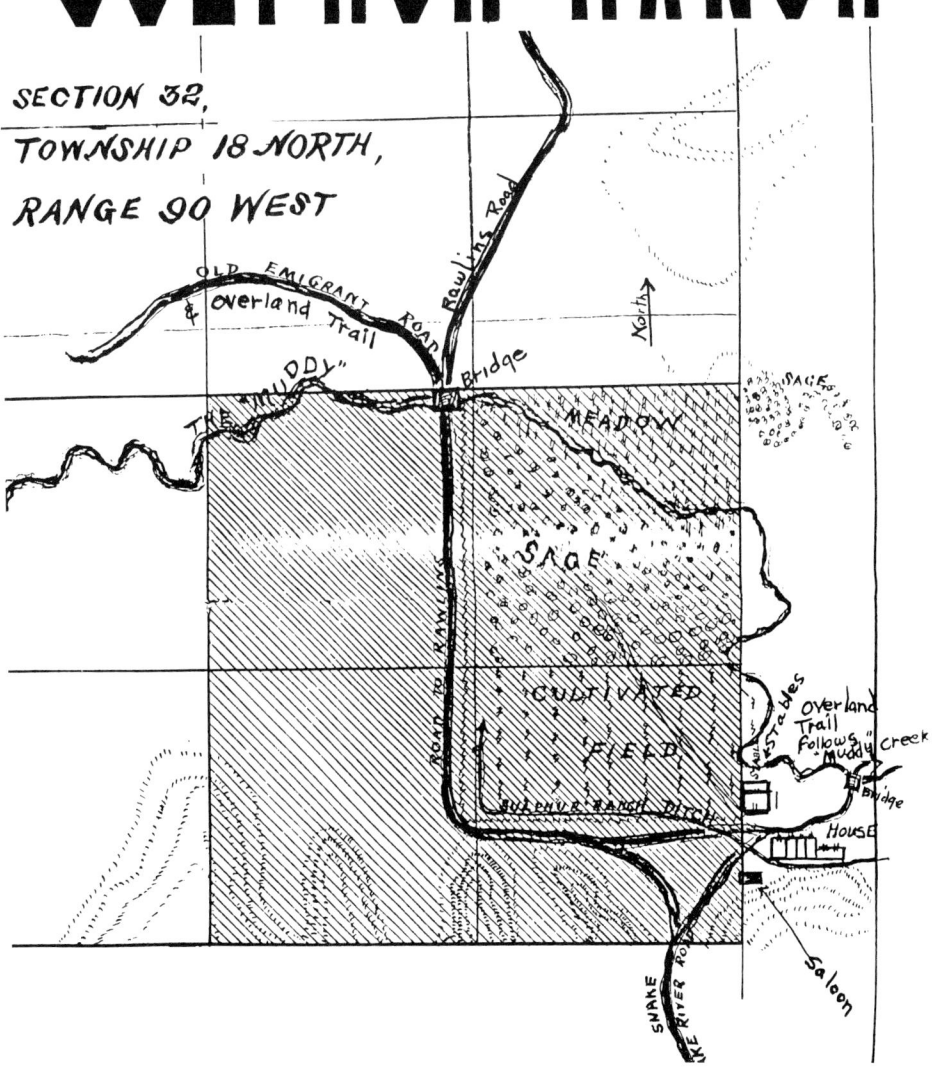

Sulphur Springs Ranch

The Sulphur house that was made from the old saloon that had stood on a slope a few hundred feet from this location. The center part was the saloon. Picture taken 1919.

The pitched roof buildings on the left is well over 100 yrs. old. It was once a saloon. It still stands. The rock building was built by Jim Robertson in 1914. He lived in it.

Sulphur Springs was the only station where the Overland Trail and the Rawlins-Meeker road crossed. The north-south trail and the Overland crossed the same bridge over the Muddy Creek.

The Overland Trail was abandoned in 1869 to stage transportation when the Union Pacific Railroad connected the east and west. Covered wagons, freight and individuals continued to use the trail however, for some time after, and even today historians, coal and oil geologists, ranchers and others find the trail a way to go up and down the Muddy Creek.

The road called the Rawlins-Meeker road was probably first used by the Indians. This area is so packed with romance and exciting stories of adventure that books could be written. If only the hills could speak, but they stand silent guardians of the past.

Sulphur was not only a crossroads for freight and stage travel, but was also used by the outlaw bands. It is on the Outlaw Trail from the Hole in the Wall in northern Wyoming, up near Kay Cee, down to Baggs, Browns Park and Robbers Roost in Colorado and Utah. Butch Cassidy, Kid Curry and the Wild Bunch, along with local outlaws, traveled along the Rawlins-Baggs road dealing with some of the ranchers for lodging and fresh horses. If one were a rancher in those days, a gun-laden outlaw would certainly have the upper hand it seems. It was a game of survival. Stories are told that some of the ranchers fared very well, financially, by providing protection in the hills, always having fresh horses close for a "quick change and a fast get away."

One ranch hand told of a pasture full of good, well-fed horses grazing one evening. In the morning when he went to the pasture it was full of gaunt, sweaty, saddle-marked horses. Nothing was said, no questions asked. It was prudent to be silent. It was a world where silence could be a matter of life or death.

Our father, Herman Bruning, told us of an incident when he was about sixteen years old and working for Jepp Peterson. A man rode in on horseback late one afternoon and had supper with the family. When bedtime came the only place for him to sleep was with our dad. Dad said the man pulled out a big roll of money and a six shooter and put them under his pillow. The following day, after the gun-toter was gone, dad found out that he had robbed a bank - dad never did know the man's name.

Freighters and Teams

Sulphur Springs Ranch

By the time the John Robertson family bought the Sulphur Ranch from Leander Boner (June 4, 1900) life had settled into a quieter pace. The Indians had given up and were living on the reservations. Sheep were being brought into the area and any wars that were fought were verbal or legal ones, over grazing rights, water rights, and stock trails. The Robertsons moved their possessions to the ranch in wagons and buggies on July the fourth, 1900. The buggy which carried our mother, Elizabeth, and her twin sister Annie from White River to Sulphur is still in our possession. Both of the girls were sick with the mumps at the time the trip was made.

For the first four years, the family lived in the house built before for the military and for the station masters, according to a family letter. Then along about 1903, they moved the old saloon building which stood a few hundred feet south from where the house is now. This was made into living quarters. Additions were built on in later years, the "master" bedroom in 1914 and an additional "company" room in the late 1920s.

The Ann and John Robertson estate kept the ranch in operation at the Sulphur Springs location until 1940 when it was sold.

The Robertson twins, Annie and Elizabeth, who drove a buggy from Meeker, Colo.
to Sulphur where they came to live July 4, 1900.

Putting up hay

Elizabeth R. Bruning
and children Ann and Gilberta, 1916

"A Sheep Wagon", Joe Fresquez was the Mexican sheepherder and camp mover for Robertsons for nearly 30 years. He taught us as children how to speak some Spanish.

John Robertson sharpening
sickle blades on a grindstone
near the blacksmith shop
at Sulphur, 1921.

From *The Denver Post* - October 18, 1903
"A Wyoming Diana!

This is the latest product of the land of the "Virginian" but Miss Annie Robertson whose skill as a huntress has earned her the name of "Diana" among her friends aspires not to fame of any kind although she has found it hard to escape the notice of the public since the news got abroad that she killed a 125 lb. buck with one shot thru the head and a downward shot at that when the deer was 150 yds. away.

She bled and dressed it and loaded it on her horse, Selim, all alone up there in the hills above the Sulphur Ranch and brought it home."

Miss Robertson bringing home her deer.

Frank Perry driver- Wm. McIntosh freight outfit of Slater, Colo. Photo taken at Sulphur Springs. Other drivers on other lines: Zeno Lamb, Teddy Hughes, Charlie Boyce, at turn of century - Rawlins-Baggs Road.

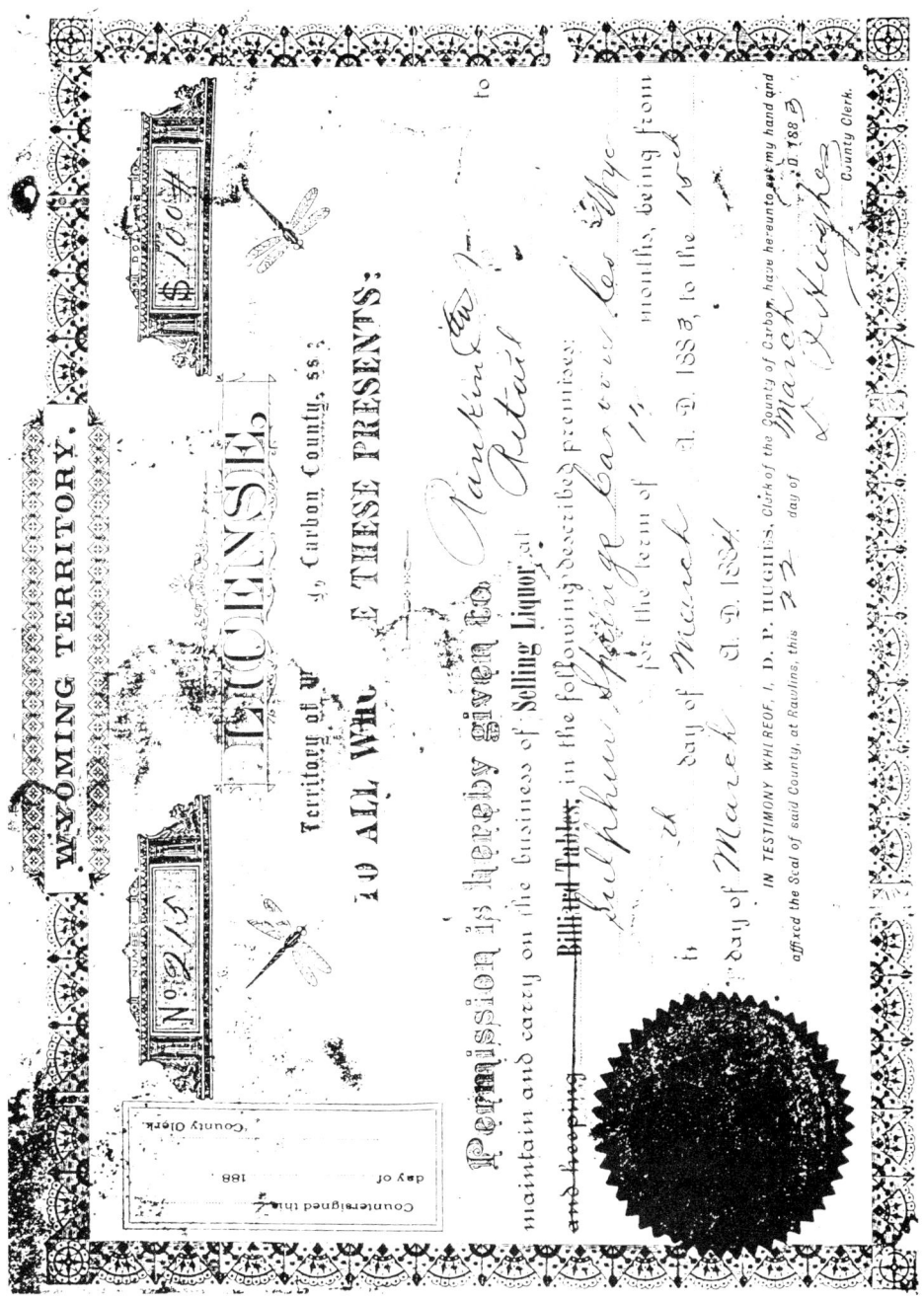

This 1883 liquor liscense was found on the wall of the old saloon at Sulphur.

Sulphur Springs Ranch

PROSPECTUS

LARSEN OIL COMPANY

[INCORPORATED UNDER THE LAWS OF THE STATE OF WYOMING]

CONTAINING A DESCRIPTION OF THE MUDDY CREEK OIL FIELDS AND THE REPORT OF THE WYOMING STATE GEOLOGIST THEREON

Every person who is interested in oil production, either as a stockholder or operator, should read every word of this prospectus. A thorough and comprehensive description of Wyoming's latest oil discovery and details in regard to the principal Company operating in the new field.

Larsen Oil Company's Drilling Rig Operating in the Muddy Creek Oil Fields, Carbon County, Wyoming.

This Drilling Rig is Completely Equipped. It Has Boiler, Engine, All Drilling and Sharpening Tools, Electric Light Plant, Fishing Tools, and 2500 Feet of Two and One-Quarter Inch Manilla Cable.

Feb. 6 1911

OFFICERS AND DIRECTORS

PRESIDENT—HANS LARSEN, Rawlins, Wyo. Mr. Larsen has been a resident of Rawlins for nearly twenty-five years. He is actively engaged in the mining of coal, the quarrying of stone and also general contracting and building, and does a large local business in lumber, coal, contracting and builders' hardware.

References: Dun's or Bradstreet's Commercial Agencies, or any bank or business house in Rawlins.

VICE-PRESIDENT—EDWARD L. SMEAD, formerly in charge of office of the Company at Rawlins, now located at Tampico, Mexico.

SECRETARY—BURTON A. SMEAD, of Garwood & Garwood, Denver, Colo.

TREASURER—J. M. RUMSEY, President of Stock Growers' National Bank, Rawlins, Wyo., for twenty-five years Cashier of First National Bank of Rawlins.

GENERAL MANAGER—J. B. CONGER, oil operator, Rawlins, Wyo., and Denver, Colo.

ASSISTANT GENERAL MANAGER—A. F. PUSCH, Rawlins, Wyo.

DIRECTOR—WILL REID, Newspaper Publisher, a resident of Rawlins for twenty-five years.

DIRECTOR—CHARLES F. BLYDENBURGH, Rawlins, Wyo., Attorney at Law, of the firm of Blydenburgh & McMicken. Mr. Blydenburgh has been a resident of Rawlins for over thirty years. He is considered one of the best posted lawyers on United States Location Laws in the State of Wyoming, and has had full charge of all legal details relative to our locations, deeds, organization, etc.

DIRECTOR—W. W. GARWOOD, of the law firm of Garwood & Garwood, Denver, Colo.

Address All Communications to

LARSEN OIL COMPANY

NATIONAL SAFETY VAULT BUILDING, DENVER, COLO.

Prospectus — Larsen Oil Company

CONSTABLE'S SALE

THE STATE OF WYOMING,
County of Carbon. } ss.

By virtue of an execution issued out of the _Justice of the Peace Court, Rawlins_, Carbon County, State of Wyoming, by _Jno. C. Friend_ on a Judgment rendered in said Court, on the _19th_ day of _August_ 19_11_, and directed and delivered to me as ~~Constable~~ Sheriff, I have levied upon and will proceed to sell on the _2_ day of _September_ 19_11_, between the hours of _9_ o'clock a. m., and _4_ o'clock p. m., at public vendue, to the highest bidder, for cash in hand, at _Cow Creek_, ~~about six miles southly~~ Cow Creek Ranch the following described property, to wit:

One Steam Engine, and Equipment Derrick Etc

Said property being levied upon as the property of _F. F. Brooke_ and to satisfy an execution issued out of said _Justice of the Peace_ Court, in favor of _James Robertson_ and against _F. F. Brooke_ for the sum of _Two Hundred_ ($200.00) DOLLARS.

THIS, the _22d_ day of _August_ 19_11_.

D. B. Campbell
~~Constable~~ Sheriff Carbon County, Wyoming.
By _W. P. Mills_
Deputy

There was lots of money looking for oil and gas in those days. This equipment was sold to pay Jim Robertson for all the coal he hauled to keep the steam engines going.

Sulphur Springs Ranch

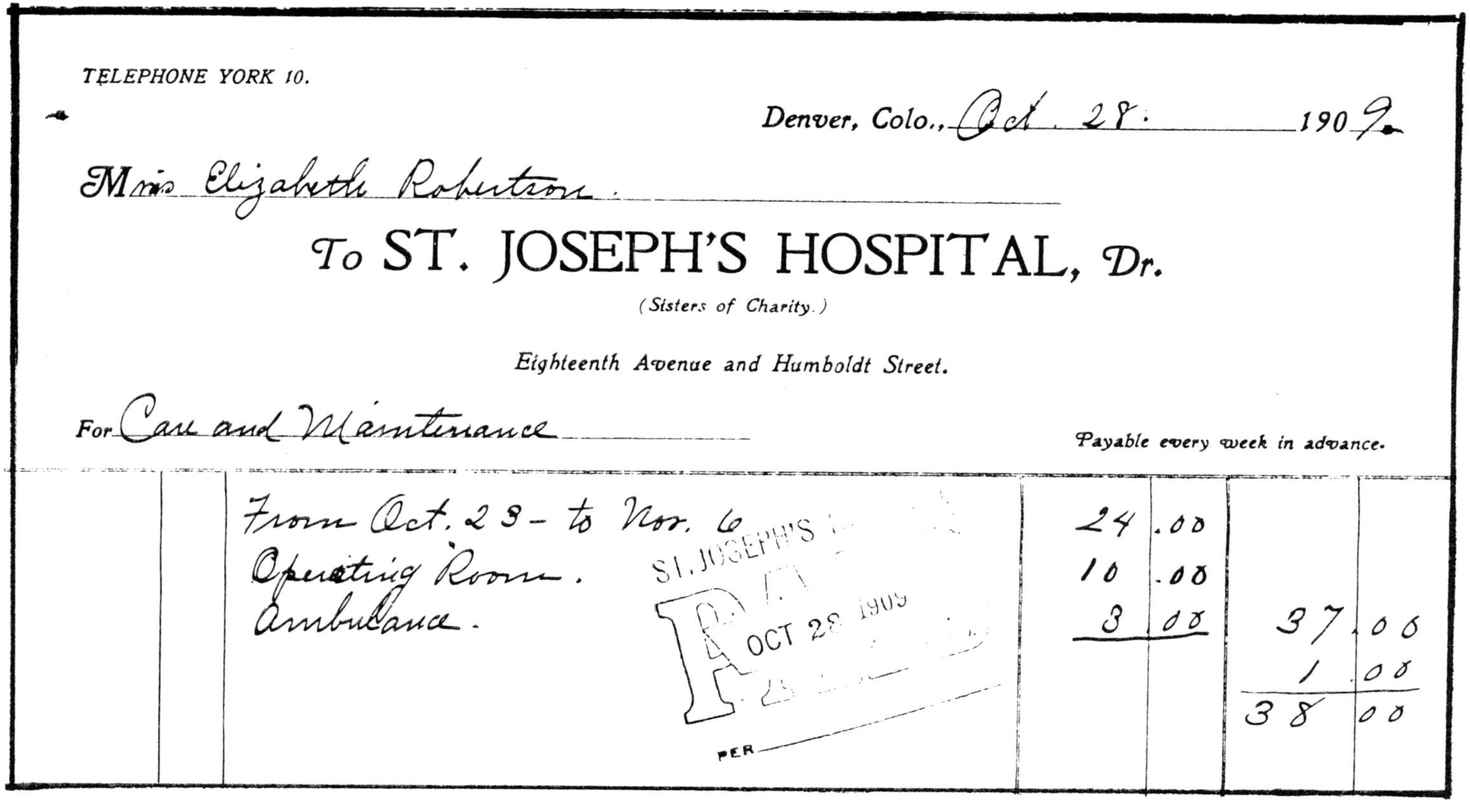

TELEPHONE YORK 10.

Denver, Colo., *Oct. 28*, 190*9*

M*iss Elizabeth Robertson*

To ST. JOSEPH'S HOSPITAL, Dr.

(Sisters of Charity.)

Eighteenth Avenue and Humboldt Street.

For *Care and Maintenance*

Payable every week in advance.

From Oct. 23 – to Nov. 6	24.00	37.00
Operating Room	10.00	1.00
Ambulance	3.00	38.00

[Stamp: ST. JOSEPH'S OCT 28 1909]

PER

Compare these costs with those of today.

Sulphur Springs Ranch

"The letter edged in black" was the customary way to report a death in those days.

> Tinlaro March 29' 88
>
> Dear Brother
> It is with grief that I have to inform you that our Father died here on Saturday March 24th at 2-10 p.m. being confined to bed a week And I trust his Spirit is in heaven and have every reason to believe that it is Dr McLagan was in attendance regularly he said disease was Congestion on the lungs And I would say that every Faculty was entirely run down to its natural termination Oh how gradually did his weakness creep on slowly but surely one staying every day with him would not notice it so soon but he was certain of it

Letter written by Jack Robertson, Scotland.

Sulphur Springs Ranch

FORM 1054

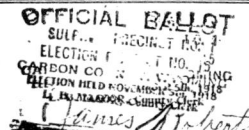

REGISTRATION

AND

POLL BOOK

OF AN

ELECTION

Held November 5th, 1918

Election District No. *15*

Sulphur Polling Precinct No. *1*

Carbon County, State of Wyoming

IN PRECINCTS WHERE PRIOR REGISTRATION IS NOT REQUIRED, THE JUDGES OF ELECTION SHALL ALSO TAKE THE FOLLOWING OATH OF REGISTRY AGENT:

THE STATE OF WYOMING, } ss.
County of Carbon.

I, *H. H. Bruning*, Registry Agent for Election District No. *15*, in the County of Carbon, Wyoming, do solemnly swear (or affirm) that I will perform all the duties of Registry Agent in and for said election district according to law and the best of my ability, and that in the discharge of my duties as such agent I will honestly endeavor to prevent fraud, deceit or any other manner of abuse of the elective franchise, so help me God (or for which I will answer under the pains and penalties of perjury).

H. H. Bruning

Subscribed and sworn to before me this *23* day of *March* A. D. 192*0*.

Mrs. John Robertson
John Robertson

Sulphur Springs Ranch

THE WILLOWS

The horses strained into their collars pulling the stage up the long sloping hill south out of Sulphur. On top in a clump of willow and berry bushes a little spring was flowing sweet water. To the east as far as the horizon lay yellow sand dunes.

There was The Willows, the next station, south of Sulphur Springs, located in a lovely spot up against a hill of willow and boxelder trees. The peaceful beauty of this stage stop was a welcome relief for the traveler since it was the only one from Rawlins to Baggs with a tree on it and not out on the open prairie.

In 1880 Joe Dentz was the proprietor of this station as well as a stage driver. According to the records he was a very popular stage driver. He and his family lived here for several years. Some of his children were born here.

An advertisement in the *Carbon County Journal* published in Rawlins appeared in September 17, 1887 reads:

"Travelers upon the White River Line will bear in mind that all leading brands of cigars are kept at the Willows Eating Station."

According to a news article in the same newspaper of December 8, 1888 Joe got into trouble trying to provide all possible accommodations for the stage station's overnight quests. It reports:

"Joe Dentz who runs a 'road ranch' at the Willow Springs Station was arrested and tried before Justice Dodge for selling liquor without a license. He was adjudged guilty and fined $65.00 and cost amounting to $20.00. The sum was paid in full."

Information from the United States Post Office records lists Stella Doty as postmistress on March 27, 1898 at the Willows Post Office.

The same newspaper reports that Mr. Dow Doty of Willow Springs was in Rawlins on business Tuesday, February 12, 1898.

A few years prior to this time it seems that the ranch foreman Dave Stewart was replaced as manager of the L7 ranch of Baggs by Dow Doty who with his brother John owned the Willows Ranch on the Rawlins-Baggs road. A man named Charley Neiman describes Doty as having been "very much of a tenderfoot." "He was foreman of the ranch for only a short time as the L7 soon went out of business."

Mrs. Gertrude Doty Randleman of Fort Collins, Colo. was interviewed in August 1979 to gather the following information about the Willow Stage Station.
Mrs. Randleman's uncle John Doty and her father Dow Doty bought the Willows Station in the early 1890's and about 1900 sold it to J.R. Rumsey of Rawlins. Mrs. Randleman was born 1896 in Illinois.

Her cousin, Mazie Doty Newell was one of twins born at the Willows. This station was about 34 miles from Rawlins and a doctor was unable to reach the place. The other twin died and may have been buried there.

Mrs. Randleman remembers when she was about in the first grade in the early 1900's being with Mr. Rumsey either coming in or going out from Rawlins in cold weather when the car broke down at 16 Mile Station and they had to stay over night. All she remembers of 16 Mile is that it was terribly cold and the blankets were heavy, scratchy wool ones.

John Doty operated the Rawlins Mercantile for many years.

As far as 1906 after the John Robertsons bought the Sulphur place there were several different families who had lived at the Willows, but we do not know who they were. Some time in there freight driver named Ralph Ryan died near the

The Willows Stage Station about 34 miles south of Rawlins. Joe Dentz proprietor and stage driver, 1880.

Willows in a terrible blizzard.

When the stage stopped running on this road the buildings were moved away. Part of them taken to the J O Ranch and as late as 1933 the rest were taken to Dad, Wyoming where they still stand.

A letter (1980) from Mazie Doty Newell - 535 Bayside Road, Bellingham, WA

>About the post offices: I hunted out of storage some old letters. Evidently there was a post office at Sulphur for many years. I have envelopes addressed to Sulphur Wyo. 1886, 1887, 1888, 1889, 1890. There are only two addressed to the Willows 1896 and 1899. There were two Willow post offices. I have seen an old picture of the first Willow post office. Perhaps Sulphur ranch was sold to someone who did not want a post office or a stop to change horses or the government did not like the situation.
>
>I cannot recall the exact distance from Sulphur to our ranch, the Willows. It was three or three and one half miles. The first Willows was about 2 miles south of Sulphur and I think the office was there for probably one and one half to two years. There was no ranch there so people must have been hired to take care of mail and horses. There was a fine spring or springs with willow trees and choke cherry trees and shrubs of some sort. Just behind the buildings was a bluff. The place was to the left of the south bound road.
>
>Going south from the first Willows was "our" Willows. This ranch together with the Cow Creek Ranch further south belonged to the Doty brothers with a $\vee\!\!D$ brand, the cattle had a dewlap for further identification. Just before reaching the ranch there was a sandy hill which

posed a problem for freighters and wagons. They frequently took the wagons up the hill separately. There was much freighting then from Rawlins to Baggs, Dixon, etc. (Snake River Valley) and even on to Steamboat Springs, Colorado. At the top of the hill on the right was a grove of trees, mostly willows, service berry bushes maybe a box elder or two. The ranch buildings were about 75 feet south of the trees.

My mother told me the first summer she was in Wyoming 1887 there was one freighter driving oxen (his last year). She was fascinated to see this and sat at the top of the hill to watch. Later the driver told my father that he had real trouble getting up the hill as he couldn't yell at his oxen as usual with a lady sitting there. When one of his oxen with horns died, he had the horns polished and sent them to my mother. I still have the horns.

The last time I was at the Willows location (about ten years ago) I looked in vain for a piece of broken pottery or some object of interest only to me. My twin sister (stillborn) was buried near the trees and two very large stones marked the grave. Even the stones were gone.

I was born there at the Willows and it was our first home. The logs for the main part of the house were telegraph poles. The army was abandoning Fort Fred Steele and they were dismantling the telegraph line.

There was an aspen grove, perhaps one fourth mile south of the ranch buildings and on the left side of the road. The road there crossed a small alkali flat.

I especially remember the aspen grove because of a very sad story. In the extremely bad winter of 1889 we lost all the cattle; only the milk cows in the barn survived. In the spring there were carcasses in the aspen groves and two carcasses wedged between the trees were still standing. The story made a deep impression on me.

The change (station) south of us was at Muddy Bridge. I remember the Overland Trail crossing near Sulphur. Even after I was grown there were some grave markers partially legible. I was told that there were five graves in the canyon.

I like living near my son, Dr. Robert C. Newell, in this very beautiful part of the United States. Ralph and I moved here in 1974 and he died in 1976. However, Carbon County always seems like my very own place.

Sincerely,

Mazie Doty Newell

PERKINS' DINNER STOP

The Perkins' Dinner Station was three miles south beyond the Willows. Charley Perkins was the first merchant on the Snake River. His original store was established in the early 1870's in a dugout on the north bank of the Snake River. He bought hides from the trappers or traded "grub" for them. He also sold feed and whiskey and was mail contractor for the route between Baggs and Meeker.

He also operated a freight line from Snake River to Rawlins and built a building about three miles south of the Willow Stage Stop where meals were served. This was called Perkin's Dinner Station.

It seems that any one might have been free to set up business along the Rawlins-Baggs road. All that was needed was to build a shelter along the road where there was also a good supply of water. The land along there at that time was open range, little land was bought, just used as long as it was needed. The buildings either tumbled down after awhile or were moved somewhere else.

MUDDY BRIDGE STATION
or
JERRY'S PLACE

Interview with Ed Tierney, Rawlins - Sid Weber, Baggs, August, 1979
and others

About 40 miles from Rawlins the station was called Muddy Bridge or just "Muddy." It was located on desolate gumbo flats where the greasewood grows thick and the wind never stops blowing. Two creeks come together here - Cow Creek and one called Dry Cow Creek which is anything but dry during a flash flood or the spring run off. These two creeks run into the old restless, relentless Muddy Creek. "The Muddy" has carved its deep mark down through this part of Wyoming with banks 15 to 20 feet high in places.

Occasionally the creek banks flatten out where a rocky earth formation affords a firm bed for crossing. Except during very high water, teams and wagons had no trouble crossing at these places. These natural earth formations dictated the direction the road took since there were very few bridges or those that were there often washed out during high water.

In the freighting days a driver named Kelsey bogged down with two wagons and teams at this station. The mud was so bad that the wagon wheels became locked and the horses had no footing. After many hours of waiting Glen Wilson came along with extra teams to pull Kelsey out.

Our Uncle Jim Robertson tried crossing the Muddy Creek here in the spring of 1912. His horses sank into the mud and water. He was able somehow to hold their heads above water until Peter Hansen came along and pulled the team out. Uncle Jim suffered for quite a while after that from the chill and exposure to standing many hours in the cold water to keep his horses from drowning.

The crossing at Muddy Station

Charlie Perkins of Dixon operated a stage line from Snake River to Rawlins. Various vehicles were used on the freight and stage lines depending on weather and number of passengers; jerkies, buck boards and stage coaches drawn by four or more horses were all in use. The coaches carried lights on the front to light up the road. One night, it is told, a driver failed to have his lights on, missed the crossing and drove his team into very deep water drowning a team valued at about $400.00, but he managed to save the mail. (The above paragraph was taken from WPA interview, Emma Jensen Blair, Februrary 1939 - Archives, Cheyenne.)

The *Carbon County Journal* printed in Rawlins reports on October 29, 1887 that G.K. Woods wishes to notify the public he has plenty of baled hay for sale at his Muddy Bridge Road Ranch.

The first public records we have on the Muddy Bridge Station are post office records listing on May 27, 1893 Clara Downing as an applicant for the postmistress job. She was turned down. On October 19, 1894 Elizabeth Wilkes became postmistress.

> "T.J. Wallace of the Muddy Station and proprietor of the Rawlins—Colorado Mail and Stage line reports on April 1, 1899 as he came into Rawlins after being out all night trying to get the stages through - 'In all the years that I've been in the stage business I've never seen the roads in such awful condition as they are this year.
>
> On March 10, 1900 T.J. Wallace died of pneumonia at the station and the body was brought to Rawlins for burial. Mr. Wallace was a popular and well respected business man and he will be greatly missed."

Mrs. Wallace discontinued the stage service provided by her husband and H. Rasmussen of Rawlins took over the Wallace outfit. Mr. Rasmussen announced "that he would soon have just first-class stock and would keep the line in the best possible condition." (News report in *Carbon County Journal*).

After the turn of the century this station took on a questionable shade of red. We can remember only hearing whispers about it from our very proper families. We heard the name of Jerry Snodgrass. She "ran" the station several years after the stages stopped running.

Since then we have learned that in addition to a very dirty stage station where meals were served she ran a whore house. The red light district of the range.

It took quite a little coaxing to get the story of Jerry Snodgrass from people who remembered her. She was eccentric to say the least. Each person interviewed had another interesting bit of information about her.

Jerry was a tall, big, rough person who wore overalls, a fur coat, high heels and many diamond rings and was "hard as nails and meaner than all get out."

She is said to have acquired a band of sheep, herds of cattle and horses by the old rustling method. The men from whom she rustled were handicapped to prosecute because "she had too much on them."

We were given quite a long list of names of men who moved in with her or she moved in with them, but probably outstanding was Dad Corlett after whom Dad, Wyoming was named. His homestead was near her place.

She suddenly left the Baggs area and was last heard of driving a beer wagon in Denver, Colo. in the 1920's.

Ironically when we visited what remains of her establishment the only things that remain are a lot of scattered rusty nails and a bed springs that the greasewood plants have grown up through and anchored to the desert floor.

We are told that this station burned to the ground.

Dad Corlette's Place today Dad, Wyo. deserted

JUMBO STOP
Interview with Sid Weber

Before the final destination at Baggs there was one more stop called Jumbo Stop. There were no buildings there - just a place they called a "rest stop." This was about 12 miles out of Baggs.

Just before coming to Jumbo Stop there is an open flat ground area on the east side of the road called Peach Orchard Flats. A freighter at one time had lost some crates of peaches off of his load and they scattered over the alkali flat. South down the road and to the west is Robber's Gulch. There once was an attempt to rob the stage at this point, but the robbers were unsucessful and left the scene of the crime.

From Jumbo Stop it is twelve miles more to Baggs where our story will end. This was not the real "end of the line," but we decided when we started this historical project to stay within the boundaries of Wyoming.

There was probably one like it at "Jumbo Rest Stop"
Photo taken at Sulphur

BAGGS, WYOMING

Baggs, Wyoming is the last stage stop in this account of the line known as the Rawlins-Baggs or White River or Milk River route. Baggs is one of Wyoming's oldest towns. It rests in a beautiful valley with the Little Snake River winding its way through. This area is "hay paradise." The ranchers, and there are many old families along here, have more hay than they can use and so are able to supply winter feed for others not on the river.

Our grandfather Robertson, Uncle James Robertson and father H.H. Bruning all used to winter sheep on the Snake River. Most of the hay they bought was from Charles Benson and others.

Baggs has an interesting history and there are many stories about the early happenings along that part of the river. It depends on what you know and what you want to say about how the stories go.

Sometime in the 1870's George and Maggie Baggs homesteaded the old Double Eleven Ranch just below the town of Baggs and ran a bunch of cattle there. This homestead was the first piece of land proved up on along the Little Snake River and carried the first deed. George Baggs later sold his cattle outfit to the Swan Land and Livestock Co., the L7 brand.

It seems to be a generally accepted fact that George and Maggie were not legally married. Maggie like a lot of pioneer women had to fight her own battles. She was said to be a rough and ready, kindly sort of person and was as much of a help running the ranch as if it belonged to her. The couple cared for and raised three orphan children.

We were told that George was an artist with a broad axe. He built his four room house on the homestead with skillfully hand hewn logs. It stood just at the edge of the town of Baggs for a good many years.

The town of Baggs is named for George Baggs, as is Dixon for Bob Dixon and Slater for Bob Slater.

Other reports tell us that if Maggie Baggs were living today she would be in the front lines of the women's liberation movement. Besides being a fairly shrewd business woman she had "roving eyes" and "a way" with the men. She was constantly interfering in business and having affairs with the cowboys around the ranch. She chose a red headed cowpuncher named Mike Sweet as her favorite.

Eventually Maggie's carrying-on exhausted the patience of even the long suffering George Baggs and he arranged for a divorce. Maggie got half the money from the sale of the cattle and she and Mike Sweet left for California. When the money ran out so did Sweet and Maggie was last heard of running some "rooming apartments" in Galveston, Texas.

There are many tales to tell about the happenings around Baggs - one tells us that Butch Cassidy and his Wild Bunch became bored hiding out at Robber's Roost in Utah and decided to celebrate. They liked the two little cow towns of Dixon and Baggs along the Wyoming border northeast of "Browns Hole" and thought they would stir things up a bit.

So Butch Cassidy accompanied by his personal retinue of eight long riders and a number of friends from "The Hole" and "The Roost" set out for Bagg and Dixon to put on a real old-time celebration and spend the Castle Gate payroll. They rode into Dixon first whooping and yelling and shot up the town. Then rode on to Baggs to finish the celebration. From *Carbon County Journal*, July 29, 1897.

It is also said that the next day they went to all of the places they had laid waste to and paid for the damages in stolen gold pieces.

"Cattle Round-up" Mess Wagon near Baggs, Wyoming

Minnie Shank's Inn at Baggs
A home away from home for the Sulphur and Hay Gulch ranchers who wintered sheep near Baggs for many years.

Everyone seems to know about Bob Meldrum and what a snake in the grass he was. Our grandfather wrote to the members of the family living away from Sulphur in 1912 telling about the brutal shooting of the well liked, popular young cowboy, Chick Bowen. Our grandfather was particularly concerned because he was a sheepman and Meldrum was a paid killer and he already had 14 notches on his gun.

First the fur trappers came into this beautiful valley laying waste to the fur bearing animals and leaving nothing constructive behind them. The miners followed in their foot steps and next the big cattle owners whose herds over grazed the lush meadows with no thought of the future. It was the homesteader, the pioneer home seeker, who stayed and "proved up" on his place that was the real solid

Baggs, Wyoming

Originally just a Bank at Baggs.

foundation upon which this community grew.

There are names of, far too many to mention, families who were on the River in the middle part of the 1800's. Generation after generation they have been successful stock people. Many of these people knew our family members who spent the winters in Baggs with their sheep camps near by.

Particularly at this point we owe a great deal to Sid and Nina Weber and Matt Weber and to Addie Corson who helped us with information that we needed to have to piece together with what we knew a more complete account of our family's lives that were lived a generation ago.

Addie Corson remembers a lot about early Baggs and its people. She has lived there since 1907. Addie is 82 years old and is still very able mentally and physically. We visited in her charming, sunny living room. Addie was born at Hahns Peak, Colo.

Mrs. Corson knew many members of our family. The Walter Leaps who lived in Baggs at the time they were married. Uncle Jim and Aunt Alice Robertson and their son Dick who lived at Minnie Shank's Hotel for a while and later in a home in town. She knew Grandfather John Robertson and Aunt Jean Robertson Tallman who owned property on Baker's Peak and spent her summers there.

Minnie Shank (Mrs. A.T.) at her "Inn" provided a home away from home for our men folk who wintered sheep near Baggs.

The hotel building itself was moved in the early 1900's from the 4 mile placer mine on 4 Mile Creek into Baggs by Mrs. Bright. She built onto it and it became three stories high.

At this time Minnie Shank was running a cafe in a frame building across the street from the hotel. She did the cooking and Addie Corson who then was only 16 years old waited table, scrubbed the floor, washed the dishes, ran errands and anything else that needed to be done - all for $15.00 a month. What few tips she received she had to share with the management. Mr. and Mrs. A.T. Shank also owned a ranch about three miles out of Baggs.

About 1912 Mrs. Shank bought the hotel that Mrs. Bright had started and she operated this place for a good many years. She had the telephone exchange center there also.

Mrs. Shank raised her grandson, Emil Blackmore. His mother had died at childbirth. Grandmother Shank sent Emil to college.

As Sid Weber and we sat visiting with Addie, stories were tossed back and forth. One when Mrs. Shank was mayor of Baggs several citizens wanted to put in a "modern" sewage system. The mayor said, "People went behind bushes for 10,000 years and they can for 10,000 more." It took a while to get a sewage system put into Baggs.

Another story about how fast things moved in Baggs - the stage and freight service was held up while the bridge was fixed at Baggs. A newspaper article states "F.H. Kelsey's teams passed thru Dixon today with the last load of timber for the repairs of the Baggs bridge which was broken down by a Bear River freight outfit over two months ago."

While grandfather Robertson, who was very "straight laced," was staying at Shank's Hotel a young man who lived in the Baggs area decided to do a little "partying" and became quite inebriated, noisy and a nuisance. So some of his friends tied him into a mail sack and sent him by the mail stage up to Slater where Mildred McIntosh, the postmistress, turned him loose. Our grandfather was absolutely horrified at such carryings on.

Mrs. Corson and Sid Weber remember that grandfather Robertson "swore" by starting the day with a huge dish, not a cereal dish, but a serving dish of oatmeal and real cream, it was a certain guarantee for a long and healthy life.

The oatmeal had to be cooked overnight to be just right. We children can remember the oatmeal too. Every morning at the ranch we had to join grandfather with a large serving of oatmeal. Today some of us can't stand the sight of oatmeal.

A man named Tom Vernon once owned half of Baggs. When he died he had only one heir, a nephew, who did not live in the area. Vernon's real estate gradually decayed and there are tumbled down houses all over town, but all the vacant lots and surrounding areas are full of trailer houses now. There are oil and gas developments all around that part of the country.

We ate lunch in a friendly little cafe in the middle of town with Nina and Sid Weber and their grandson, Clint Weber, and a young man named Ron Wille. Clint and Ron were working at the Blue Gap Natural Gas well about 15 miles north of Baggs. It has taken nearly 80 years to see the harvest being reaped from under the earth's crust that all of our people had invested in and went broke trying to develop. They had such high hopes for success, but the drilling goes much deeper these days.

Baggs ends the stage-freight line as far as we are taking it. It actually serviced a lot of Northern Colorado down as far as Meeker. Other people interested in history have written about this.

At the completion of our efforts to record this small area of history we realize that there can be very few, if any, authentic accounts of life as it was over the last one hundred and seventeen years still to be published. The majority of those people who had a story to tell have either told it or passed on without leaving any records and their place has been taken by circumstance by historians who can only reconstruct and hypothesize.

We have made every effort to reconstruct the events of this account as they really happened to us or our families and friends.

L to R - Matt (Dutch) Weber, Sid and his Wife Nina Weber. There have been three generations of this family ranch near Baggs on the Snake River.
Much of the material for this book came about through their help. They knew our families.

Showing the wood stove inside a sheep wagon.
Courtesy Carbon Co. Museum

THE CANYONS AND HOMESTEADS IN BETWEEN WHERE PEOPLE LIVED

Jepp's Canyon
Squaw Canyon
The Slide
Snow Shoe Gulch
Hay Gulch
J O Ranch or Cow Creek

The first five of these canyons are on the west side of the range of hills now called the Atlantic Rim.

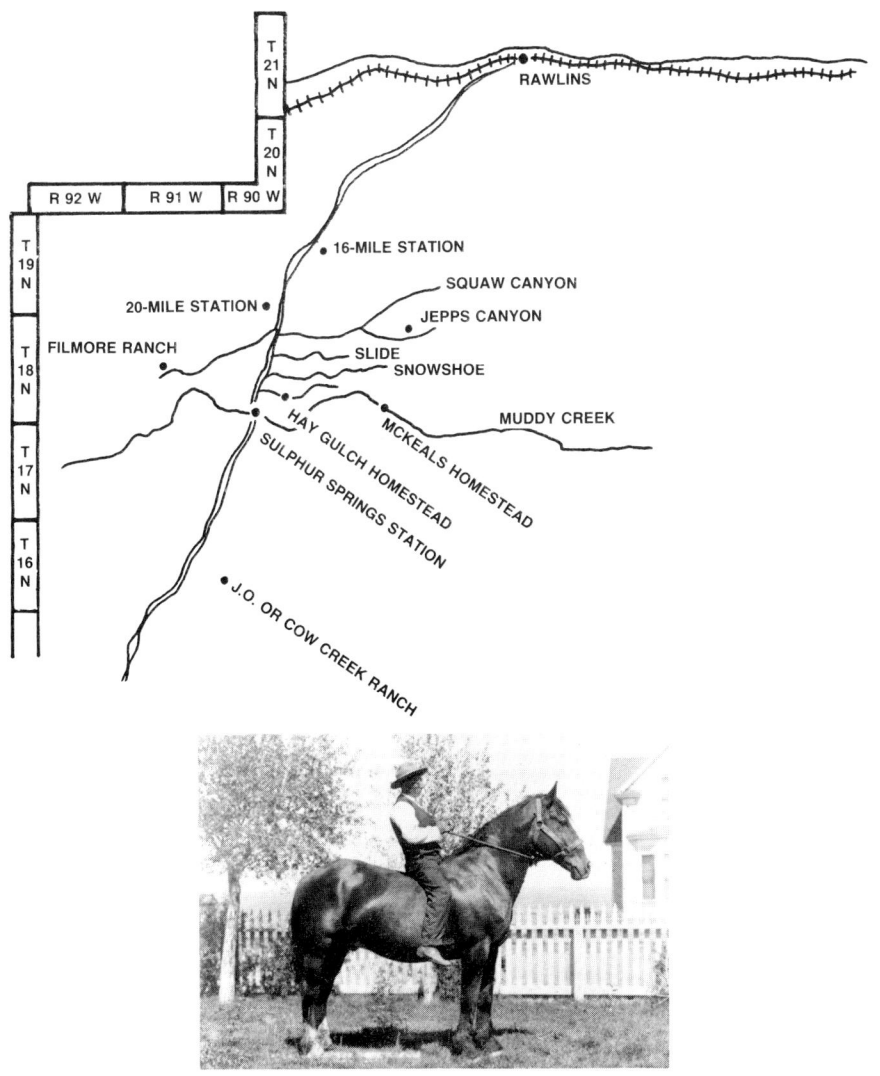

Jepp Peterson, the horse raiser

JEPPS CANYON

Southwest of Rawlins, about 22 miles on the east side of the old Rawlins-Baggs Stage Road runs a range of high hills that sweep on down into Colorado. Every now and then there is a canyon with a clear stream running down the bottom of it fed by springs and run-off water. These steams feed into Alamosa Creek which in turn runs into the Muddy Creek and that winds its way by a very crooked path into the Little Snake River at Baggs.

These canyons or gulches were natural sites for squatters and homesteader. The homesteader with a good water supply on his place had a chance of winning against the often fierce environment. Very few dry farmers lasted a year.

So secluded are some of the smaller draws and gulches coming into the main formation that they are hardly noticed. These were choice locations for the moonshiners during prohibition days. On horseback or the modern mode of transportation, motorcycles, one may come across scattered barrel staves and rusty boilers that are evidence of a once thriving business.

Tucked back into the hills in the wide canyon where runs Separation Creek a man named Jepp Peterson built a home. The canyon was fertile. Grass grew belly high to the animals. Chokecherry, black currant and serviceberry bushes were abundant. Beaver had dammed up the stream into little ponds. Their stick houses indicated their domain.

Jepps was a typical pioneer place, small log cabin, log barn and corrals. He had come from Denmark, like Jim Hansen, and also like the latter raised horses and cattle. They supplied the freighters with the good strong horses they needed to pull the heavy wagons.

The lure of the American west and the urging of the people already settled in Wyoming brought many more relatives and friends from Denmark. Iver Hansen, a nephew of Jepp Peterson came and Thyra Jensen. Iver and Thyra were soon married and lived at Uncle Jepp's place, but a tragic incident claimed the life of Iver only one month after the wedding. Millicent Miller (Goffar), Jim Hansen's neice, went out to stay with the greiving young widow for awhile.

Later Thyra Jensen Hansen met Skerner Rasmussen, who worked for the Ferguson Mercantile Store in Rawlins and they were married.

One fall when Jepp's cattle were ready for market, he took a load by train to Omaha, Nebraska. During his stay there in a hotel he was accidentally asphyxiated by gas fumes leaking from a gas light fixture in his room.

Jepp never married and after his death his place was only occupied now and then by itinerant cowboys, one of them being Bill Byers who often rounded up and sold unclaimed wild horses.

Bill Beyers (Biars) was a well known bronc rider. He was the first cowboy to ride the famous bucking horse called "Pin Ears" at a rodeo in Baggs. Some other bronc stompers at a later time were Pete Olsen, Jim Karstoft, and by the way his wife, Jessie Alameda Karstoft, was no shabby rider herself, and Jack Tapers.

And now the 90 years have taken their toll. The corrals have disappeared and only a few logs and a bit of the foundation of the cabin and barn remain.

Jepp Peterson's Place "then" about 1900

and now 1979

Jepp's Canyon

SQUAW CANYON

Just past the mouth into Jepps Canyon a small narrow canyon takes off to the north. The stories that have come down tell of the canyons getting its name from an Indian squaw who lived there in the early 1880's. There was and still is, a small coal mine in that area, from which it is said she mined and sold coal to the nearby ranchers.

An account written by Henry Bunch of Baggs, Wyo. in 1937 gives an account of an experience he had in the early days.

"In the spring of 1883 I was living at my home in Iowa. Several of us heard of a placer development in Route County, Colo. on Fortification Creek. A man named Calicott came to town trying to sell stocks in a company developing a claim in this area. He succeeded in disposing of ten shares to ten different people in our locality. I was one of them. I was one of five of the group to go out to inspect the property.

We landed in Rawlins May 28, 1883 coming by train. When we arrived in Rawlins the ground was covered with a wet snow.

We looked around town for some transportation to Fortification Creek. We were lucky to find some freight teams loaded for Meeker ready to start, and we made a deal for them to haul our outfit to Snake River, we paid them five cents a pound and we had the privilege of walking along with them, which did not turn out to be a very hard job. We left Rawlins the 29th of May, and the first day made four miles, and kept that gate for five days arriving at Separation Creek 22 miles from Rawlins in 4½ days.

At Separation Creek lived a Frenchman and a Squaw, we made a deal with him to bring us on into Fortification Creek, as the freight teams were too slow. The Frenchman had an old mule and a buckskin pony with a light wagon, and we took turns in driving and walking.

We were two days getting to Snake River. There was a Company of Soldiers here under the command of Colonel Trotter and it was known as "Camp on Snake River." We arrived here about noon and camped overnight. The next morning when we got up we found the ground covered with snow and as the Frenchman had taken up his abode with the Wilson Brothers who were running a Saloon nearby he became pretty well loaded, we could not get him started, so about noon we pulled out without him and went about four miles and camped to await his coming. He came in about dark and sure did some swearing which he was proficient at. It took us two days to arrive at our destination and we were glad to get rid of the Frenchman."

THE SLIDE

A gulch between Jepp's Canyon and Snow Shoe was only known to us as "The Slide." Water runs down that gulch the same as the rest. It flows into Alamosa or Alamoosa (found spelled and pronounced both ways) Creek and into the Muddy Creek.

The terrain suggests a massive slide although it is all brushed over now. The following account was found in the August 18, 1888 issue of the *Carbon County Journal*:

> "We were informed by Mr. A.W. Fullie of the Alamossa Gulch, that place known as 'The Land Slide' at the west branch of the gulch, was a spectacle of wonderous beauty.
>
> When the enormous mass of earth and rock was rended from the mountain side it exposed a huge seam of coal 18 feet thick and nearly one fourth mile long. Last week during that extraordinary storm that passed south of this city (Rawlins), the bridge on the Rawlins and White River road was washed out. The muddy stream that had been dry for days arose above its banks and overflowed the upper bottom lands for yards in width.
>
> The bridge across Alamoosa was washed away and a torrent of water as wide as Snake River rolled down its sides.
>
> A huge flame broke from the hill of exposed coal. The immense vein had been ignited by lightning. The entire mountain side was a scene of blazing beauty.
>
> Every once in a while there was a terrific explosion filling the air with earth, rocks and lumps of coal.
>
> Many curiosity seekers are flocking to view the scene."

There was no evidence of all of this during our time, but once when Dad was on horseback in that area he discovered a small opening in the earth with steam drifting out of it. He took us up there to see it, but we can't find anything like that now.

Slide Canyon

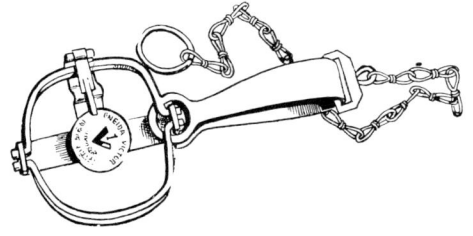 

SNOW SHOE GULCH

Another bridge to cross on the Rawlins-Baggs road. This bridge crosses the stream coming down Snow Shoe Gulch. There was never a stage station here.

We have never known for sure why Snow Shoe Canyon was given this name, but it was said that there had once been found a pair of snowshoes hanging in a tree up there somewhere.

We always have such wonderful memories of a patch of whispering Quaking Aspen trees growing near the water. There is no sound so mysterious and plaintiff as the sighing and moaning of wind through aspen leaves.

There was a spring with cold, clear water. This was our favorite picnic spot. The families from Hay Gulch and Sulphur Springs went there many years to enjoy the natural beauty of the place and a sumptuous 4th of July picnic.

Our names were carved into the white bark of the aspen trees until the beaver cut them all down building more dams in a frantic, but hopeless effort to save the water.

Through the years the water table in all of that country has dropped considerably. Many once free-flowing springs and streams are nearly dry.

There are no more beaver and no more aspen trees in Snow Shoe Canyon.

Efforts were made a few years back, according to an article from "Beaver Management and Ecology in Wyoming" by James Grasse and Euvern Putnam, 1950-1955, to transplant and support areas where beaver can contribute much to man's welfare. James Karsoft, a government trapper in the Rawlins area transplanted some beaver into Snow Shoe and Jepp's Canyon. They had a rough go of it because the water was disappearing from these streams. The beaver would travel from one canyon to the other as a dam would dry up or as one would fill up with water. Finally in an effort to find water the beaver left the canyons and followed Separation Creek to the Union Pacific Railroad tracks. Many were killed crossing the tracks, John Hansen tells us.

Beaver have been known to make long migratory trips through cities, over mountains and across deserts, but such migrations are not the usual thing according to Misters Grasse and Putnam.

HAY GULCH

Just another gulch - no, not to us. This was our home for many years. It looked like all the other gulches. The headwaters came out of a high walled canyon that opened out, now and then, into natural hay fields and finally onto flat sagebrush land.

Our father and mother, Herman and Elizabeth Bruning, chose this canyon for a homestead in 1915. There was plenty of water then. A lovely cool spring of good tasting water that our father walled up with rock and wood. This spring supplied us with water and refrigeration. We hung the buckets of milk from strings tied to the nails on the walls and floated the watermelons on top of the water.

The ranch house was built on level ground just above the spring. The water had to be carried up hill in buckets to fill the reservoir in the old Majestic cook stove and our drinking water bucket.

The Bruning Hay Gulch homestead adjoined our grandparent's, Robertsons, ranch at Sulphur. We soon had worn a foot path, a mile and a half long, over the hill visiting each other. There were times when wagons and buggies were needed and the road we created is still there.

As the casual observer looks across the hot, dry sage covered land he sees nothing but desolation. The homesteader found that nature had provided some of the richest top soil there is under that sagebrush. It took a lot of back breaking hours to clear away enough brush for the most wonderful vegetable garden any of us have seen since. If it hadn't been for the water with the soil this could not have been so. Included is a photo of a field of rye hay grown on land cleared by hand of sagebrush on our ranch. The hay grew as high as our heads. An appropo quote from one of our grandfather's letters: "There is no salary like a good crop of hay or a good garden."

Our father, with the help of Charlie Dow of Rawlins, built our house in 1916-17. While the family lived at Sulphur, father hauled cedar posts from "down" the Muddy for fences and boards from an abandoned tar paper shack to start the buildings on the homestead. We lived in the tar paper shack with a tent along side of it until we could occupy the new addition. The shack was incorporated in the new structure and served as the kitchen dining area.

That house was so well built that it still stands, firm and strong despite the woodpeckers, the weather, pack rats and the vandals. It is now 72 years old and has had no care since we left it in 1940. Many of the ceder posts are still strong and upright in the ground.

We three Robertson granddaughters have each separately written our personal accounts of memories and impressions of life on the ranches. these will appear later in this account.

Hay Gulch

Our mother,
Elizabeth Robertson Bruning

Our father,
Herman Henry "Dutch" Bruning, Jr.

Bruning winter camp - 1928
Sheep feeding near Baggs

Our Brands listed in 1916 Brandbook — plus a couple of Jens Hansen's

Brand		Location			Owner
ꙅᴐ Reverse B-Lazy J	...	LRC		LSH	H.H. Bruning, Rawlins, Wyo.
JB	...	LRC		LTH	Mrs. T. Bruning, Rawlins, Wyo.
NP	...	LSH			H.H. Bruning, Rawlins, Wyo.
A̲	...	LRC	BS	LSH	Charles Bruning, Rawlins, Wyo.
─┼─ ear mark	...		BS		John Robertson, Sulphur, Wyo.
U̲ (U-bar)	...	RHC		RSH	James Robertson, Sulphur, Wyo.
U̲̇ (U dot bar)	...	LRC		LSH	John Robertson, Sulphur, Wyo.
PH	...	Cattle-horses			Jens Hansen, Filmore Ranch
⋈	...	Cattle-horses			Jens Hansen, Filmore Ranch

In describing the location of brands upon animals the following abbreviations have been used:

J for jaw   N for neck   S for shoulder   H for hip   R for ribs   T for thigh

BS for back of sheep

Prefixed by L for left; R for right; B for both; E for either; designates the side. The letter H following the location of brand signifies horses, the letter C Cattle. The word sheep is written out where space will allow. If the location is described thus LSH   BS   LRC it signifies left shoulder of horses, back of sheep, left ribs of cattle.

Hay Gulch

Branding Bruning "⌶O" sheep at
Sulphur shearing pens - 1938
reverse ⌶—O

Bruning cattle

Cheyenne 012460   4-1003.   R 90 EXAMINED

The United States of America,

To all to whom these presents shall come, Greeting:

WHEREAS, a Certificate of the Register of the Land Office at Cheyenne, Wyoming, has been deposited in the General Land Office, whereby it appears that, pursuant to the Act of Congress of May 20, 1862, "To Secure Homesteads to Actual Settlers on the Public Domain," and the acts supplemental thereto, the claim of Herman H. Bruning has been established and duly consummated, in conformity to law, for the west half of the northwest quarter, the southeast quarter of the northwest quarter, and the northeast quarter of the southwest quarter of Section twenty-eight in Township eighteen north of Range ninety west of the Sixth Principal Meridian, Wyoming, containing one hundred sixty acres, according to the Official Plat of the Survey of the said Land, returned to the GENERAL LAND OFFICE by the Surveyor-General:

NOW KNOW YE, That there is, therefore, granted by the UNITED STATES unto the said claimant the tract of Land above described; TO HAVE AND TO HOLD the said tract of Land, with the appurtenances thereof, unto the said claimant and to the heirs and assigns of the said claimant forever; subject to any vested and accrued water rights for mining, agricultural, manufacturing, or other purposes, and rights to ditches and reservoirs used in connection with such water rights, as may be recognized and acknowledged by the local customs, laws, and decisions of courts; and there is reserved from the lands hereby granted a right of way thereon for ditches or canals constructed by the authority of the United States.

IN TESTIMONY WHEREOF, I, Woodrow Wilson, President of the United States of America, have caused these letters to be made Patent, and the seal of the General Land Office to be hereunto affixed.

GIVEN under my hand, in the District of Columbia, the TWENTY-FIFTH day of JUNE in the year of our Lord <u>one thousand nine hundred and TWENTY</u> and of the Independence of the United States the one hundred and FORTY-FOURTH.

By the President: <u>Woodrow Wilson</u>

By <u>M. P. LeRoy,</u>   Secretary

<u>L. Q. C. Lamar,</u>
Recorder of the General Land Office.

RECORDED: Patent Number <u>759140</u>   6-6020

16/72

Deed to the Herman H. Bruning, Jr. homestead in Hay Gulch
Sec. 28, T.18, R.90, filled in 1915, proved up in 1920.

Bruning homestead deserted and weathered but still standing strong. 72 years old.

What is left of the spring box that provided drinking water and refrigeration.

Hay Gulch Homestead - 1922
Field of rye high as our heads grown without irrigation.

Bruning's new Model T
Ann & John Robertson looking it over - 1919

Taken in 1931
Tom Middlemass moved
camp for Brunings

Where the tall corn grew-
Hay Gulch garden - 1920

Hay Gulch

THE J O RANCH
OR COW CREEK
Written by Ed M. Tierney

Just a few miles off the Rawlins-Baggs road to the east between the Willows Station and the Muddy Bridge Stop is the J O Ranch.

Barrett Littlefield homesteaded the land where the J O Ranch buildings are now along about 1878 or 1880. This was sold to Ora Haley on June 20, 1887. On April 12, 1893 Haley sold the property to John and Dow Doty. J.R. Rumsey was a partner. Mr. Rumsey was president of Stockgrowers National Bank in Rawlins at the time. Rumsey had borrowed heavily on the land and could not pay off the notes Harry Britenstein, E.M. Tierney, Mr. Daley and Mr. France purchased the land September 25, 1899 and E.M. Tierney purchased their stock in 1900.

Herman H. Bruning was foreman for Tierney until 1921. Abe Stratton was foreman from 1921 to 1925.

William Tierney became manager in 1925 and owner-manager in 1937 when grandfather Tierney died. Major stockholders were Edna Rasmussen and Joe E. Tierney.

The J O was sold to George Salisbury of Snake River in 1958 when Bill Tierney retired.

Littlefield and Haley each in turn built some of the buildings and others were moved from the Willows Station when it was abandoned.

Tom Greives of Snake River owns the place now.

The sheep wagon where a sheepherder and a camp mover lived the year around.

An "Overland" one of the first automobiles around that country.

J.O. Ranch Buildings 13-miles south of Sulphur Springs just off the Rawlins-Meeker stage road

The J O Ranch or Cow Creek

2 above - J O Ranch wool clip sacked and ready for market.
Shorn sheep in lower picture. Herman Bruning foreman - 1912.

JOHN ROBERTSON FAMILY
HERMAN HENRY BRUNING FAMILY
Summation

Sulphur Station, winter of 1900. Center group is the Robertson family. L. to R., 1st woman, Ann Robertson Leap; 3rd women, Ann Stewart Robertson. Next to her with the scotch cap is John Robertson. The woman in the right foreground is Elizabeth Robertson Bruning. The rest are freight and stage drivers or passengers.

THE AUTHORS' GRANDPARENTS

Ann Stewart Robertson
Taken about 1904

John Robertson
at Sulphur Springs early 1900's

Theresia Zimmerer Bruning
taken about 1911

Herman Henry Bruning, Sr.
in Rawlins, Wyo. about 1885

The Robertson Family Life

"Father came to America with Mother and us four children about May, 1883 from Lundy, Scotland. We lived in Orange C.H. Virginia about 6 months. Then went to live on a 600 acre farm near Orange called "The Yalton Place." It was a fine old place, but the soil was much depleted and when two years of drought came, things went badly for us with money short. In three years, we left this place and moved later to West Virginia (Huntersville). By this time, Father had lost much of his money that he came here with and was anxious to get settled somewhere before it was all gone. He answered an "ad" in a livestock journal for a sheep ranch for sale in Meeker, Rio Blanco County, Colorado. We then moved to this place about 1888 and stayed there until 1900, when we moved again. This time to Sulphur on the Muddy Creek south of Rawlins, Wyoming, where in 1920, Mother died and in 1926, Father passed away from that place of residence.

"They fought all the battles of life together - a fine upright pair. We are proud of them."

Signed,
Jean Robertson Tallman
daughter of John Robertson

Jean Robertson Tallman

Clay Tallman: Head of Dept. of Interior during Wilson Admn. Named head of legal force Stanolind Oil in 1930. Headquartered in Tulsa Okla.

Married November 23, 1909.

Alice Emerson Robertson
and James Robertson
Married February 17, 1921
Ranchers at Lay, Colo.

Ann Robertson Leap
and Walter E. Leap
Married March 5, 1908
Operated a ranch near
Baggs raising registered horses

Elizabeth Robertson Bruning
and Herman Henry Bruning, Jr.
Married November 29, 1910
Ranched southwest of
Rawlins until 1940

Eva and Dr. Fred Kuykendall.
Eva is the daughter of Lillie Bruning
Turpin, granddaughter of H.H. Bruning,
Sr.

Willie Bruning
taken about 1891

(1) Charles Bruning; (2) Gilbert Turpin;
(3) Lillie Bruning Turpin; (4) Rollin Turpin;
(5) Herman H. Bruning, Jr.; (6) Eva Turpin
(Kuykendall).

Nelle Bruning Coe employed at
the Post Office in Rawlins in
1901.

THE BRUNING FAMILY

Both Theresia and Herman Henry Bruning, Sr. came from Germany.

On Oct. 15, 1864, while being only 16 years old, Herman enlisted, as a private soldier in the Union Army with the New York 25th Calvery, under the asssumed name of Henry Baedel and age 19. He served the last 6½ months of the Civil War. When he died in 1896 it was many years before grandmother Theresia could prove his identity and get her pension from the government.

| B | 25 Cav. | N. Y. |

Henry Baedel

Rec't, Co. K, 25 Reg't N. Y. Cavalry.

Appears on
Company Muster Roll
for Nov & Dec, 1864.

Present or absent... Present
Stoppage, $ 100 for
Due Gov't, $ 100 for

Remarks: Assigned to Co.
Dec, 18" 1864.

Book mark:

B. M. Kennedy

| B. | 25 Cav. | N. Y. |

Henry Baedel

Appears with rank of Priv. on
Muster and Descriptive Roll of a Detachment of U. S. Vols. forwarded
for the 25 Reg't N.Y. Cavalry. Roll dated Hart Island, N. Y., Nov 24, 1864.
Where born Germany.
Age 19 y'rs; occupation Harness Mkr.
When enlisted Oct 15, 186 .
Where enlisted Brooklyn.
For what period enlisted 1 year.
Eyes hazel; hair bro.
Complexion dk; height 5 ft. 0 1/4 in.
When mustered in Oct. 15, 1864.
Where mustered in Brooklyn.
Bounty paid $ 33 33/100; due $ 100
Where credited 3 Cong. Dist. Brooklyn.
Company to which assigned
Remarks:

Book mark:

H. W. Reed

In 1866 Herman Henry Bruning started West. After speculative pauses in Missouri and Colorado he went into the Gold Hills, Atlantic City and Sweetwater mining areas of Wyoming. In 1873 back to Nebraska City to marry Theresia Zimmerer, then back to Missouri where in 1875-76 his name was listed in St. Joseph, Missouri city directory. In 1875 he went alone into the Black Hills, 1877 finds the family in Cheyenne Wy.

In 1879 Bruning homesteaded near St. Mary's Stage Station in Sweetwater County, Wyoming. In 1881 Theresia and the children came to Rawlins and Herman went to Miners' Delight, Wy. near Atlantic City where gold had been brought out in good quantities.

Shortly after this venture into the gold fields the family lived in Cheyenne where he worked for a saddle and harness maker named Frank Meanea. He had learned this trade in Germany. In 1884 they moved to Rawlins where he started his own business.

On July 4, 1884 a fire that threatened the whole town of Rawlins destroyed Bruning's saddle shop along with many other businesses. Later in 1886 he built another building and started up business once again.

Herman Henry, Jr. was born September 21, 1884 in Rawlins where he grew up and attended grade school. He was twelve years old when his father died, at which time he left school and began working, first for the Union Pacific Railroad and later for ranches. It was only a short time later when he became a rancher himself.

While searching through the old files at the Carbon County Museum, we found this advertising the *Carbon County Journals*.

Our Live Business Houses - A listing
H.H. Bruning (Sr.)

"This gentleman has been a resident of our city for the past six years and is so well known to our citizens that a recommendation from us is unnecessary. Launching out two years ago in the manufacture and dealer in harness, saddles, chapparajos, etc., he has built for himself a large lucrative business; he is a public spirited, courteous, conscientious, business man and is everyone's friend."

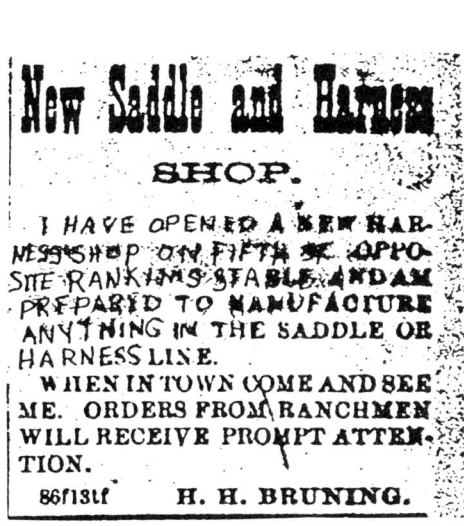

Carbon County Journal
September 3, 1887
Rawlins, Wyo.

Carbon County Journal

"In April of 1891 Herman Bruning had just put the finishing touches on another one of those Candlish patent sheep wagons sold by Junquist and Hocker. This is another one of the arts at which Mr. Bruning cannot be excelled."

NELLE AND LILLIE

On March 23, 1889, Nelle and Lillie Bruning opened a candy and cigar store in their father's building on 5th street. The *Carbon County Journal* advertised April 20, 1889, that the Bruning sisters had just received a big lot of fine choice candies, nuts and fruits.

L. to R. Lillie and Nelle Bruning owned "The Bruning Girls Candy and Tobacco Store" in Rawlins in 1889.

L. to R. Mary and George Coe of Lancaster, PA. George is Nelle Bruning Coe's son and grandson of the Herman Bruning, Srs.

ANN BRUNING BROWN

After reading and re-reading family letters, I am deeply appreciative of the physical and moral stamina of all of the members of my family. I owe to them all of my inherited ability to deal with crises and have found the strength to cope with a good many crucial events in my life. They were a proud, self-reliant and independent people. A bit of advise my Dad left with me "Be alert, pay attention to what you are doing" I think of it often.

My mother, Elizabeth Robertson Bruning and me about 1913 at Sulphur. The horse was named "Blue".

My Grandfather John Robertson and me about 1913 at Sulphur

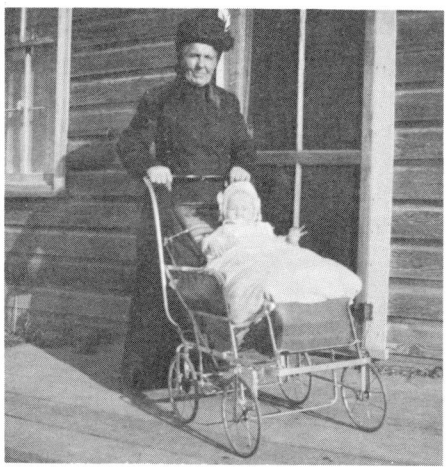

Grandmother Robertson with Ann
as a baby—1912, Sulphur Ranch

I was the first child born to Elizabeth and Herman Bruning. My parents were living at the Sulphur Ranch and my father was foreman at the J O Ranch 12 miles south. About the time of my birth my parents moved into Rawlins where I was born February 24, 1912. The Rawlins-Baggs stage had been discontinued so we stayed in Rawlins all winter to be near Dr. T.J. Swisher, the family doctor.

In the winter of 1913 it was nearly time for my sister, Gilberta, to be born so my mother and I went to live with Aunt Ann and Uncle Walter Leap in Fairfield, Idaho. I want to quote a letter from Grandmother Robertson that gives a vivid picture of everyday life at the Sulphur Ranch in the winter time:

> "On February 18th and 19th the snow was very deep and it was swirling and drifting so that a person could not see across the yard. It was something fearful.
>
> The boy, Pat that was herding the sheep we had at the ranch did not return at dark. Jim (my uncle James Robertson) went out at night to try to find him and the sheep. Finally, after walking for miles and giving up, he stumbled onto Pat in the open meadow west of the ranch nearly frozen to death. He had lost the sheep. The men came home and the next morning Uncle Jim started out to look again for the herd. The wind had gone down some and he finally found them where they had drifted into a fence corner 2 or 3 miles from the ranch, they were alive but just barely."

A faded letter of the same date from my Grandmother to me as a baby is very precious, which shows the closeness and love in our family.

> "To Baby, My Dear little granddaughter I am awfully glad to hear of you and of how well you are beginning to walk, talk, and sing. I would love to see you and talk to you. I am sure you will keep Aunt Annie and Mommie real busy taking care of you. I think about you every day. Do you remember the cookie fight you and Grandpa had? You beat him and got the cookie. Tell me when you are coming back to see me and I will have a great big bucket of cookies waiting for you. I must stop now and get breakfast, but I will write again. With much love and kisses

and cuddles to my dear little baby granddaughter. May God Bless you."
Grandmother

A note at the end of the same letter from my Grandfather:
"Hello Boss (he called me that for awhile) I am sending you a little gift from Rawlins tomorrow."

Yours very truly,
John Robertson

Another letter from Grandfather to Aunt Ann Leap:
May 21, 1912

"Today Maam and I are in Rawlins to the christening of Ann, the little baby of Lizzie and Herman Bruning, tomorrow. So you see we are on our Majesties best interests - so clear the way!"

There are a good many things that I remember and they will probably stay with me as long as I live.

Some of the things that developed patience and endurance were trips from Rawlins to the ranches in a wagon drawn by a slow team, such as coming from Rawlins in our first motor car, an Overland, and having to wait for hours in the hot sun half way home for a team to pull the stalled car in.

Then, going range-branding with my Dad, riding my black horse, Sox, (named so because he had white socks on his hind legs). We went all day long without any of us having a drink of water. Sometimes we would come across a spring of cool water, but lots of days we didn't.

As I write this and think back I was terribly "water" conscious. I guess because it was very scarce and precious. The water was either muddy or strong soda or sulphur tasting. A cool clear spring was a gem in the desert. Even the water out of the clear spring at Hay Gulch was very hard. Soap curdled in it. On wash days we added lye or a commercial softener to get a suds. This, along with the horrible task of rubbing ones knuckles raw on the old wash board, followed by ironing with an appropriately named "sad" iron - but there was nothing nicer to smell than a washing blown dry on the clothes line.

We had a rain barrel below where the eaves of the house came together. This caught enough rain water to wash our hair.

Women on early-day ranches were amazing. The amount of work they tackled and accomplished is beyond belief. When the men were out with the sheep or cattle they had the milking to do at home. Maybe go out to shoot some sage chickens or rabbits or even a deer or antelope to feed the family. Carry water a long way in buckets for drinking and household use. Do the family washing on a scrub board. churn the butter and bake the bread. Often chop the wood, mend clothes, take care of the ranch stock as well as their own children.

When the shearing, branding or fall round-up crews came in there were gigantic meals to prepare and mountains of dishes to wash before going to bed. Their days started early, breakfast for the crews who often started out at day-break. Much of the food that was prepared came from our gardens or a mail order house or the stores in Rawlins. I remember eating dried loganberry pie or dumplings. Much dried food was ordered from a mail order catalog. My Dad liked pickled herring and that came in wooden buckets.

Somehow through it all my Grandmother lived to be 78 and my mother 72 years of age.

When I was young it was embarrassing to tell people I had grown up on the homestead at "Hay Gulch." When we started living in Rawlins in the winter so we

Ann Bruning Brown

children could go to school, we found it confining to live in such a structured life. I hated to come to town to school and wanted to stay at the ranch all the time.

Looking back on my life there is a lot to be said about growing up the way we did. We learned to be creative and self-reliant because we had to. I can never remember being bored as some children complain about today.

As long back as I can remember I liked to draw. The first drawing I did was on a slate. My Mother could draw very well and I enjoyed watching her, especially the horses she drew. When I finished high school, Mother especially wanted me to go on to school. My Aunt Jean asked me to live with them where I attended the University of Tulsa and received a BA in Fine Arts. Later, I helped make a living teaching and sending my own children through college at Wyoming University.

On April 25, 1937 I married Wilbur R. (Rap) Brown in Rawlins. We were both enrolled in art classes in Laramie at the University.

"Rap" was from Buffalo, Wyoming. His high school chums nicknamed him "Rap" after an old-timer there, a squaw man who lived with the Arapahoe Indians. He was an artist in his own right. His specialty was pen and ink renderings of western subject matter.

During World War II my husband was with the military Red Cross in North Africa and Italy. After his return to Wyoming at the end of the war we moved to Worland where "Rap" was in the insurance business until his death on September 9, 1969. I taught art in the schools there retiring in 1975.

We have two children, Donald R. (Herky) Brown and Sandra (Sandi) Brown Brome.

Our family built an adobe house in Worland, making the adobe bricks from local mud. It created a lot of interest in that part of Wyoming because it was so different. We enjoyed living there, it was cool in the summer and warm in the winter.

W.R. "Rap" Brown and his son Donald R. Brown are members of the Cloud Peak Masonic Lodge #27 in Wyoming

Ann B. Brown is a member of the Wyoming and Colorado Chapter of G.A.R. Auxiliary

Our daughter, Sandi, married Robert H. (Bob) Brome. They have two Children, a daughter, Andrea Elizabeth and a son, Trent Robert Brome, my grandchildren.

My son, Don R. Brown, is in the real estate appraising business in Cheyenne where he owns a home. We all enjoy his cabin at Lake Creek in the Snowy Range Mountains above Laramie. He has been on the ski patrol a good many years at the Medicine Bow Ski Run. Sandi Brome and children live in Arizona.

At this writing, I am living in a townhouse in Laramie. I am enjoying "the fifth generation," my grandchildren as much as my grandparents seemed to enjoy the three of us at the "Hay Gulch" and Sulphur Springs ranches.

The townhouse reminds me of a prairie dog town, 65 little individual places side by side within a two block area. We each pop our heads out of our doors in the morning to see if the newspapers have come.

My land has been reduced from 4000 acres to a 15 by 20 foot patch of lawn grass. Each townhouse owner tries for some sort of identity. A name on the mail box, a hanging planter of profuse blossoms or mine is one of the old wagon wheels from the ranch placed at my front door. *Ann Bruning Brown*

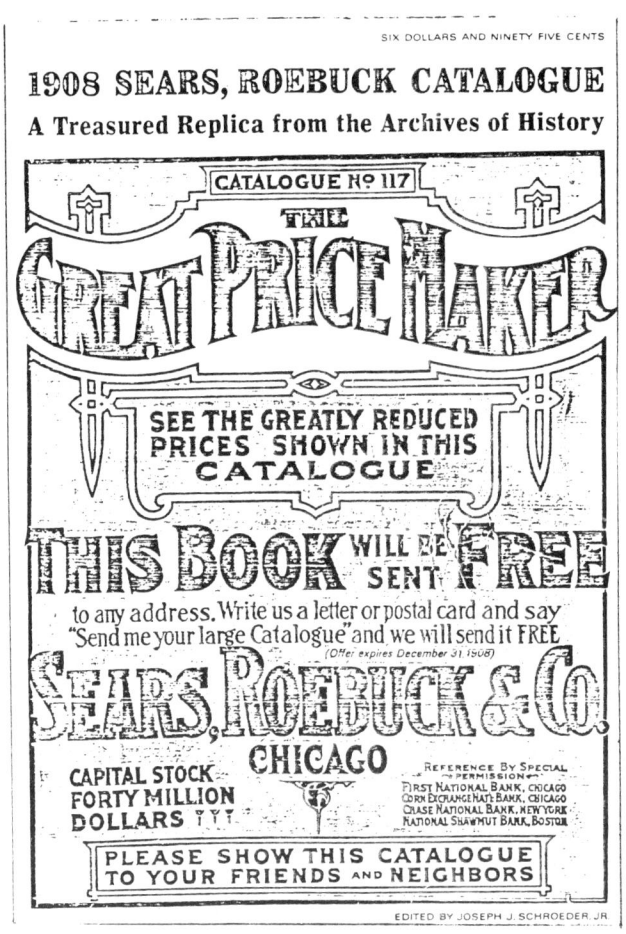

GILBERTA BRUNING HUGHES

Now that we have worked many years and reared our three children I can stop and take time to reflect back through the years of my childhood. It has been interesting to be a part of the history of the Sulphur Springs Stage Station area and the heritage of the Bruning-Robertson families.

A letter from grandfather Robertson to Aunt Ann Robertson Leap after I was born, April 25, 1913 in Fairfield, Idaho where the Leaps lived at that time reads: "Well, if it doesn't beat all - another girl! Lizzie (my mother) I think you are out to fill a kirk." Kirk is the Scotch word for church. I am the second child born to Herman and Elizabeth Bruning.

When I was about a month old our Dad went to Fairfield from the J O ranch to take his family home. We stayed with our grandparents, John and Ann Robertson on the Sulphur Springs Ranch most of the time. Dad was manager of the J O at this time and commuted back and forth from Sulphur. This ranch is about twelve miles south of Sulphur.

Another old letter written about this time from grandfather to Aunt Ann says, "Maam is sewing nowadays for children. These two children are surely smashers - they are dandy you bet!" "Maam" is the affectionate name grandfather called grandmother.

In 1901 grandfather Robertson bought grandmother the first model sewing machine put out by the Singer company. Another old letter found dated 1912 says, "Mother is happy with her new little glass churn. It holds a five pound bucket of cream at a time."

When the house was built in 1917 on the Bruning homestead at Hay Gulch about two miles north of Sulphur we moved into our new home. We spent the winter of 1917 here.

The last trip into Rawlins was made usually in November, depending upon the weather. The families would purchase food stuff and other supplies to last until they could get back into town in the late spring. I remember a big box of oranges and long strings of wieners. A few Christmas presents were bought at this time and saved for us until later.

Snow is deep and winters cold in Wyoming, and even as a child I can remember how difficult it was for our folks to feed and care for their livestock. The cattle were fed up the gulch from the house in a more or less protected area and hay was hauled on a sled from the ranch to the feeding grounds. We girls enjoyed going with our folks on the sled and being nestled down in the hay. Occasionly a cow would get down in a snow drift and would have to be shoveled out or pulled with a team of horses.

Christmases were not traditionally festive occasions, but they meant a lot to us. The folks would put Ann and me on a cow-hide sled and it was pulled by a lariat rope tied from the hide to a saddle horn and we would all go to Sulphur to spend Christmas Day. Dinner ready everyone sat at the big dining room table and grandfather would repeat the grace he said before each meal:

> "Lord look down upon us at this time in mercy. Pardon our sins, speak peace to our souls and grant us a blessing to this present refreshment. May we eat and drink to thy Glory, for Jesus sake Amen"

In another old letter we found written by Aunt Ann it says:

"The little prayer our beloved Mother taught us to say at her knee when we were little children:

> 'Gentle Jesus meek and mild Look upon a little child
> Fain I would to thee be brought
> Gracious God forbid it not.'"

This little prayer was in turn taught to us by our own Mother.

We enjoyed Christmas Day with our slates and dolls and of course special on this day were grandmother's buttermilk sugar cookies and hot Scotch scones.

After the long hard winters Spring was welcomed with a new lease on life for man and animal. Many wild flowers came into view all through those old sage brush hills - Mariposa Lillies, Indian Paint Brush, Columbine and Wild Rose.

Beside barns, corrals and a cellar built on the ranch, Dad also built a storage dam up the canyon from the Hay Gulch house. This water was used for irrigation. A well was dug for household water and the spring water was carried in for drinking. We girls liked "irrigation day" so we could play along the wet ditches making mud sculptures and pottery.

No other children lived anywhere near us so our playmates were lambs, calves, cats and kittens and at one time rabbits that Uncle Charlie Bruning brought to us. We never lacked for something to do or to play with. Chores also had to be done - carrying in firewood, gathering eggs and feeding the chickens, keeping lamp chimneys clean and keeping the lampwicks trimmed. Sometimes we helped with the cooking and baking which at times was a disaster! Extra water had to be carried into the house for our Saturday night baths in a big wash tub.

In the Fall the two families went chokecherry picking. With a lunch prepared we would all get into a big wagon and drive to the Sand Hills where cherries were plentiful. In the afternoon we returned to the ranches with tubs full of berries to be made into jam and syrup.

Gypsies occasionally stopped at Sulphur on their way to Rawlins or Baggs. They always wanted a meal and while they were in the house they had to be watched closely - they were known to be "Light fingered!" They traded Dad something for a wagon at one time. The old "Gypsy wagon" now sits in my backyard.

In 1918 we went into Rawlins to go to school. This year on September 30 our sister, Louise, was born. She is the last child born to Herman and Elizabeth Bruning. Dad worked in the Union Pacific shops that winter. He and his brother, Charlie Bruning were due to go into the service in World War I. The war ended just before Dad was to go and Uncle Charlie died in the terrible flu epidemic that winter. When school was out we returned to Hay Gulch for the summer.

Grandma Robertson was a small Scotch lady with a heart of gold. She turned no one away who needed a meal or a place to stay. She worked very hard over the years and in 1919 her health began to fail. The good doctor, Dr. T.J. Swisher would drive the thirty miles from Rawlins to the ranch to give her what medical aid he could. The folks later brought her to town to care for her until she passed away in 1920. Grandfather tried to operate the ranch alone then for four years and in 1924 Ann and Walter Leap sold their ranch near Riverton, Wyoming and came to take over the management of the Sulphur ranch and to help him. He passed away in 1926. The Leaps stayed on the ranch then until it was sold in 1940.

From the time we girls started to school our family spent the winters in Rawlins, but the Leaps stayed at Sulphur the year around.

Mike Cronin and Earnest McKeal had little homesteads up the Muddy Creek from Sulphur. Everyone helped each other during the long winters. McKeal and the Leaps would take turns riding horseback into Rawlins a few times during the winter when the weather was permissable. It was a long cold ride. They would go in one day, stay a day or two and then ride the long way back. Often the Leaps rode down the Muddy Creek to the west to the Henry Baur ranch to pick up the mail or to get a ride into Rawlins.

About 1923 a grass fire destroyed the barn, shop and corrals at Hay Gulch. Heartsick from seeing everything he had worked so hard to build go up in flames, Dad lost interest in the ranch. The barns were never re-built. The ranch then was used as a stock headquarters and lambing grounds and a place still for us to spend our summers.

Depression years were bad with low prices and hard winters. The life of a stockman was one of blood, sweat and tears a lot of the time, but with great preseverence and just plain "guts" they made it and there were better years ahead. Dad remained in the sheep business until 1940 when he retired and sold the ranch and livestock.

I went to business schools in Denver, Colorado and Tulsa, Oklahoma and later took a course in cosmetology in Denver and worked for a time at this profession. On April 28, 1941 I married Lewis E. (Mickey) Hughes in Ogden City, Utah. He was an Engineer on the Union Pacific Railroad and retired in 1970. He passed away on August 31, 1975.

We have three wonderful children. Sharron, now Mrs. Rick Parr, who, with her husband, owns a Phillips 66 Station on Interstate 80 just out of Sutherland, Nebraska.

Douglas Clay, married to Colleen Michie is Marketing Manager for a computer software firm in California.

Debra, now Mrs. Mac Black. Mac is with the Game and Fish Department in Powell, Wyoming and Debra is printing composer for the school system in the same city.

Our grandchildren are Stephen and Stacey Parr; Melissa, Hillary, Katherine and Keeley Hughes; and our three step-grandchildren are Mary Jane, William and Teresa Black.

I still reside in Rawlins close to my friends and keep in close touch with all of the family.

Yes, my memories are many - riding in open free country, no fences acting as barriers across the sage brush country we loved. There were moon light horse back rides, hearing the Whippoorwills call in the early evening and the coyotes howling to each other at night and in the early morning the songs of the meadowlarks. Some may see this as a lonesome life, but to us it was the greatest life anyone could experience. Childhood memories related here and in other parts of this book are very dear to me and not to be left unmentioned are the treasured years raising our children. I am grateful and indebted to my parents, grandparents and aunts and uncles for the knowledge I gained from them and the stamina to conquer difficult situations in life. There is an emptiness now that all the "old folks" are gone, but memories of them will always be with me.

Gilberta Bruning Hughes

Gilberta and Lewis (Mick) Hughes

"THE OLD GOVERNMENT COAL MINE"

The accompanying picture shows Gilberta standing at the opening of the coal mine about a mile east of Sulphur in the canyon wall of the Muddy Creek. This mine was referred to as "the government mine" evidently used when Sulphur was a military headquarters.

Dad would blast the coal down and then when the dust cleared we would go in and load up the coal cars and push them down the track to a place where we could dump the coal into a wagon below. The coal was hauled to Sulphur and to our Hay Gulch ranch by team and wagon or by truck.

Coal was hauled from here for a good many years for ranch use and for the steam engines at the oil well sites in the area about 1903 to 1912.

In 1939 Lee Stackhouse and some other men from Rawlins were attempting to mine coal commercially at this location and without proper safety precautions. Five men were killed when the mine caved in and it was forever closed after that unless someone decides to re-open it in this day of the energy crunch.

Gilberta helping to mine coal at the "Old Government" mine used by surrounding ranchers. Located about 1 mile east of Sulphur Ranch on the Muddy Creek.

"The Old Government Coal Mine"

HOWARD C. PARMELEE.   STANLEY B WELD

PARMELEE & WELD,

CONSULTING AND ANALYTICAL CHEMISTS AND ASSAYERS.
SUCCESSORS TO POHLE & PARMELEE.
1755 ARAPAHOE STREET.

P. O. Box 1421.
Tel. Main 1460.

DENVER, COLO., Dec. 11th, 1903.

Mr. A. H. Stewart,
    C I T Y.

Dear Sir:-

    Following is the analysis of the sample of COAL submitted by you yesterday. From the figures obtained we are justified in considering this coal to be superior to many brands of coal now on the market, and equal to the best that we have ever examined. This statement, of course, applies to coals of the same class. The total fuel value is high and the moisture about equal to the average; while the ash is quite low. The coal burns to a clean white ash and will not coke.

    MOISTURE---------------------- 8.15
    VOLATILE MATTER--------------- 42.35
    FIXED CARBON------------------ 44.90
    ASH--------------------------- 4.60
                                            100.00%

    Total Fuel Value-------------- 87.25%

                                                         Very truly yours,

Charges $5.00   *Parmelee*

Mr. A.H. Stewart owned some coal land adjoining ours. We three Robertson granddaughters still own 40 acres of coal land on the Muddy near Sulphur.

LOUISE BRUNING ERB

A black crepe bow hanging on the front door and a casket in the front room. On that late November day in 1920 at 206 W. Buffalo Street in Rawlins, Wyoming, a little pioneer lady, Ann Stewart Robertson, who had left her beloved Scotland 38 years before, had died. For a two-year-old child this was an indelible impression-my grandmother, I only knew in death.

And my grandfather, John Robertson, who lived for six more years, I remember only as a stern man with a short white beard and a Scottish accent. I never remember any nice "grandfatherly" relationships with him. When I, Louise Josephine, came along a few years after my two sisters, and another girl at that, I guess he wasn't impressed.

At the time of my birth in 1918 our family life was emerging from the pioneer way of living into the advent of the automobile. Horses still played an important part in our early lives. That was still the time when they were used to pull the mower, the rake and the hayrack when haying season came. A horse drawn fresno was used to scoop out little catch ponds for water or huge reservoirs for the large bodies of water. Horses were a definite part of the sheep business. But the height of our young exciting times came when we'd get to help with branding the calves and occasionally get in on a wild horse round-up.

To me, summer times on the Bruning and the Sulphur Springs ranches were long pleasant days, miles and miles of open space to ride horseback, a feeling of aloneness with no fear, a total independence and a healthy respect for nature and her whims. I always liked to pause on top of a high hill and watch the little whirl winds spiraling the dust high in the air as it skipped across the sagebrush flats, or off in the distance see a rain storm forming.

Weather then held the controlling hand. In summer, rains turned the roads into sticky gumbo. One stretch, no longer than one mile, on the road to the ranch once took us four hours to negotiate. The long, cold, stormy Wyoming winters were cruel. Some winters, when snows were heavy, stockmen's losses would be high.

On the first of September each year we were back at our home in Rawlins where I eagerly looked forward to school. All my next years through graduation from high school were spent taking for granted the clean pure air and pleasantries of Wyoming except for the incessant wind.

The desire to study and do more took me away from Wyoming in 1936 and I have only returned to visit since. Coming from a naive life in Wyoming and plunging into a world of intensities, crises, exactitudes and all kinds of people was difficult. I went to college for one year at Greeley, Colorado then into nurses training at Children's Hospital in Denver, Colorado for three years. I can truthfull say that my nurse's training was the most important and rewarding experience I ever had. From it I gained an awareness of all aspects of living.

In 1940 after my graduation as a Registered Nurse, my parents sold all their holdings in Wyoming and moved away. My ties with the ranch ended then. It was the passing of and era in which my life was closely entwined. My parents had taught me a freedom, a discipline and a resourcefulness that has kept me continually learning and exploring new activities.

Also, in 1940, I married my school classmate, Lester D. Erb, who had graduated from the Engineering College at the University of Wyoming and was working for R.C.A. in New Jersey. War years were spent on the east coast. Then with a determination to live in the west again, we came to Denver, Colorado in 1945 and have lived here ever since. My husband started a business of his own, now called Flame Spray, Inc., and after many growing pains and hard work it has successfully endured 42 years of operation.

We have two children. Our son, Lee Alan, is a graduate of the University of Colorado in electronic and electrical engineering. He has his own custom design and consulting electronic engineering business in Boulder, Colorado. They have two darling daughters, Larisa and Lacey and a son, Lane.

Our daughter, Lynette Carol is now one of the managers of her father's business.

When Lynette was small she loved horses like I did. Even in this populated area we had a place to keep them so she was able to experience the fun of riding and the companionship of her horses like I did. She is a good horsewoman and seeing how well her horses worked for her showed how well she trained them.

I guess a parent always like to relive the happy times of their lives through their children.

Seventy years is but a flash of time in the eons of this world but my 70 years of life has touched several dramatic eras. I consider it quite thrilling and a privilege to have a life that has touched pioneer days and ways, and experience and benefit from the advanced technologies of the past 30 years.

Louise Bruning Erb

Lester D. Erb

RICHARD STEWART ROBERTSON

It has been the good fortune in my life to have been a part of some of the early day settlers of Colorado and Wyoming. My parents, James Robertson, born in Scotland on January 1, 1878 and Alice May Emerson, born in Rawlins, Wyoming on August 12, 1886. Mom and Dad were married on January 17, 1921 and on November 21, 1923 I came along to join the Robertson family.

My first home was a sheep wagon. Since I was born in Denver, Colorado I was returned to the Lay, Colorado area, first on the Moffat Railroad over Corona Pass to Steamboat Springs, then by stagecoach to Craig, where I would guess by car to the ranch, where Dad wintered his sheep. From that time until I was about six years old, our home was the wagon, a place in Baggs, Wyoming and our beloved Bakers Peak summer land. After the big depression which took its toll on my family, as it did all the people, we were back and forth between Bakers Peak and the Emerson home ranch at Lay, Colorado. The old Pick Ranch was an historic landmark taken up in 1876 by my Grandfather and Grandmother Emerson. This history of this ranch is beautifully written by Val Fitzpatrick in volumes 1,2,3,4 and 5 of his books, *The Last Frontier*.

Boner Stage station was traded for a ranch at Meeker, Colorado. Since all of my grandparents had passed on before I was old enough to remember them and the families had adjusted to the life, Aunt Ann and Uncle Walt were at Sulphur Ranch engaged in ranching and cattle business. Aunt Lizzy and Uncle Herman were in the sheep business at Hay Gulch. Dad and Mom were based at Baggs, Wyoming and the Pick Ranch.

As I grew up I have intermingled memories of all of those places.

Of Sulphur Ranch, I carry fond memories of riding for cattle, feeding the lambs and sharing the lives of my cousins, Gilberta, Ann and Louise, and of course aunts and uncles. I think the most outstanding memory I have of Sulphur Ranch is that at the age of nine I killed my first deer and a few days later I killed my first antelope. This started a tradition, as I used a 30-40 single shot Winchester rifle; now, today, all my boys — Jim, George, and Monty Bill — have all killed their first deer with this same gun. It hangs on the wall in my home today in mint condition, waiting for the time when my grandchildren are old enough to carry on that tradition.

As I grew up, I went to a country school at Jackrabbit near Lay, Colorado, Tulsa, Oklahoma and Regis High in Denver, graduating from there. I took over the ranch at Lay, while Dad had one near Maybell, and upon his death in 1945, I operated both ranches raising cattle.

I married Chloe Eller Bunker on June 1, 1949 and in the 17 years until her death we had five children, James Clay, George Edward, Mary Beatrice, Monty Bill and Elizabeth Ann.

We sold the Pick Ranch and moved to Craig, Colorado where I engaged in Earth Moving Contracting. Chloe taught vocal music in the Craig school system and we raised the five children.

Upon Chloe's death on August 9, 1966 I continued in the construction business. I now live at 575 N. Rose Street in Craig, Colorado.

I am semi-retired and enjoy my family. James Clay and his wife Terri, married June 17, 1972; their two children Catherine Iris born July 4, 1973 and Jamie Alice born July 16, 1976. Mary and Matt Vassek married June 19, 1970 and their three children, Matt III born October 8, 1970, Martin Stewart born February 25, 1973 and Melody Chloe born July 5, 1974. George and his wife Brynelle, married August

12, 1978 live in Alamosa.

In closing, I wish to relate the joys, but mostly the sadness in the passing of all of the family who are now gone, because they, through their love, created a wonderful life for me and have left such an emptyness without them. I only hope that I can leave with my family that feeling of gratitude for their love and achievement that I have for those gone by. And that God will in some way make this world a place that they can enjoy their stay on earth as I have mine.

R. S. Robertson

Richard Robertson about 4 years old. "His home was a sheepwagon"

Richard S. and Chloe Eller Bunker Robertson. Married June 1, 1949

WINTER AT SULPHUR RANCH
Ann Robertson Leap's Diary
1931-1932

Nov. 11— Our first snow for the season. Had cold bad weather for days.

Nov. 17— We went to Rawlins with "Whitey" (our beef). It was storming bad when we got as far as 16 MILE. The roads are awful.

Nov. 18— We came home over the drifted snow. Had a hard trip and it will be our last in the car till spring. Car was smoking like it was on fire when we got home. We had to stop to cool it off a lot of times on the road.

Nov. 19— We started to get calves in to wean. It has been very disagreeable since the storm started.

Nov. 20— We turned Fan and Sis out for winter on the range.

Nov. 21— It was disagreeable until this date when it came a big cold blizzard from Northeast. This storm started the night of the 20th and howled and blew all night.

Nov. 21— The pretty little black kitten got in a coyote trap with both it's front legs. It's poor little legs were frozen. We held them in cold water for an hour then rubbed them with coal oil and lard.

Nov. 22— Cold but clear. Cattle came down the canyon and hung around.

What it was like in the winter.

Nov. 22— These are days of many worries both great and small. We are wondering how Jim* is making it moving out of the mountains at Baker's Peak and how Herman* is getting on moving his sheep to winter quarters. He passed here with his bucks Nov. 19th He is moving his ewe camp and buck camp himself. I am worried day by day how we are to make it with the hay hauling from McKeal's*. These things take all the joy out of life.

Nov. 24— Herman left here for his sheep. He came yesterday. Had fared pretty good thru the Northeast storm. Poor Herman looked sad going up the hill this morning in the cold headed for another long winter in camp. Not a pleasant thing to look forward to. It's sure a hard life.

Nov. 29— Poor Kate got on her back in a hole just like Lad did the later part of Aug. We have no team. Walter* got on Jim's horse and rode to McKeal's for help and a team. I got things ready as far as I could and was too nervous to sit and wait so I got on Baldy and went in search of Lizzie's big black team. I was lucky to find them at the Soda Springs. I slipped up gently and caught them then I went to Hay Gulch and put their harnesses on and led them to Sulphur getting here about fifteen minutes before Walter and McKeal. We hauled Kate out of the wash with McKeal's team. They sure are good pullers. Poor Kate couldn't get up so we hauled her to the corral and got her up, but had to hold her up. We finely got her to stand and we led her about and then put her in the barn, but she soon went down and stayed down. I think she has pneumonia from being in the cold damp ground so long. What a day we have had!

Nov. 30— Kate still alive but seems unconscious. The men (Walter and McKeal) started to haul hay from McKeal's, 10 miles up the canyon and I'm alone and very worried for the roads are bad. This is a bitter cold night. An owl hooted.

Dec. 1— They got here at 1 o'clock this PM. with the first two loads of hay. They upset a number of times and got stuck on some of the hills. There isn't enough snow yet for good sleighing. McKeal's hay rack is so wide it got stuck on a rock on the sandstone dugway and knocked the end off. They're going to change his rack to a narrower one he has. An owl hooted here tonight—this means storm.

Dec. 2— They went up to McKeal's again and will load up today and fix the rack and come down in the morning. They fixed some holes in the road on their way up today. I've been punching the cattle around today and cutting water holes and tending all the little animals at the barn. My calves did fine today. They staid out in the pasture all day and were nice to get back in the corral this evening. I'm alone again tonight. How I hate being alone these cold nights to get up in the morning and start fires. My rheumatism is bad this winter and it's hard for me to get around and do my chores. I wonder how everybody is tonight?

*Jim Robertson, Herman Bruning, Walter Leap, Ernest McKeal

Dec. 3— Walter and McKeal got home at noon. They'd have made it here at 11 but they upset one load up here in sight of the house. Kate died about 2 P.M. today. This is a pink sunset tonight. Before sunset there was a

Earnest McKeal, a good neighbor who homesteaded east of Sulphur on the Muddy.

What is left today of Earnest McKeal's cabin which still stands along the Muddy Creek about 7 miles east of Sulphur.

The remains of the Osborne Place on the Muddy Creek between Sulphur and McKeals.

rainbow all over the sun — a complete rainbow.

Dec. 4— After a week of beautiful clear warm days and cold clear nights we woke this morning to find a snow storm going on. The little old owl knew his business and last night when we went to bed I looked out at the clear beautiful night and the stars were twinkling so fast and pretty. I said to Walter, "It's sure going to storm — it always does when the stars twinkle and when the owl hoots." The men went back to McKeal's and it had cleared and looked like it would stop snowing but at noon it started in bad again. I went down to the Rocky Ford to bring the bull up here as he's very lame and falling off pretty bad. I was out all afternoon in the storm getting the bull then the calves in and as one of them had sneaked away with it's mother, I went down past Alamosa Gulch and was until 5 P.M. getting all my chores done. Came in tired, wet, cold and hungry to a cold house, wondering what's it all about any way.

I saw a wood pecker this afternoon. There's lots of snow birds today. The first I've noticed so far this season. They fed until dark. Yesterday I noticed the badgers were digging out their holes. Guess they're getting ready for this storm. The cattle are drifting down the creek.

I look every day for Jim. I wonder what is keeping him so long. He was to be back in two weeks. He left here Nov. 14. I hope he got moved out of the mountains without mishap. Charles Back (Charlie Back) passed here today taking a bunch of horses from Pete Hansen's to Jim Hansen's.

Dec. 5— They got home O.K. with their big loads of hay. Didn't upset this trip.

Dec. 6— They went back to McKeal's for more hay. I'm alone and awful busy.

Dec. 7— They got on fine today until they got to the bend in sight of the house near the bridge and McKeal's load turned upside down and about went in the creek. They upset and righted it once and then started it up only to turn clear over. They let the boone pole loose and then pulled the rack and sled right side up and put on part of the load. Made two loads of it. I'm still wondering how all my dear "buddies" are and hoping to hear. The owl hooted a long time tonight and it will sure snow. Old owl never misses.

Dec. 8— It's a wintery looking day today. Jim and Bus and Hart came today from Rawlins and bro't letters and news that every body is well. I'm so glad.

*Bill Hart and Bus Kelly were hired hands.

Dec. 9— The owl hooted last night and this morning a fine snow storm is in progress. They landed safely with two big loads of hay and went back up to McKeal's after dinner so as to load in morning and get in extra loads. Jim couldn't go today with his car for it was too blustery to see the road.

Dec.10 — They got home at noon with their loads without any trouble. Jim started to Baggs at 10 A.M. The car sure had to kick to make the hill. Hart and Bus rode after him in case he got stuck and they could pull with the saddle horses but Jim was going right along the last they saw of him. I'm hoping he gets back here with the sled and team Sunday so I'll know how he made it in the car. He's coming for his saddle horse "Dutch."

Ann Robertson Leap's Diary

Dec. 11— I'm alone tonight at the house. Bus and Hart are across the road in the other house. I got the "Guernsey" colored cow's calf up this P.M. and tied her in the barn. She's awful wild but will soon tame down. We have all but one calf now. It's snowed off and on all day. Weather just can't settle. It's not cold only snowy. It keeps laying it down. Looks like we might have quite a little snow. This has been the mildest fall and winter so far we've had for years. One sheep didn't come home tonight and I was sure the coyotes had it but when Bus went up to put out his baits he found it on the ice under a high bank where it had fallen and knocked it goofy. He got it home. It's very blind. Water awful high in creek, all over ice.

Dec. 12— They got here O.K. with their hay and went back to McKeal's. A Mexican from Rock Springs came looking for horses for Guy Rife. He found his horse (a buckskin pinto) at the outside willow up in Sand Hills. Got here in eve. It's very cold and clear tonight.

Dec. 13— They arrived O.K. again. Jim came at 2:30 with Jean's team (Nig and Johnnie). Mexican left this morning.

Dec. 14— Walter and McKeal went up to McKeal's for more hay. Will load today and come down tomorrow. Jim left for Baggs with his saddle horse. It's a cold day — cold and clear. it was 20 below this morning at 8. Fan and Sis came toddling in for feed today. I felt so sorry for the little things. I'm feeding them. I know they'll want to stay all winter now. I rode Sis down to chop the water holes. I saw a big badger and a coyote trotting along not far apart across the creek. Had a nice little ride and it did me good. The water is low in creek.

Feeding cattle at Sulphur

Dec. 15— They got here at 11 A.M. with their big loads of hay and had dinner and went back to come again tomorrow. I went down to Rocky Ford and took Fan and Sis but they followed me back. They want to stay here and eat. I rode Johnnie. It was awful cold last night in the house I about froze in bed. Didn't sleep it was so cold. The wind blew and altho I had a good fire in the stove it was awful cold. At 8 this morning I looked and it was 20 below. The wind made it seem lots colder.

Dec. 16— Walter up set on hill just as they came in sight and started down at the first bad place, otherwise they made it fine. The sunset tonight was pink and it looked cloudy before sunset like it might storm soon.

Dec. 17— They went up for more hay today and I rode doen the creek to see if I could find the R/R cow and calf. I met them coming home with another cow and a yearling steer and yearling heifer. I saw all the cattle except 9 today and I think they're up the creek. I took 40 head down to the Rocky Ford crossing and left them. Put the R/R cow in the lower pasture with more cattle. It's been cloudy all day but sunny between times. Think it is making ready for a storm. Sun set was red and look like more moderate weather coming. Cattle act uneasy and are drifting about.

Dec. 18— They got here today at 11 A.M. with the last two loads of hay. They got here without upsetting. I'm so glad this "haying" is done.

Dec. 19— We just straightened up today and set everything in readiness to get out coal. I made the Xmas plum pudding and steamed it.

Dec. 20— They got out a little coal (McKeal and Wiley). Walter arranged things around the ranch. Killed turkey for Xmas.

Dec. 21— —Walter went up to mine and helped McKeal and I went down to the lower water holes and looked at the cattle.

Dec. 22— Walter and I went up to the mine. Walt and McKeal shot down more coal and we got a nice load and so did he. It snowed a soft mild snow like spring-time and we had nice sleighing.

Dec. 23— Walter went back up to the mine and they shot down two more big loads. I washed the turkey and cleaned up the house. This was a nice day.

Dec. 24— It's kinda cold today but not bad. I scrubbed the floors and baked bread and stuffed my turkey so I'd have everything in readiness for Xmas. We heard Madam Schuman Heink singing "Home Sweet Home" and "Holy Night" tonight over the radio from New York. She also gave a little talk.

Dec. 25— We just had a grand day. Never saw a milder day on Xmas day. I kept the doors open most all day. Mr. Hart and Bus and McKeal were here for Xmas dinner at 5 P.M. They spent the evening and we had a very pleasant time. The bull dog had a gay time of it playing around among us all. He's a cute wise little dog. He and the pet lamb come with McKeal from his ranch. The lamb didn't get to come this time for he hurried off on horseback but it follows a sled like a dog.

Dec. 26— Walter and I made hens nests today and worked around the place. It's been rather cold and windy all day but nice inside the hay shed. Hart and Bus got a load of coal for themselves.

Dec. 27— We're just sitting around today resting. Hart and Bus went hunting. This morning before sun-up the sky was clear and a big red cloud hung near the horizon and looked like a hill back of the cellar was a great big golden mountain. After sun-up the wind got up and it blew all day. In the evening when we were doing the chores (Iwent out with Walter to do chores) a storm started that gave promise of being quite a big one. It's cold and windy. Hart and Bus got back just before dark very cold and having had no luck. They saw four deer up on top the Sand Hills that went to Horse Gulch. We've had such mild beautiful weather that for several days there were big places opened up in the creek. I'm hoping this storm is like the ones gone by so we'll be able to get our mail soon for McKeal is going to Rawlins from his ranch tomorrow *if it's a good day*, and he's got a bunch of letters to mail for us. My rheumatism has been bad lately so I'm afraid maybe we'll have storm. The sunset tonight was stromy and a snow storm in progress. Looks like it might be bad. Awful windy all day.

Dec. 28— We went down to the lower fords (Rocky Ford) and broke the water hole and then came back and picked up 42 head of cattle in the field and took them up the creek. It's been a beautiful mild day and the cattle that were up the creek were up on top of the rough hill tops north of the creek grazing like summer time. There's lots of good safe water holes open up the creek.

Dec. 29— It's storming today. Was at it when we got up this morning. We staid in and churned. The sunset looked rather stormy, a dark red and cloudy. it didn't lay down much snow. It has taken 3 days to melt enough snow to wash.

Dec. 30— This had been a beautiful clear day but cold. I washed my big bunch of sheets and pillow slips and four big white table cloths. Some of the cattle we took up the creek Mon. came back this P.M. Walter drove them back where we left them Mon. He saw cattle up on the rugged hills eating like summertime. The sky was purple and gold around the horizon tonight. A clear beautiful sunset.

Dec. 31— I washed more today. It was awful cold to hang out the clothes in the cold wind.

Jan. 1— It's cold still today and snowed some. I got a lot of the washing in off the line.

Jan. 2— We rode after the cattle most all day. Found a bunch away up the north gulch of the 2 Fork draw. They were looking fine. We bro't them down the canyon as far as the upper slide. We rode up the 2 Fork draw but saw only 3 horses then we rode back and picked up our cattle and started them on and went up in the draw north of the Emigrant Fork and got six more. They were in good feed. We slid off the hills thru drifts and across washes but made it fine. Saw hundreds of Alaskan Robins along the creek. Walter rode Baldy and I rode Johnnie. He's fine in snow and gulches. Cattle on top of the high hills.

Jan. 3— We went back up the creek today to get a cow and calf. Bro't two thin cows and the calf home. Had rotten time with the cow and calf in the willows up above the Buck pasture, but finely got them out and home. Cattle look fine.

Jan. 4— We puttered around home today, cleaned the stove and cared for stock. We're wearied for mail. Wish McKeal would come and bring us mail.

Jan. 5— We worked around with things about the place. Bus went up to McKeals

Jan. 6— to find out if he'd gotten back from Rawlins with mail.
It's storming today and Bus didn't come back. We stuck around down here and cared for the calves and Walter drove some of the cattle back up the creek.

Jan. 7— We started to feed the cattle up the creek today. Bus got back but McKeal hasn't gotten home yet from Rawlins so we have no mail yet. 12 head of the cattle were up on top of the hill above the rim rocks. Didn't get all the cattle to feed lot, they stuck around in the brush and wouldn't go up after the sled of hay. It's stormy cold day. There's a great big rock on the road above where we feed that's bigger than 2 cook stoves. it rolled down the hill some time between when Bus went up and when he came back. It blocks the road and we feel lucky we have our hay hauled before it got there. The water holes are open and fine.
I came home and made a prune cake.

Jan. 8— We got all the cattle on the feed lot today. Mr. Hart and I drove them up and Walter bro't the hay. This is a nice mild day, clouds look like rain clouds. It's thawing and nice. A pretty pink sunset filling the canyon with gold. It's moderate tonight and I think we'll have some fine weather.

Jan. 9— Got our mail today via McKeal and everybody is happy and sad too for it's both good and bad news we have. All my folks are well but Uncle Charlie is very ill yet, just dying by inches and Dale (Harold Leap's son) is bed fast at McPherson, Kansas threatened with T.B. so Leah tells us in a card in this mail. Such a fine bunch of mail, I don't know which to read first. I read part of each, then go over them the 2nd time and finish reading them thru. I rode Johnnie up to punch the cattle on to the feed lot and Walter drove the hay sled.

Jan. 10— Walter and McKeal went up and fed the cattle and I took all the calves up past the spring, over the hill where they'd get lots of feed. They came home full as ticks. Got a good drink on way up and then again of way home. I'm trying to get letters ready tonight so when this storm stops Bus can go for the mail at Cow Creek Ranch. Lizzie is sending it to Dad P.O., for Iverson (Mrs. Hays' son-in-law) who is at the C.C. Ranch, to get and have at ranch for us to get.

Jan. 11— Walter and I went up on the sled to feed the cattle. They were all at the water hole on a riffle. We never have to break it. It stays open all the time. It's up from the upper slide under the rocky hill where the road leaves the grassy flat and starts around the bluffs of the creek. They go across the creek at the slide and bed down in the heavy brush around the old creek bed where the creek used to run before the sand slid down and changed it's course. They can get a drink at the spring at the green spot also.

Jan. 12— This has been an awful windy nasty snowy cold day all day. The wind was blowing hard when we got up and didn't let up till dark tonight. Hart and Bus fed the cattle so they could have the team to get themselves some coal. I tho't I'd wash, but it took all day to melt the ice for water so I'll wash tomorrow — maybe. We got 5 eggs today. The pullets are starting to lay. We sure have lots of snow. It's just kept at it till there's lots on the ground but the south hills are blown so if it ever gets clear and warm they bare up quick.

Ann Robertson Leap's Diary

Jan. 13— Spent a rotten day. Everything went backwards. I tried to get at my washing this morning but didn't get to it until 2:30. I finished after many interruptions at 7:30. The calves were mean to get into the pasture and I had said I'd put them in so the cattle would go with the hay sled for they had come down. There was a little hay at the corner of the stone building and as Spottie brought them out of the corral they spied it and poor Spottie bro't one or two or as many as he could start out of the knot around the hay and I was waiting in the lane to head them into the pasture. It's an easy job as a rule for Spottie knows just what is wanted. There's lots of snow but it didn't lay down any more today. Hope the storm is over. It was an awful bad night last night.

Jan. 14— Stormy. We just did the feeding as usual.

Jan. 15— Walt and I went up and fed and Bus and Hart went to look at their baits. Stormy and windy.

Jan. 16— Walt and Hart went up and fed and I took the calves up to pasture. I walked up and the snow was waist deep in places and the little calf trail was awful narrow and hard to walk in. The calves dig in and eat rye grass and willows and all kinds of brouse. Spottie went with me and I enjoyed getting out altho it's a windy cold day it's always sheltered up in the calf pasture behind the hills. I heard a chick-a-dee.

Jan. 17— I didn't do anything today only helped Spottie turn the calves out and he likes that job and works so cute for me. I stand in the lane and he runs the calves out of the corral and across the road into the gate then comes running for his pats and a hug. He's a cute little stumpy tailed dog and is a lot of help to me. The wind blew awful hard all night last night and piled the snow high in deep drifts. It's been a cold drifty day all day and still it's blowing tonight. We sure have lots of snow now. Walter and Hart went to feed and I stuck around home.

Jan. 18— A clear cold day, the morning was mild but the wind got up around noon and it was cold. Bus didn't go today for mail. It's not warm enough yet for him. I am desperately anxious to mail my letters and and to get mail. He sure is a "weak sister." I wonder if we'll have to go ourselves, yet he wants to go to Rawlins instead of Cow Creek Ranch so he can putter around town awhile. This sure is an awful way to get our mail. I'll be glad when spring comes and next winter I hope there will be some other way to get our mail that will be more reliable.

Jan. 19— A beautiful day but Bus still hangs back. Oh this is a shiftless way to get our mail. Such a good-for-nothing never lived than Bus. I got my letters ready and here I wait. I went last winter my own self (a mere woman) in many a cold windy day, a lot colder than we've had all this winter. He says he'll go tomorrow. I've heard that till I could do damage to his skull. We went up to feed the cattle and they were taking a nice nap in the warm sunshine.

Jan. 20— *At last!* at last! Bus has gone with the mail. It was a gorgeous sunset last night and this morning it was snowing, but cleared warm and beautiful by 9 o'clock so old Bus dug out. Mr. Hart went as far as Hay Gulch with him to help him get on his way. I wonder when he'll get back with our mail. This is the 1st soft feeling day we've had. It's like early Spring and the sled slipped along so fine. The first really good sleighing so far. It's cloudy this P.M. but soft and thawy. There were 2 big sun dogs

Jan. 21— this evening.

Jan. 21— Another beautiful day. It was snowing when we got up this morning but cleared up about nine and was a fine day. Bus didn't come today as we figured. Well this sure is a hard way to get mail. I wonder if the weather ever will suit that Bus enough so he can come back.

Jan. 22— It was nice morning but turned to a bad stormy day but Bus had just started back so he came home. I'm sure glad to hear from my dear ones and to know all are well. Poor Herman, Lizzie says, is having his trouble earning his mutton chops. He's at Dry Cow Creek Bridge with his sheep in the high sage brush. Toward evening the wind was higher and the snow flying.

Jan. 23— This morning the hills look rough from the drifting and awful high wind in the night. Walter's birthday and I'm busy getting my chicken roasted and cake and ice cream made. Have Mr. Hart and Bus over to eat dinner with us. We opened our Christmas presents that came in the mail. A nice box of cigars for Walter from Clay. A nice box of candy to both — from Jeannie Ogilive and a nice fruit cake from Uncle Charlie and Olive. All were carried twenty-two miles on horse back and arrived here in fine shape altho there are many deep drifts, the horse had tough going thru. We had a pleasant evening all together. It's a cold clear day.

Jan. 24— Another cold clear day, really very cold. McKeal came down to visit and Mr. Hart and Bus came over and the men told stories of their kid days all very funny and we spent a pleasant evening. I have a cold that is settling in my left eye like I've had so often the last three years. Bus has a cold too.

Jan 25— Another mighty beautiful clear day but awful crisp and cold. One of our coldest days...McKeal went home today. He said when he came down yesterday he had to walk nearly all the way to the 2 Fork Crossing so much snow. My eye is worse today and has spells of stinging and watering that's awful. I'm to try Boric Acid in it tonight. Maybe that will help. Got 9 eggs today.

Jan. 26— A nice morning and looked like we might have a fine warm day, but towards noon the clouds began to come from the west and north and by mid-afternoon it was an awful cold blustery afternoon. High winds and disagreeable. The evening and night was cold and windy but at sunset it felt more moderate. Got 7 eggs today.

Jan 27— A nasty blizzardy day. Very cold and disagreeable. Mr. Hart went up with Walter. I'm sticking near the fire. My eye is all better today so I guess the Boric Acid did the job. This afternoon the sky shows blue in places and there's spells of sunshine.

Jan. 28— Cold and windy all day. I didn't go out of the house. Mr. Hart went up with Walter. Walter came home awful cold. The snow drifed a lot all day. Walter says the water has been awful low in the creek now for three weeks. They have to draw it with a bucket on a rope and water the cows and horses in a tub. I've tried to do my mending today but I about froze at it. I'm trying to get it done.

Jan. 29— Another awful cold windy day. They came home very cold. Walter had to get off the sled and walk going up to keep warm. How this cold nasty weather hangs on! We're all hoping Feb. will moderate this weather and let us have some nice days. We're all very weary of cold and winter, wishing for Spring to come, trying to make the best of it. My cats and Spottie too wish Spring would come.

Jan. 30— A blizzard was raging when we awoke this morning and it was a bad old day all day. Awful cold and windy. This late afternoon a great sight met our winter weary eyes — two dear little brave *Robins* — real ones — and what a joy and hope they gave all of us! They were chirping about like summer-time and the snow flying about them. They lingered about the black currant bushes and picked at the dried currrants hanging on the branches. We hope they know Spring is near or at least a moderate time. The snow drifts are big and wide and I wonder how we'll make it getting out of here for mail next time. Walter has a cold and I'm worried for fear he gets real sick. Bus got this cold at Cow Creek from Fred Rasmussen who was at C.C. when he was and he had a bad cold. We have all been pretty free from colds till now.

Jan 31— It's more mild but quite dull and some windy yet today. One Robin is still here and I do hope it can manage to live. I've put out tallow for the birds. Walter spent a rather bad night and has quite a bad cough. Bus came over this morning and offered to go feed the cattle and I'm glad to let him so Walter can stay in and get his cold broke up. At about 1:30 this P.M. there was a big sun dog north of the sun.

Feb. 1— Well the wind was whoopin' 'er up this morning early and it blew all day, but the clouds drifted away and by noon it showed signs of breaking away. This evening the wind isn't quite as bad but bad enough. There's a sun dog north of the sun this evening and it's clear and not a lot of clouds. Today the sun fairly burst out at times so bright it was dazzling to the eyes. I saw one of the Robins this P.M. Walter is lots better today and was able to do chores at the barn. Bus fed the cattle again for him. I had a bad throat and head-ache all night last night. My head still aches and my cheek bones ache, but I'm lots better. The old drifts look deep I tell you. Can't see the cellar only a board that sticks away up and the top of it is all that shows now. The sunset was pretty, only a dark cloud hung on the horizon where the sun set and there was a sun dog north of the sun.

Feb. 2— Last night was a terror. It blew something awful and rained and snowed and plastered the doors and windows shut and this morning Bus came and dug out our door as we were shut in unless we'd torn the screen door up. It laid down nearly a foot of snow. Today is a changable day. It acts like it was trying to clear and then it clouds up and snows. This morning the hills up the creek looked blue like bluing water. It did clear enough for the old ground-hog to see his shadow a minute (if he could dig out to see anything). This is a bad winter and we wonder how the sheep men are faring.

Feb. 3— Still it's a wintery snowing day. We are all getting well from our colds, but I still feel rotten bad, so weak and useless. Mighty glad Walter is better. He had a bad old cold. maybe if the sun would ever shine we'll all feel better. It's been dull and cloudy so long that we're all dull with the weather. Sure lots of snow. It snowed quite a little last night again. It looks like the Arctic Region out side and I've been inside so long I'm ready to go thru the ceiling. This sure is some job holding down the Fort till we do something. I wonder what? Summers are wonderful here, but Oh Ye Winters! Aren't Ye cruel!! Walter saw a bunch of horses at the mouth of Alamosa last night and thinks it's Pet and her colts and Fan, Sis and Pilot. The colors were right for them. They've been up along Herman's fence all winter. Am glad to see them dig out for new range. They came home to visit us this evening and stuck around and ate hay out of the feed sled and then all pulled out again for the range. Herman's old Nig horse is with them but my 2 yr. old mare is missing. I sure hope she has just cut off with the balance of Pet's summer bunch. Hope she hasn't got in a ditch like her mother (Kate). Fan, Sis and Nig are pretty thin. The others (Pet, her colt and Pilot) look fine. They've sure had to dig for a living. Wind keeps a howlin'.Feb. 4— Walter said the road up to Slide feed lot was worst it's been. All blown in. It still blows a gale and sends the snow flying and piles the drifts highter and higher. 2 P.M. Oh the surprise! I just heard Spottie barking and looked out and saw he was looking like he really did see something so I stepped to the door and looked up on the hill and there was a man on horseback leading an extra horse. My heart stood still. It's news but what kind! I called to him how the best way to come thru the drift and when he got his horses wallowed thru and got to the gate I asked if everybody was well and he assured me they were. What a relief! He had just come for Bus as Bus has a job waiting him to start on the 8th. The man was Iverson from Cow Creek Ranch and he told us he had been in drifts over the horses backs and had had to tramp the snow down to help his horses thru. We are rejoiced to know everybody is well. Herman sent us that word and he is right at Dad P.O. with his sheep and has his feed at Dad. He wanted Iverson to bring him the black team and sled if he tho't he could but it's impossible to get a team with a sled thru this deep snow. I am sorry we couldn't have known sooner about this then we could have gotten the team and sled to him. I saw the Robin again today. How the wind is blowing tonight!

Feb. 5— Bus and Iverson left at 10 A.M. and such snow those poor horses do have to dig thru. I took a picture of them in this first drift. The wind blew so hard all night and still is that there's lots of high knobs showing bare this morning. I hope it blows all this snow to the North Pole if its got to blow all the time. How I long for Spring to come. I've staid in so close I'm awful weary. Time drags when I can't get out every day and it sets me to thinking how it will be if we are still here when we are old. My thots go back to dear Massie here.Feb. 6— Last night was an awful windy blustery night and plastered up all the buildings with packed snow. This morning it was still whoopin' 'er up. Oh will this wind ever stop! It slacked up about 11 a.m. but it's at it again this p.m. The snow is plastered up against the house so close this winter. It usually whips out a circle around. We'll sure have water every place when this melts. Our door is snowed up about 3 ft. every morning now. We took the screen off so we can dig ourselves out in the morning. At 5 p.m. it started to snow little round snow turning to flakey snow and it looks like it might give us a heavy fall before it stops. It clouded up a misty looking cloudiness around 2:30 or 3 p.m. Walter said the creek is raising today. The water has been so low in the water hole for weeks that they have been drawing it with a bucket on a rope. It usually moderates when the water raises in the creek. The wind has gone down this eve and the snow is laying down fast. Here's hoping it's the last big storm of the long winter.

Feb. 7— It was blowing to beat time when we got up and was cloudy and the snow flying before the wind, but at 9 A.M. the sun popped thru at times so dazzling bright. It cleared as the day grew. Walter and Hart went up and fed as usual and I stayed home. I'm awful tired of staying in the house. I never was meant to stay inside. I'm more interested in the stock than I am in my house work. After dinner I went for a stumbly walk thru the snow down to the bridge. It's a wintery sight every place. Snow drifted over all the buildings and great big drifts behind the willows. The stable is beginning to be wet and when the drifts around them melt they'll be full of water for weeks. I always hate the break-up for we never have any place to put a young calf or lamb. We all got busy this evening and pulled the snow off the north side of the Hay Shed. It's 3 and 4 ft. deep and hard. We got a lot off but will have more tomorrow. It's sure a weight up there. Had a thawy afternoon and beautiful pink and blue sunset. The sky around the north was purple and looks like we'd have moderate weather now. The owl is hooting tonight and the night is wonderful and clear with stars so bright and twinkling. I'm afraid we have another storm in store for us, for the-old owl knows and the stars never twinkle so bright but that it storms.

Feb. 8— Well, it's cloudy again this morning but quiet, but I think the owl was right last night for it doesn't look promising today. The storm was not bad. It's a silvery night.

Feb. 9— This has been a very wet day. A wet rain-like snow falling part of the day. The snow is awful wet and heavy but has settled a lot. The country looks wet. The new moon is square on it's back. Walter dug into the cellar for spuds today. The snow being wet didn't drift in as fast as he could shovel it. The cellar is all under snow. A beautiful sunset.

Feb. 10— It's been a blustery day all day. High wind and at 3 P.M. a regular fright of a spring-like snow that plastered all the house up and sifted inside and shut all the windows up. Walter and Hart just got home before it. Walter went into *the barn* to feed his team and there was the first lamb of the season. A fine black faced ewe lamb. Have it in by the kitchen stove just now. Pet and her bunch are over on the hill across Alamosa today. A little bare spot there.

Feb. 11— Another blustery day. As I write this it's a regular blizzard going on. Walter went up alone this morning to feed and the cattle were all holed up under the high bank at water hole. Mr. Hart has a tooth ache so he didn't go. Oh we are so weary of winter. We only hope it will be an early spring or our hay won't last. Such a worry. How I wish we had a home some where where we wouldn't be at the mercy of the climate. I have stayed in this winter more than I ever did and I'm so weary. I haven't felt so rugged this year. My hip and leg have hurt all winter. The storm is so bad just now (5:30) that I can't see past the rock stable. It's a fright! We've had so much of these storms I don't see how the stock live.

Feb. 12— A kinda blustery day but not so cold. Walter and Hart found two yearlings snowed in (had gotton in in the night) where they'd slid down a bank.

	They dug them out. It stormed and blew when they were up feeding and off and on all day.
Feb. 13—	Another blustery day and rather cold. Oh I'm so tired of winter I could blow up. It's done nothing but storm and BLOW since Xmas. I hope it gives us relief soon or our hay won't last and then it will be all over for us. Just looks like all this snow can't melt till June. I wonder, will it get us and Herman too.
Feb. 14—	Another blustery day and cold. It's snowed and drifted by turns all day. Poor old Nig (Herman's horse) has given up digging for his living and the poor thing has come here for help. I'm going to feed him oats and maybe we can save him. He's awful thin. Hay is so precious I don't know what to do. We've got to get old Sis in too right away.
Feb. 15—	The owl hooted last night and this morning looks like mid-winter. Darn such hard winters. They'd break a horse's heart. I never saw it stay so cloudy for so long at a spell as it has this winter. We couldn't brag about the sun shining all the time in Wyoming this winter. If the sun doesn't shine pretty soon I don't know what will become of all of us. It's even gotten on Walter's nerves. 1 P.M. Well the sun has popped out. I'm almost afraid to say so for fear it hides again. I took a ride up to the top of the hill north on long dug-way.
Feb. 16—	A big northeast blizzard going this morning when we got up and continued until well into the afternoon. Maybe now that the wind has got around in that side it will let up and give us a change. They couldn't go feed until 1:30. It looked awful white looking up Alamosa toward the Divide last night and the snow is deep and crusted terrible.
Feb. 17—	This was a sunny day but cold and windy. Drifted most of the time. Mr. Hart saw a bunch of sage chickens going up the creek so we hope the long winded bluster is over. I saw Fan and Sis and Pet today over on the hill side north of the lower pasture. I washed today and it was sure cold hanging out the clothes. I can step over my clothes-line as easy as I can get under it. Can't hang any long article on it any more.
Feb. 18—	At Last! A beautiful clear quiet day. Oh, how fine it is to see the sunshine. It was fine all day. I went up with Walter in the hay-rack to see the cattle. They look good thru it all. I can't see much difference in most of them since I last saw them, sometime in January. The road is built up about 3 ft. and deeper in lots of places, all the way up the canyon. Never saw more snow on the south slopes. We saw Pet and her bunch out on the hill today in sight of the house and they were taking a much needed nap. The first time they've laid down in weeks.
Feb. 19—	Another great day. So sunny and fine! Coyotes are howling all around on the hills. They've been mighty quiet all thru our stormy days. It's so clear and shimmering today. Such a vast whiteness all about. I went for a little run on my skiis and it sure fine going only once in a while I hit a soft pocket. The snow is awful choppy but the skiis fly along on it. I went down to the lower field where I could look off up Alamosa and it sure looks snowy and white as far as I could see.
Feb. 20—	Another clear beautiful day. I went up to the cattle with them today. The sled scooted along fine. Lots of coyote tracks along the way. I dreamed about dear Massie* last night and Lizzie too. I sure hope all are well. It's awful to be shut away from all my dear ones and wonder

day by day how they all are. An air plane passed low over us this morning and we all ran out and waved our hands and hollered at them. I feel frantic at times wondering about everybody and helpless to learn till this infernal crust softens on the snow.

Feb. 21— A beautiful day and we're all mighty glad of it. I went up with the men again to feed the cattle. It was so nice and warm that I didn't put on my heavy coat going up but coming back we both put on our coats as there was a breeze. I went up on the hill again this evening after supper and skiied around and slid down the hill. Spottie and little Tom went with me. They think it's lots of fun to run after me down the hill. it just looks like the snow could never melt away, there's so much of it.

Feb. 22— Fine day again — warm and quiet. Four airplanes have past over here today. I wonder why so much air travel. Wonder if we're at war with the Japs or have they settled satisfactorily so the U.S. won't go to war with them. If only we had our Radio Battery charged we'd know these things. Purple and gold sunset tonight. Am so glad for the purple means moderate weather.

Feb. 23— Another beautiful day and Mr. Hart came up to tell me he heard the black birds singing down among the willows. It's a slight breeze blowing like a chinook might be starting. I sure wish we could have a chinook and make it possible for us to ride out and find out how everybody is. I feel like I couldn't hold out much longer and look at all this everlasting whiteness.

* "Massie" was Mother Robertson

Feb.24 — Had a little chinook today and the snow sure has settled quite a bit. This is the best day we've had so far to settle the snow. I stayed home all day and cooked up things so I can get out for a day or two. The days seem endless, but they do pass.

Feb. 25— Early this morning it was cloudy and a thin fall of hail like snow fell, but by 9 A.M. it was beautiful and sunny and warm and the black birds were singing down among the willows. I went with Walter to feed the cattle and Mr. Hart tried to get to some of his coyote sets, but could only get to Herman's corner and that by going down along Alamosa creek. There was a little breeze like a chinook today and the south slopes are baring some. The beaver are out of their holes feeding around. The cattle are beginning to scramble around on the side hills a little and feed on sage brush.

Feb. 26— Fine thawy day and the road up to feed lot is rotten. I went with Walter and Mr. Hart went on the skiis to look after his traps. The cattle look fine.

Feb. 27— A great hot day and the cattle are happy. They're rustling quite a lot now. McKeal came this P.M. and says the water is running down the hills and the creek — is "busting up."

Feb. 28— A wonderful thawy hot day. The snow settled lots today. McKeal went home so as to start to Rawlins tomorrow. I didn't go up with Walter for McKeal went with him. He had quite a hard trip down here. Awful deep snow.

Feb. 29— It was beautiful and thawed a lot today, but I could hear a wind coming that sounded like a thunder storm might be coming. I washed and got my duds out on the line and we ate dinner at 4 P.M. (still have just 2 meals a day) and as we ate it started clouding up like a shower and I hurried and took in my clothes. It started spitting hail like snow and tonight it sounds like quite a storm might be in progress. Hope it is just ushering March in and it won't last long. The hills looked bare on all the south slopes today and the horses all went away up on top. A lot of the cattle went on top the high ridge today again. Yesterday was the first time since we started feeding that they've gone up on top. They broke out a new feed lot today.

Mar. 1— The storm didn't amount to much — about an inch of snow fell, but it was cold all day and pretty blustery and drifted, but toward afternoon it cleared and the evening was clear and crisp. There were 44 head of cattle up on top of the high ridge near the feed lot this morning. They're doing fine and can get lots of feed up there — bunch grass and shad scale and sage and it helps a lot with what we feed, and is saving hay. I saw a bluebird today. Walter and Mr. Hart went up to feed and I stayed home and baked bread, pie and cake and ironed a little. This cold spell has checked the thaw and driven all the water into the ground.

Mar. 2— Walter and Mr. Hart took the sled with the wagon box on it up with the hay today. It's been a cold windy disagreeable day. All the cattle were waiting on the feed lot today. I staid at home and puttered around doing a deal of nothing. I've sure been lonesome today. This winter is endless. They drove all the calves across the bridge and up around by the old Government Coal Mine. They fed out good and a lot of them climbed on top of the hill.

Mar. 3— They went up to feed and there were 22 head of cattle gone that they couldn't find. It's not been a nice day. Windy and cold. I stuck in the house and looked up seeds I'll be needing for my garden.

Mar. 4— A rotten cold windy day. I rode up with the men to feed the cattle but I got awful cold. The 22 head of cattle that were missing yesterday were on the point of the high ridge over looking the feed lot and came running down when we got up there. This sure is a cold old day altho it's clear. Walt got into the cellar for spuds today. It's covered over yet and a job to dig in.

Mar. 5— 10:30 A.M. Got up this morning to the tune of a raging wheezing blizzard. Will this winter ever let up! I'm so sick and weary of winter I can hardly live. It's been ages since I last heard from anybody. A month now since we had mail and then it was Lizzie's old letter dated Jan. 20 and Jeans' Jan. 16. Every time we think it won't be long till we can break the trail out of here and go for mail it turns loose and gives us the dickens. Sure hope McKeal makes it back and has good news from all. This is a bad storm and I hope it's the wind up of the winter for we've all wearied, wearied of this winter. This is a tough old hard boiled life. There was a sun dog north of the sun as it set last night and I said to Walter "I'll bet it's storming when we get up tomorrow." That old sun dog looked wild and cold.

Mar. 6— A blustery day. McKeal came with our mail and it's a great relief to know everybody is well. Such anxious days! Lizzie and Ann write us the sheepmen are having a terrible struggle. Poor Herman has needed this team and here Iverson said he didn't want the team without the sled. The horses didn't come home till noon today. They were away up on top of the big hill northeast of the house. 16 of the calves stayed up there too tonight. May be home by morning. They can get at lots of feed up there so don't think of home and Purina. The cattle are on top of the high hills now.

Mar. 7— Another rotten day. When oh when I wonder will this awful winter end! I'm so weary and worried about everybody and wondering if we'll have enough hay to make it thru with our stock. Such a worried life this is! Walter, Hart and McKeal all went up to the cattle today. McKeal laid over today. I'm wondering if Jim will be here for the black team. Lizzie said he might. I hope he can get here without breaking his neck. These drifts are awful. Walter is to break out of here and take the team to Herman's camp as soon as ever he can if Jim doesn't come. It snowed so hard in the night that I have to stand on my tip toes to look over the drift that is plastered against my kitchen window to see up the hill road. The drift around the house is a whopper now. This is awful. With the terrible general depression and prices of all live stock down to nothing and on top of all that, this awful winter. And they've got the spring mud and water to drag thru yet after all this hard winter in the deep crusted snow. There will be terrible losses. We heard thru Mckeal that a man from Filmore had been out west on the Desert and reports sheep dying like flies. Old Nig didn't come home this morning for his feed. There were only 15 calves that came home for feed this evening. The others stayed up on the hills. Only half the cattle too came to the feed lot altho they were in sight of the feeding when the men threw off the hay. New moon lies right on it's back.

Mar. 8— It's a cold northeast wind this morning. Nig hasn't showed up yet. There were only 51 head of cattle on the feed lot this noon. The others stay up on top of the ridge, and feed on the bunch grass.

This P.M. Walter and McKeal went south on the road as far as the Willows to see how the road was. They walked and led their horses. Part of the time the horses could walk on top the crust and often fell thru but they made it there and back in 3½ hours. Mr. Hart went with me over to Hay Gulch to get the horse blankets and nose bags for the big black team. We were planning to send McKeal down to Herman west of Dry Cow Creek with the team so we were getting everything ready. Mr. Hart and I tried to get to Hay Gulch via the main road but the snow is up to the horse's breasts and crusted so it's terrible on a horse. We got half way between the Soda Spring and Herman's gate and had to turn back and instead of coming back over the big drifts we climbed a hill and got on the ridge and tied our horses — heads to saddle horns — and I skied and Mr. Hart walked — for the crust held him but not me. We got the things and came home by the hill road. It was awful deep even if it does face the south but we made it. The snow to the north is lots deeper than toward the south, but it's all deep enough. Nig (Herman's horse) hasn't showed up yet. He didn't come home for his feed yesterday morning either. We can't find even his tracks. We think he must be dead for he's been coming daily for his feed. He came here a while back and had given up the fight to dig snow. He's awful poor.

Mar 9— This is a clear sunny cold day and we hope our bad weather is over. Walter rode Baldy up to the cattle and took Purina to feed on the hills. No hay as the cattle are all on top of the high hills. They're doing fine on bunch grass. The south slopes on the rugged steep hills up the creek are bare so they can get at the feed.

Well I got on Baldy a little while ago and rode up in the pasture to look for old Nig. Not finding him inside the pasture I rode up the north side of the creek and looked over the banks and saw where the ice was broken up so I looked over near the bank and there poor old Nig was in the creek dead. He must have slipped off the rough bank. Poor old horse was trying to live and would have pulled thru if he hadn't fallen in the creek.

Mar. 10— Another clear but cold day. Walter saw all the cattle today. Two calves were on top of the barn this morning when we got up. They just walked on the drifts and on to the top of the stables. Spottie has been on top of the milk house all day. Just walks on from the drifts. The drifts are plastered up against all the building. This doesn't happen often. Usually there's a circle around that is clear to the ground — not so this winter. The cattle are feeding on the high ridges as the south ridges are blown bare. We stopped feeding hay the 8th, only feed Purina.

Mar. 11— Another clear sunny very cold day. Walter took Purina up to the cattle and they were all there but the four that has been away for awhile. They're on a low ridge north of the sand stone dugway. Half the calves came home tonight and the horses didn't come home for their oats. Walter walked up on the ridge southeast of the house to the sandhills to see Susie and her two colts. Susie is thin and so is her 2 yr. old colt. We're hoping Lindberg's baby is safe at his home and unharmed. We are so anxious to get our mail for news of the little curly head.

Mar. 12— We rode up to the cattle today and they were scattered all over the hills feeding. We gathered them together and fed them Purina and watered them. We then went up to the sand stone dugway and on up that ridge north and found the three head that have been missing for a week. They had slid off the big hill and couldn't come south any farther for snow so were snowed in. All tho' they were in a nice open place with plenty of feed but no way to get to water. Walter walked and got them out. I led the horses down the hill and the cattle followed and we got them back among the cattle. The cattle are a little thin but I hope they live for we haven't hay enough to feed them. Have to save all the hay we have left for any early calvers. Oh this is an awful life. Never know how we're to come thru these infernal winters.

Mar. 13— Walter and Mr. Hart went after Sis and Fan today and now I learn Mr. Hart went yesterday — skiied — and found Pet and her fine yearling colt down. Well today Pet is dead and the yearling too far gone to save so they shot her. That makes three horses I'm sure of that I've lost since last Fall that I got from Dad. (The two mares I got from Dad and the colt was one of the mares). Fan and Sis and Pilot are awful thin, but we may be able to save them. We have them here in the corral and will feed them hay and grain and try and save them. This last severe storm has finished things. These horses looked fairly well when we saw them last. I notice it was Feb. 3 we saw them last. Poor things, I'm just sick over this. Darn a place you can't raise hay on to feed all your poor dependent dumb brutes with.

Mar. 14— I went up the creek with Walter today to feed Purina to the cattle. We called them and they came stringing down off all the high hills. They got a good drink and look fine. Mr. Hart went on foot with two sacks of hay to feed Susie and her colts, but as poor as they were they were scared of him coming and left and went away down the country so we think they must feel better than they look.

It was hot all day and a chinook wind blowing. Lots of ground on the exposed sides have bared up. At 5 o'clock it clouded up and looked like it was going to storm. Just a little snow fell for a few minutes on the hills and the cloud passed on. Oh, I hope this is the break up!

Mar. 15— Another beautiful day, a chinook wind and the snow is getting rotten. Water has run down the hills on the south slopes. We didn't go up to the cattle today, but will tomorrow. Can see a lot of them on the hills feeding. There was just the faintest sign of a sun dog on the north of the sun tonight. I sure hope if it storms it's just as faint a storm as the sun dog. The men dehorned one calf today. Will start dehorning right away if the weather stays fine. Calves didn't come home tonight.

Mar. 16— Walter went after the calves and was gone so long I was worried to death, but finally here he came with them all but nine. They were away up on the high hill and in good feed. We started right in to dehorn them as soon as he got here and dehorned twenty one. Mr. Hart helped us. We stretched them out and tied them tight and got on fast. We have the dehorned ones in the hay shed out of the wind. It started to snow while we were finishing this evening, but I don't think it is going to be bad. I had my dinner ready to set on the stove and I came in and got it quick so we did a little after. We have only two meals a day yet, so have our 2nd meal at 3 P.M.

Mar. 17— We finished dehorning in three hours today. It's a wet blustery day but not cold. We worked in the hay shed. It's like April Showers today, little round hail-like snow fell in little squalls all day. A bunch of the cattle came down this afternoon and tried to get on down the creek, but only as far as the hill this side Alamosa and had to turn back.

My hands are bruised from holding the rope today and yesterday, but I'm not not tired. I think the men are more tired than I am, of course they did the hardest.

Mar. 18— Walter rode up the creek to see about the cattle. He found our black and white steer in the bottom on the creek on the ice and it couldn't find a place to get out. Walter drove him to where he got up the bank. The others are OK. Some of the calves came home but not many. Thry're doing fine after their dehorning. It was a warm cloudy day and little squalls of hail-like snow fell.

Mar. 19— Mr. Hart and Walter rode all around the Dam Canyon ridge to look after the cattle. It's rained a fine mist-like rain off and on all day and this evening it's raining right down pretty hard. Am afraid it will turn to snow and if it does it will be heavy old snow. I hope if it does it's the wind-up of this terrible long stormy winter or it surely will be the end of all the stock men.

Mar. 20— A deep snow covers all this morning and it's still snowing great big flakes. It was quiet this morning when we got up — just snow falling softly and steadily. About 9 A.M. the wind got up and it's a dense blizzard. I sure wonder how the sheepmen can survive — if it freezes after all this wet storm the sheep, cattle and horses are surely doomed. This is a cruel old country. Our cattle were fine yesterday, but I wonder how they're faring now. They're scattered all over the ridges and in this storm it is impossible to gather them. Suppose they'll come crawling out of hiding as soon as they can. Well we've saved 12 days hay which we can maybe pull them thru with now.

Mar. 21— What a day! I've walked miles, inside this house watching and worrying. The men have broke trails all day to get the cattle out of the places the storm drifted them into then piled banks of snow behind them so they couldn't get out. One cow passed out of the scene of action. Such a terrible storm this was. It was only a thawy misty day until near night when the heavy rain started and turned in the night to a deep snow then the wind (north-west) got up and fixed things for sure. Everybody is worried and cranky tonight. They saw all but 21 cattle so we don't know yet how much of a loss we have. The men were all in when they got home in the evening for they had to walk and lead their horses thru all the deep drifts to make trails so the cattle could make it out.

Mar. 22— The work horses left last night and it took till eleven today to dig them out when they'd crossed a gulch and their trail had drifted shut. They've been so good about coming home when we didn't need them. The men loaded the hay rack with hay and ate a lunch and went for all the cattle that are up on the hill from the bridge. Will feed them across the bridge then I'll take the team with the sled and go up to where we can feed the others. The men will ride the saddle horses on ahead so as to have the cattle at the watering place where we'll feed. It was five o'clock before we got the first bunch here. The men had to break trail again and get some of them out. As I sat watching out of the window to see if they were coming I saw seven head of cattle coming on ahead by themselves so I kept watch of them. When they got to the top of the hill where the trail turned down they cut across and the lead cow went down into a deep wash, but as she was fairly strong she wiggled about and got turned around and out then little "Shorty" tho't she'd try her luck but she didn't fare so well for she's awful weak. I watched for a time then got our old Nig and rode up bareback to see just what was going on. Little Shorty was stuck fast and couldn't move. I tried to help her but couldn't without a shove. She was head down and was bloating up fast so I had to hurry. As I had no saddle on Nig I had to walk home and lead him. Got my shovel and set it where after I'd got on Nig from the sled I could reach it. I sure had to move a lot of hard snow to get Shorty out. I first lowered her hind quarters so she wouldn't pass out before I had time to dig a trail ahead of her. Finally got her out and home. We put this bunch of cattle in the little pasture across the way (the old alfalfa field) so they would'nt run away and as it was a clear evening we felt they'd be fine. We then went up to the Ford at Coal Mine and threw out hay for the cattle Mr. Hart was bringing off that ridge. We hurried home and did up all the chores. Mr. Hart found 18 up there so we're still two short and as yet don't know if they've been snowed in some where and died or if they're safe. Such a frantic day we've had! Everybody going out at break-neck speed to save the cattle.

Mar. 23— Got up to the tune of a big blizzard and the cattle are huddled in a tight pack trying to live. Gosh but this is awful! We fed down in the willows at the old feed lot so they'd have shelter. The men took feed up to the ones above and every thing got cared for. The sun-set looked promising as north of the sunset above the horizon it was clear and blue but all signs have failed us this winter. We are short three head of cattle yet and tomorrow if it's humanly possible we will hunt for them. While the men did the chores I moved our bed back into the dining room. I'd moved it into our bedroom Monday but we slept cold and to worry and work feverishly all day and lie awake at night just was too much so I moved back into the warmest room. It's just been a terror of a storm today. The snow is awful deep and wet.

Mar. 24— Another blustery day turning to a regular blizzard in the P.M. I drove the sled team up and Mr. Hart rode up with me and then walked up the draw east of the Coal Mine crossing (north side of the creek) and Walter rode Baldy. He rode up the ridge but couldn't find the missing cows. I drove up to the upper feed lot and looked along under the high cut bank to see if they might be snowed in there, but no, so I drove back and waited for Mr. Hart. Walter came back on the road and went up to the Emigrant Ford west of the Two Fork Crossing and rode up the ridge form the Sand Stone Dugway to see if they might have slid off the high ridge down into that rough country and he found them snowed in but O.K. They could go north but not south. He broke trail and got them to feed on the ridge where the bunch grass is good. We feel relieved to know we're only out one in all this terrible storm. Only one died. Mr. Hart and I came home and here were the cattle stringing up the road; had gotten out of the field. They're a restless lot. The calves had broken the gate down and were spewing out thru the hole. We watered first the calves then the cattle and put them in and fastened the gate. We put the cattle in the little alfalfa field till Walter came when we put them in the little lamb pasture behind the corrals so they can't leave and will be in shelter. It was a blinding storm while we worked to get the cattle in shelter. I was wet down my neck and tired and hungry and I'm sure the men were equally so for they had worked all day in the snow and wet. I hurried in as soon as they didn't need me any longer and got our own food ready. We're out of milk for the present and it's hard to find things to cook. Haven't had time to dig our cellar out so we can get out potatoes and we have not had potatoes since the storm.

Mar. 25— A clear cold day. Just fed and cared for everything as best we could. I stayed inside and petted my sore face. The men's faces and eyes are burned too. Mr. Hart got a coyote in his trap.

Mar. 26— I went up with Walter and fed at the crossing so Mr. Hart could have time to skin his coyote. The cattle were stuck along the creek feeding on tender willows. It was a hot and awful bright sunny day and our faces got more burned. This sure is a hard time for us. We're not sure if we'll have enough feed to get thru for altho' it's clear today it doesn't look settled. If it doesn't clear up in a few days we'll have some losses for we only have a wee butt of a stack. Saw a bluebird today. The first bluebird that came sometime back either died or left. Just a few blackbirds and one bluebird so far now. The men dug out the cellar

Mar. 27— and got spuds and while they were doing that it snowed like the dickens.

Mar. 27— A rotten day. The cold wind is whoopin'er up and it just looks hopeless out side. The snow is as deep as it's ever been all winter and this continual bluster looks like we surely are doomed. We surely are having a stuggle. I sure have spent a hellish day today. The men have been out struggling with everything and I stayed inside.

Mar. 28— We went up to the feed lot with our little dab of hay for the upper bunch and found them all gone. We trailed them up to the upper feed lot where we fed in winter and found twelve head only on the feed lot. The rest are scattered all over the hills. It's a lot better day today but Gosh! the snow! It's over everything. Walter and I went alone up there today. I just have to get out of the house. What a pitiful little dab of hay we have to save the day with in such weather as we're having. It's sure a tough old winter when it kills horses like it's done this winter.

Mar. 29— Our big milk cow has a calf (a heifer) this morning and I'm sure glad for we sure need the milk awful bad. It snowed about two inches in the night and it's a rotten stromy windy day. Gee I wonder will we make the grade or are we doomed. 3:30 P.M. We just got home from breaking trail for the cattle and this day will stand out in our memories as a terrible day. We took the cattle (all but the ones that will calve in a few days) up the country. We dropped them at the watering place and then rode on to open up a trail. The snow is belly deep in most places and deeper in some and when we got on the rye grass flat this side the Two Fork Crossing poor old Baldy went down and we thot he was going to die and he may yet. We all three pulled and hauled and got him up and got the other two horses ahead to make a trail to a bare spot. Baldy went down the 2nd time and it was a long time before we got him up. He was rolling and was in snow 3½ to 4 ft. deep. We were sure desperate for Baldy is our stand by. We got him up at last. While he lay there we took the saddle off and when we got him to the bare spot we led him around for quite a long time to cool him off. He was foaming and I'm afraid it's an attack of Azoturia which is nearly always fatal, altho there is hope when one gets them in time.

Mar. 30— Another Blustery wet snowy day. A high wind is blowing and it's been awful bad all day. Our poor cattle are out to live or die. Baldy is better this morning, but looks awful tucked up. Oh it's heart-breaking to see our stock, everything is hungry and poor and we have no more feed. I sure hope the storm will stop before everything on the place is starved to death. Mr. Hart and Walter have worked so hard and schemed every way to keep all the stock alive. We sure are doomed to lose a lot of cattle and some more horses. It is terrible to be shut in here and helpless to help ourselves. All the many state highways costing millions and here we are out here without a road or mail. We read to each other in the evenings so we can go to bed with something besides cattle and horses on our worried minds, but 3 A.M. finds us lying wide awake with a terrible feeling of helplessness and desperation in our fevered minds. I wonder will this storm *ever* stop. It's been steady at it since the night of the 17th when it started a light rain turning to a hard rain toward evening and to a heavy snow in the night.

Mar. 31— A wonderful thawy hot chinooky day and the hills are baring a lot. Such a relief, but we are bound to lose some of the weak cattle yet. I washed quite a washing today and it was fine for drying.

Apr. 1— This morning the robins, killdeers and bluebirds were here and act like spring was here. The creek is starting to make sounds of flowing water. This has been a hot day. McKeal came this P.M. for our mail as he's going to Rawlins. I'm sure glad for we'll soon hear and I hope and pray it's good news.

Apr. 2— Walter rode up the creek to the *Osborne Bridge* to look over the feed and the cattle. He found them still trying to live. They feed on something and fill up. The last ones he saw were on the hill north of the Emigrant Ford. McKeal went home at the time Walter went up the creek and he will go to Rawlins tomorrow. It has thawed an awful lot and lots of ground is baring up looking toward the north. The creek is filling with water at the Bridge.

Apr. 3— It's another thawy day but not so warm. Walter has taken a little Purina up the country to feed any cattle that have come onto the creek.
I heard my first Meadowlark today. It sure sounds fine.

Apr. 4— I took the skiis after I finished up my morning work and went up in the hill (south) as far as the Springs. From the old sheep camp place I could see over lots of country and it's awful white. It looks to be baring up pretty good down at the Balance Rock ridge also that flat and on down the creek toward O.P. Olsen's cabin it's pretty bare looking. I saw something on the road on farther that looks like a dead horse in a snow drift. I am going to see as soon as I can get a horse thru these drifts. It was too far for me to walk and ski. I walked where the snow had blown off and where it was thin for my skiis aren't very strong and they had to bend too much where the snow was thin and loose. Walter and Mr. Hart went up the creek and bro't 22 head of cattle down and put them over on the hill between here and Herman's ranch. Little spots in the upper meadow are showing up but there's an awful deep patch of snow on both sides the gate so we can't get cattle there yet for quite a while.
Gideon's heifer has a calf up the creek and Walter is to take her some hay and Purina this evening. This sure is an anxious time with all these little things coming. The stable and hay shed are filling with water and there's no place to put little new calves. The country looking south and even looking north is awful white yet. I hope this nice weather continues so we will have a chance to get thru. The men keep the cattle punched around on new places so they'll have something to eat all the time. It's sure a job too for they can't get thru lots of places to get to bare ridges.

Apr. 5— A new calf up at 2 Fork Crossing. I stuck around the house all day and tho't about the awful deep drifts toward the south of us. The men went up the creek to ride around the cattle to see they were all on feed. It was a cloudy day, looked like rain.

Apr. 6— There was 4½ inches of snow this morning to greet us on rising. It was warm and melted all day. The men punched the cattle around to feed. I stayed inside all day. The cattle were all right and feeding.

Apr. 7— Another little calf was born out here in the lot. The men went out up to the Coal Mine Ford and got a bunch of cattle and put them on hill north of here. I sewed.

Apr. 8— The men went up the creek and looked over the cattle. They saw another cow with a calf up the Middle Hill of the Dam Canyon. The cow with the straight out horns. She has a heifer calf. This has been a cold day but clear and has thawed lots. The new moon is on it's back again. I sure hope it won't be as stormy as the last two moons that have both been on their backs and it stormed so much. I sewed all day again today. Have made two pair of riding breeches the last two days. The birds are singing lots every day now.
(to about the 2nd I think. For aways back I'm a day ahead on dates)

Apr. 8— McKeal came bringing bacon and ham and MAIL. Oh how glad we are to get our mail again, and to know everybody is well altho Herman is and has had a terrible winter and now McKeal is to take the team. Herman sent a fellow up the 2nd and the fellow said he got as far as the Red Cabin (Willows) and that the gulch was full of snow and he was afraid to tackle it so he turned back. The men rode up the creek and looked around the cattle. I sewed some.

Apr. 9— McKeal started at 9 o'clock this morning. Walter going with him to help him thru the drifts. Walt went as far as Kelsey's Gulch and as they seemed to be getting into lots less snow he turned back. He was gone 6½ hours and I simply walked the floor for I didn't think he'd be gone so long. It's always something to worry one's life away out here. Well Walter finely got home and they had made it alright. The horses could walk on top of the crust lots of the way even the big heavy team.
Walter saw Paint and altho she's thin she can run like a scared wolf. He also saw Susie's two colts. The 2 year old is pretty thin but the yearling is fine. Susie must be dead, she wasn't with them. Mr. Hart took Purina up to a cow with a calf up the creek.

Apr. 10— McKeal got back at 5:30 O.K. and had gotten to Herman's camp O.K. which was on the divide between Dry Cow Creek and Dad P.O. We're so glad Herman has the team. He's awful blue and has lost quite a lot of sheep and is having a fearfully hard time even yet as the 20th of Mar. storm about killed his outfit. His team and saddle horse are worn out and so is he. What a life! Just get a good start here and along comes on of these infernal hard winters and sets you back years and years. McKeal saw Smokey (Lizzie's horse) so they have one left too and I'm sure glad for they sure need them. They saw one sorrel mare dead up near the Willows. Fine weather.

Apr. 11— McKeal went home today and is to go to Rawlins around the 25th so I will get mail ready to send again. Walter and Mr. Hart went up Dam Canyon and looked at a bunch of cattle and on up to the 2 Fork Crossing. All they saw are doing all right. I hope we never have to go thru the like again. It's just too cruel. It's a mild kinda hazy day but warm and thawy. The drifts are settling lots. The creek was out of it's banks yesterday but must have cut thru the drifts that were clear across the creek down in the meadow for today it's away down. It was backed up. Oh yes that fellow that Herman started up here after the team lied to him about the snow at the Willows for he didn't come nearly to the Willows. He just came as far as the Lake and sneaked back with a lie to square his weak self.

Apr. 12— Still a nice thawy day and the cattle are still alive. Walter misses one of our Holstein steers and we think he must be dead but they can't find him. He was very poor and may be in a hole.

Apr. 13— Another nice day. The men went around the cattle as usual today and found Snowball's mother dead. How I wish I could ride out too, but our saddle horses are so thin and tired that I must stay at home and save them for they have just the three head in here and must change off to save them.

Apr. 14— It threatened rain all day today and thundered but only a drop or two fell. We are sure glad it didn't snow for we'd sure have a big loss. We have a cow with a little young calf here, feeding her, and letting the calf suck another cow to help it to make a go of it. She hasn't any milk and the poor little calf was starving, so the men carried the calf on Johnnie and drove the cow to get them here. We're feeding her Purina and think she'll make it. It thawed an awful lot today.

Apr. 15— A beautiful drying day. I never saw snow melt faster. There's been a regular river between the house and the barn coming from the gulch south of here. It hasn't broke thru yet west of the yard but seems to be this P.M. It broke thru before night and the water stopped running between the house and barn. The barn is so full of water that we've closed it up so nothing can get in it and drown. The cattle are pulling out up the creek themselves and doing lots better. We've got nine calves up to date. One of them is from the Gideon cow we've wintered. The whole meadow is bare of snow. It just went like a flash. I never saw snow go so fast. And aren't we glad!

A very bad winter on stock. Have had colder but never a steadier winter.

Apr. 16— It is a grand windy drying day again today and how the snow drifts settle. It begins to look like we'd be able to get to town soon. I can hardly wait. Nobody knows how I look forward to my first trip out of this snow locked place in the spring. I can hardly wait, it seems so awful long since last I saw a woman or heard a woman's voice. The last time was Nov. 18, 1931. Isn't that a long time? Just five months. I try to keep interested but it's hard to do so long for there's so much I want to ask about and hear about. I'm alone all day every day and I just cook the best meals I can while I'm trying to forget it all. Maybe it's a good thing for the men I am trying to keep interested for then they get good eats. And I hate to cook so awful and hate to stay shut in close.

Apr. 17— We spent a restful day today. The first day the men haven't gone around the cattle for a long time. We three walked down to the end of the meadow to the watering place to get an axe we left there the fore part of winter but the creek was too high for us to get our axe so we poked on back. The meadow is getting dry in places. It's threatened rain some today.

Apr. 18— I churned today in my little glass churn, the first butter we've had since along in Feb. (early part). The men went up Dam Canyon to see two weak cows they've been watching. Found one with a nice steer calf and the other one dead. She got on her back. This cow is awful weak and thin altho we've fed her twice a day all winter. She was not thrifty all winter. We have to help the calf with our milk cows so as to save it as she hasn't much milk. This sure is a hard old time for us. It's just terrible to see everything poor and have no feed to help them. Will feed her Purina and may save her. These Southern cattle are the "Bunk" for this cold country. They have no vitality at all. The men ate a lunch and went on back up the creek to see how the others are. Our saddle horses are poor and we have nothing but oats and turn them in the Buck Pasture to rustle. Have to ride them all day every day. I wait here and worry for fear they'll come home with the news we have lost cows. I'd rather ride out with them and see. I hate to stay here and cook and worry.

Herman came walking in dragging his tired team along behind him. We were sure glad to see him.

Apr. 19— Herman left today. I took him as far as the gulch this side O.P. Olsen's cabin down the creek and led his horse back. We saw Fan, Sis, Pilot and Archie, also a horse we think is Sweetheart down west of the Balance Rock. Walter and Mr. Hart went up on the hill for a jig of hay to help feed the cows we have here. They had quite a time getting thru the drifts. Herman walked from where I turned back to the C Y Corrals and Bridge. he was to meet his sheep outfit and count them over the Bridge.

Apr. 20— We three took Herman's team over to Hay Gulch and turned them loose and then went down to the house and got 2 sacks of Purina he said we could get. We packed them — one on each side — of Nig, tied on with a long rope over the saddle. We went over via the Dam and back by the road. Got thru the drifts all right. It blew awful hard and rained. Awfully high winds all day.

Apr. 21— It's been raining off and on since around five A.M. today. We hope it just rains and doesn't snow. The creek was out of it's banks this morning. An awful lot of snow went during the high wind yesterday. Our nice cow that raised two calves for us last year had a calf today. Bull calf. The old cow they bro't down from Dam Canyon with her calf the other day is dead this morning and we have to give this cow her calf. At present we're letting it suck one of the milk cows till this fresh cow can take it. She always lands an extra calf to raise with her own.

Apr. 22— It started snowing hard at around five o'clock this morning. Was just a white skiff when I looked out at four A.M. and wasn't storming, but soon the wind came up a little and the snow started — big flakes. It snowed six inches, but was warm and after awhile it rained and was a real Spring-like day.

My little blue Kittie had four pretty little kittens today and she's awful proud and "talks" a heap about her babies when I go and look at them.

Apr. 23— This is a rotten cold, raw, wet, dirty day. Looks like we might have a bad storm yet before it stops. Our last little lamb came today and is a lively nice big black face lamb. This is the only one we have saved. The others died. We're all terribly sick of "Weather." Gosh what a lot of it we've had! Still it snows and looks so awful wintery and cold. just looks like we never would get spring and warm days. We all stuck close to the fire.

Apr. 25— A fair day and looks like the storm will let up. The men went around to see how the cattle were making it. Everything seems to be doing all right. The wind started up this evening and sounds awful bad like a storm was coming.

Apr. 26— Such a night as it was! Nearly blew the house away and it's a rotten cold windy day. So weary and wintery. We're not doing anything only trying to get warm some where. I wonder if winter is going to last always. We're sure having a time keeping our milk cows fed something to keep them going for they can't go out on the hills and feed. This is an awful time. We're feeding an orphan calf with the milk cows milk that we need so badly ourselves. The barn is still full of water and the hay shed and there's no place to put little new born animals to keep them warm and dry.

Apr. 27— Snowing when we got up and cleared up and I was able to dry a few of my clothes and get them in off the line. I washed a big washing. Walter helped me all day and we got a lot done. In the afternoon about 2:30 it started to snow and kept it up all night. Mr. Hart went up on the hill (south) to look around. He found the cow that we turned out last with a calf. The cow was spry but the calf was dead. Too much wet and cold and too little milk.

Apr. 28— Another miserable wet snowy day. There's about 8 inches of heavy wet snow and it's still dull and storms by spells. I wonder how many calves we'll have when we get thru trying to have spring come. I had to wear my leggings to put out my washing today, the snow is so deep. Lots of drifts come above my knees.

Apr. 29— Another wet stormy day but warm. In the late afternoon the sun came out and I hope the storm is over. It's a terrible thing to be out of feed for all our animals and them so thin and weak. We are also getting very low on food for ourselves. Having to feed an extra calf makes us too short on milk so I can make butter. We'd have had plenty for a long time yet if we hadn't had to change our arrangements right in the middle of winter and take an extra man. Goodness knows he's earned all of it, but it just makes it hard having to make different plans after we were snowed in here. Had we known in the Fall we'd have made our plans differently. Our sheep are too thin to be mutton and I'm nearly out of ham and bacon and with no feed to feed a sheep so we could have mutton it looks like I might have to kill my hens. Such mud and snow we have! I hope it dries up quick so we can get to town and replenish our store.

Apr. 30— McKeal came today and is going to try and go to town Wed. He's to come here Tues. and he and Mr. Hart will go in Wed. in his wagon. He's to go after his team Sunday. The weather has been trying to clear all day and we're sure hoping it clears. The cattle have had a tough old time. We didn't go any where or do much today. It's awful nasty under foot.

May 1— At last it's May and it's a beautiful day. Has thawed an awful lot and the hills are all bare that were before this last storm. The old drifts are melting lots too. Walter and Mr. Hart went up the creek with McKeal to look around the cattle to see if we had any new calves. There's no new ones and we're mighty glad of it. I went up on the hill (south) to look at the meadow and the cattle up that way. I put the big cow with straight out horns and her calf and some young stuff down in the meadow where the grass looks pretty good. They're sure hungry and just went after the feed.

May 5— The first car over the road. Herman came from Rawlins. There's a big drift at Separation Creek and one 4 miles from here.

May 9— Two cars passed going to Savery. We rode today and got in Archie. Fan and Sis and Pilot are looking a good deal better. We turned them back to get fat on the range.

****

Winter of 1935-1936 Selections

Dec. 26— On Xmas Day I roasted a fine 25 lb. turkey and we had invited all the neighbors we have — two men — McKeal on his old place now the Enberg place and a one armed man from the Cow Creek Ranch. We five, Walter and I and the hired man, Courtney and the neighbors sat down to the big turkey and all the fixins.

Dec. 27— Well Walter and Courtney (our hired man) went into Rawlins Dec. 16 and back Dec. 18. The Weber boys were here after their cattle when Walter got home. Ernest McKeal drove down each day and did the chores for us while Walter was gone.

I was just getting on my horse to go break the water hole open in the Meadow when Fred Chadd came to get some of Enberg's cattle.

Jan. 31— A pretty good day. McKeal left for his ranch. Walter and I stayed inside. I sewed and Walter read to me part of the time. There's a big circle round the moon tonight and the owls are hooting. Must be going to storm. The fire burns blue too.

Feb. 22— A chinook wind. I went with Walter to feed lot. It's warm but cloudy. Mrs. Baur (Clenna) came plunging in thru the drifts at 3 P.M. bringing mail. Oh what a relief! They got so worried about us that she came. She had an awful hard trip up from OP Olsen's cabin. Lots of snow. Mr. and Mrs. Henry Baur and daughter Jean live west on the Muddy.

Feb. 23— A storm is whoopin' it up this morning so Mrs. Baur can't go back. Walter will go as far as the deep snow with her when the storm stops. Cleared at one P.M. but too late for her to go. Started again at sundown. About 6 inches of wet snow fell today. It's to be hard going for Mrs. Baur.

Feb. 24— A nice warm day after noon. Cold but clear forenoon. Walter went as far as the second bad gulch with Mrs. Baur. Snow very deep. She will be o.k. from there on as snow lessens all way down creek to Baur's. Walter got back in three hours.

Mar. 5-6— We've lost a day. We're not sure whether it's the 5th or 6th. Won't know now until some one comes and tells us. I set two hens today.

CLOSING THOUGHTS

As we close our account of history of the Overland Trail, The Rawlins-Baggs Freight and Stage Route and our family life on the Sulphur Springs and Hay Gulch Ranches, which covers about one hundred and twenty seven years, we hope that everyone interested in pioneer history will help to preserve the memories and tangible bits that remain.

Most of the places recorded by photographs in this book are now gone — just a few sticks and stones remain to show where they once stood. Only the smell of sage after a rain stays the same and the blue birds still fly.

THANK YOU

I wish to thank the many people who gave their information, encouragement, support and advice on writing of the Overland Trail.

I especially want to thank my husband, Les Erb, for his many photographs, his technical advice and his patience.

Open range is a thing of the past

INTERVIEWS

1. Mr. and Mrs. Judd Blodgett, Rawlins, Wyoming
2. Lawrence Braig, Rawlins, Wyoming
3. George B. Coe, Lancaster, Pennsylvania
4. Addie Humphreys Corson, Baggs, Wyoming
5. Mrs. Pheobe Cross, Rawlins, Wyoming
6. Peggy O'Neil Gates, Denver, Colorado
7. Mike Goffar, Rawlins, Wyoming
8. Millicent Goffar, Rawlins, Wyoming
9. John and Jennie Hansen, Rawlins, Wyoming
10. Eva Turpin Kuykendall, Greeley, Colorado
11. Clifford Leggett, Baggs Wyoming
12. Lelia Corson Leggett, Baggs, Wyoming
13. Mrs. Irene Marvin, Rawlins, Wyoming
14. Ella Rasmussen Pedersen, Rawlins, Wyoming
15. Roy Rasmussen, Rawlins, Wyoming
16. Mrs. Gertrude Doty Randleman, Ft. Collins, Colorado
17. Mrs. Nellie Robertson, Rawlins, Wyoming
18. Mr. and Mrs. Charles Sanger, Jr., Saratoga, Wyoming
19. Edward M. Tierney, Rawlins, Wyoming
20. Nina and Sid Weber, Baggs, Wyoming
21. Matt Weber, Baggs, Wyoming
22. Jessie Karstoft, Rawlins, Wyoming

The above listed persons were interviewed by the authors and compilers of the materials for the Carbon County, Wyoming information for "Wagon Trails and Folk Tales".

23. Jack French, Ft. Collins, Colorado
24. Gene Mikelson, Julesburg, Colorado
25. Jim Stretesky, Julesburg, Colorado
26. Martin H. Schloo, Ft. Collins, Colorado
27. Richard Baker, Ft. Collins, Colorado
28. Mr. and Mrs. Evan Roberts, Livermore, Colorado
29. Jim Anderson, Livermore Colorado

The above listed persons were interviewed for information on the Overland Trail in Colorado.

30. Mildred Wood, Laramie, Wyoming
31. Marge Richardson, Laramie, Wyoming
32. Russel Tanner, BLM Rock Springs, Wyoming,
33. Goldie Pitcher, Arlington, Wyoming
34. Alice Bronsdon, BLM, Rawlins, Wyoming
35. Mick Kazer, BLM, Rawlins, Wyoming
36. Sheila Bricher—Wade, Wyo. Recreation Comission, Cheyenne, Wyoming.
37. Debbie Chastain, Saratoga, Wyoming

The above listed persons were interviewed for information on the Overland Trail in Wyoming.

38. Walter Edens, University of Wyoming, Trek associate.

BRIDGER PASS OVERLAND TRAIL - BIBLIOGRAPHY

Bib. No.

1. Alter, J. Cecil; *Life of James Bridger,* 1925, pg. 512.
2. Tallman, Jean
3. Ibid.
4. Ibid.
5. Ibid.
6. Ibid.
7. Ibid.
8. Alter, J. Cecil; *Life of James Bridger,* 1925, pgs. 59-60.
9. Tallman, Jean
10. Ibid.
11. Morgan, Dale; *Jedediah Smith,* 1964, pgs. 160-161.
12. Alter, J. Cecil; *Life of James Bridger,* 1925, pg. 70.
13. Powell, James Wesley; *The Exploration of the Colorado River and Its Canyons,* Dover Pub. pgs. 141-143.
14. Alter, J. Cecil; *Life of James Bridger,*1925, pg. 69.
15. Kinnaman, Daniel; *A Little Bit of Wyoming,* unpublished manuscript, pg. 12.
16. Gowans, Fred; *Rocky Mountain Rendezvous,* pg. 13.
17. Tallman, Jean
18. Kinnaman, Daniel; *A Little Bit of Wyoming.* unpublished manuscript, pgs. 54-57.
19. Ibid., pgs. 62-66.
20. Ibid., pg. 42.
21. Root and Connelley; *Overland Stage to California,* 1950, pg. 18.
22. Fredericks, J.V.; *Ben Holladay the Stagecoach King,* 1940, pgs. 67-68.
23. Root and Connelley; *Overland Stage to California,* 1950, pg. 217.
24. Ibid., pg. 220.
25. Ibid., pgs. 220-221.
26. Sedgwick County (Colorado) Historical Society.
27. Frederick, J.V.; *Ben Holladay the Stagecoach King,* 1940, Appendix F, pg. 290.
    Root and Connelley; *Overland Stage to California,* 1950, pgs. 102-103 and Map.
28. Root and Connelley; *Overland Stage to California,* 1950, pgs. 324-325.
29. Monahan, Doris; *Destination: Denver City,* 1985, pg. 115.
30. Krakel, Dean; *South Platte Country,* 1954, pg. 20.
31. Gray, J.S.; *Cavalry and Coaches,* 1978, pg. 68.
32. Cremony, John; *Life Among the Apaches,* 1868, Bison Books 1983, pgs. 180-184.
33. Ibid., pgs. 193, 266-267.
34. Ames, C.E.; *Pioneering the Union Pacific,* 1969, pgs. 315-316.

35 Thompson, John C.; *Wyoming State Tribune,* Cheyenne, WY., Jan. 24, 1943.
36 Frederick, J.V.; *Ben Holladay the Stagecoach King, pg. 212.*
37 *USGS Hutton Lake 7.5 series 1963.*
38 *Headlee, Richard; unpublished manuscript.*
39 *Richardson, Bill; 1984, Interview.*
40 *Tanner, Russel; 1986, Survey of Site Along the Overland Trail.*
41 *Brown, Hester A. Rogers; In Albany County WY Autobiography.*
42 *Finfrock, Dr. J.H.; Diary.*
43 *Hull, Lewis Byran; Co. K 11th Cavalry, 1864, Diary.*
44 *Coutant, C.G.; Interview with Dwight Fisk.*
45 *Kinnaman, Daniel; A Little Bit of Wyoming,* unpublished manuscript.
46 Ibid., pgs. 158-159.
47 Allen, Capt. Aspah; Commander of Co. B 9th Kansas Cavalry, Official Report.
48 Kinnaman, Daniel; *A Little Bit of Wyoming,* unpublished manuscript.
49 Tallman, Jean
50 Ibid.
51 Root and Connelley; *Overland Stage to California,* 1950, pg. 311.
52 Headlee, Richard; 1978 Research for National Register, Albany County.
53 *Rawlins Republican Newspaper,* Rawlins, WY., Aug. 28, 1933.
54 Tierney, Edward; *Annals of Wyoming,* Oct. 1961.
55 Ibid.
56 Frederick, J.V.; *Ben Holladay the Stagecoach King,* Appendix G, pg. 300.
57 Hafen, Leroy; *Overland Mail,* 1926, pg. 320.
58 Tanner, Russel; BLM Archeologist, Interview.
59 Kinnaman, Daniel; *A Little Bit of Wyoming,* unpublished manuscript.
60 Wyoming Recreation Commission, Research for National Register, Sweetwater Co.
61 Reynolds, Adrian; *Annals of Wyoming,* Oct. 1962, pg. 241.
62 Ibid., pg. 242.
63 Tanner, Russel; BLM Archeologist, Interview.
64 *Annals of Wyoming,* Vol. 3, July 1925, No. 1, Published by State Department of History, Cheyenne.
65 Ibid.

ALSO SELECTED REFERENCES

Reference Books:
Beadle, John H.; *Western Wilds & The Men Who Redeem Them,* Jones Bros. & Co., Cincinnati-Chicago, CR 1877, pg. 53.
Betenson, Lulu Parker; *Butch Cassidy, My Brother,* Brigham Young Press, Provo, Utah, 1975.
Burroughs, John Rolfe; *Where The Old West Stayed Young,* William Morrow & Co., N.Y. CR 1962.
Kelly, Charles; *Outlaw Trail,* published by the author, Salt Lake City, Utah, 1938.
Leckenby, Chas. H.; *The Tread of Pioneers,* Pilot Press, Steamboat Springs, CO, 1945.
Moody, Ralph; *Stage Coach West,* Thomas Y. Cowell Co., N.Y. CR 1834.
Rankin, M. Wilson; *Reminiscence of Frontier Days,* Smith-Brooks, Denver, CO 1935.
Siringo, Chas. A.; *A Cowboy Detective,* published by the author, Santa Fe, New Mexico, 1912–Ch.15.
W.P.A. Wyoming; American Guide Series, Oxford Press, University N.Y., N.Y. CR 1941, pg. 239.

Reference Articles:
Bury, Susan and John; Compiled and Edited, *This Is What I Remember.* Printed by *Meeker Herald,* Meeker, CO 1972.
Carbon County Museum; Newspaper files *Carbon County Journals* beginning 1879.
Grasse, James & Putnam, Euvern, *Beaver Management & Ecology in Wyoming.*
Hunter, Vickie; Hamma, Elizabeth; *Stage Coach Days,* Lane Book Co., Sunset Books, Menlo Park, California.
Kinnaman, Daniel; *A Little Bit of Woming,* unpublished manuscript.
Lander Clipper newspaper, July 6, 1906.
McAuslan Edward R.; *The Overland Trail in Wyoming,* Reprint from Wyoming Geological Association, 1961, pg. 327. Also *Sulphur Springs Stage Station, Wyoming Annals,* Oct. 1961.
Post Offices of Wyoming Nat'l. Archives Records, group 28–July 25, 1868 and Dec. 31, 1975.
Wild Life Magazine; pen & ink drawings; Wyoming Fish & Game Department, 1953-57, Cheyenne, Wyoming.
Wyoming Annals, Wyoming Historical Archives, Cheyenne, Wyoming, Vol. 33, Oct. 1961; Vol. 3, July 1935; Vol. 16, pg. 93.
W.P.A. Wyoming Writers' Project Files–Wyoming Historical Archives.

INDEX
BRIDGER PASS OVERLAND TRAIL

A

Abbott-Downing Company 12
Adams, Clarence E. 100
Adams, Effie 121
Adams, Madeline 110
Adams, Roy B. 100
Adams, W.R. 121
Aingen, S. 83
Alameda, Jessie Karstoft 150
Alamosa Creek "Alamoosa" 150, 153
Alamosa, CO 187
Alamosa Gulch 191
Albany County Historical Board 39
Albany County, WY 38, 39, 41, 59
Allen, Capt. Asaph 52, 60
Allen's Guide 1858 98
Almond Station 98
American Bison or Buffalo 73, 115
American Ranch or Kelly's Station 20
Andrew, Lt. Col. George 9
Annals of Wyoming 49, 87, 96, 98
Antelope Station 20
Apache Indians 28, 29
Arapahoe Indians 27, 46, 48, 53, 60
Arikara Indians 4
Arizona 28
Arkansas River 10
Arlington, WY 42, 45
Artemesia Tridantata 61
Ashley Falls 7
Ashley, Wm. 4, 6, 7, 8, 25
Astorians 5
Atchison, Kansas 12, 22
Atlantic City, WY 106
Atlantic Rim 6, 69
Augur, General 48
Auraria 10

B

Back, Charles 191
Bacon, John 83
Baedel, Henry (Herman Henry
   Bruning Sr.) 169, 170
Baggs Creston Hwy. #789 90
Baggs, George 144
Baggs, Maggie 144
Baggs Rawlins Stage Road 106, 113
Baggs, WY 109, 144
Baker, James 7
Baker, Jim 110
Baker, Pvt. 41
Baker, Richard 33
Baker's Ferry 36
Baker's Peak 146, 186

Balanced Rock 83, 84
Bannock, Idaho 23
Barrel Springs Draw 91
Barnes, Demas 47
Bartleson, Mr. 9
Bath Ranch 39
Baur, Clenna 215
Baur, Henry 215
Baur, Henry M/M 215
Baur, Jean 215
Bear River 5, 11, 14
Bear River Freight Outfit 146
Bear River Station 11
Bear River, CO 114
Beaver Creek Station 20
Beckwourth, Jim 7, 8
Bellingham, WA 139
Bengough, Clement S. 42
Beni, Jules (Old Jules) 17, 34
Bennett, Ed 65
Benson, Charles 144
Benton, WY 120
Beyers, Bill (Biars) 114, 150
Biars, Bill (Beyers) 114, 150
Big Bend Station 25
Big Hollow 40
Big Laramie Station 27, 39, 40, 102
Big Pond Station 96
Big Thompson 26
Bijou Station 20
Bishop, L.C. 66
Bitter Creek 7, 9, 36, 94, 96, 98, 102
Bitter Creek Mutton Monarch 116
Bitter Creek, WY 95
Bitters Bottles 25
Black Bear 48
Black Butte 96
Black Butte Coal Co. 96
Black Butte Station 96
Black, Debra (Hughes) 180
Black Gus's Cabin 77
Black Hills 36
Black Hills, Dakota Territory 170
Black, Mac 180
Black, Mary Jane 180
Black Squirrel Creek 9
Black, Theresa 180
Black, William 180
Blackfeet Indians 4
Blackmore, Emil 146
Black's Fork 4, 9, 99
Blair, Emma Jensen 141
Blake, Paddy 76

Index

Blodgett, Judd M/M 217
Blue Gap Natural Gas 147
Blydenburgh, Charles E. 132
Boalt, Lt. John H. 57
Bodine, George 50, 70
Bolton, Isadore M/M 66
Bolton-Saratoga Road 71
Boone's Station 25
Boner, Elizabeth 122
Boner, Leander 121, 122, 128
Boner, Lee 121
Boner, L.N. 122, 123
Boner Stage Station 186
Bonner Springs Station 30, 31
Boulder Creek 25
Boulder, CO 185
Boulder Ridge 39
Borderai 9
Boston Medical and Surgical Journal 55
Bowen, Chick 145
Boyce, Charlie 130
Braig, Dora 113
Braig, Joseph 113
Braig, Lawrence 113, 114, 217
Braig, Nellie Robertson 113, 217
Brandley, E.J. 100
Brandley, Lt. 60
Brandley, Mary (Mrs.) 100
Bridger, James 4-9
Bridger Pass 6-9, 11, 36, 75, 77
Bridger Pass Station 58, 72, 75, 77, 89
Briggs, Cal 87
"Brighamites" 50
Bright, Mrs. 146
Briley, P. 86
Brink, P.C. 88
Britenstein, Harry 162
Brodt & Rasmussen 113
Brome, Andrea Elizabeth 177
Brome, Sandra (Brown) "Sandi" 177
Brome, Trent Robert 177
Brondson, Alice 90
Brooke, F. 133
Brooklyn Bridge 104
Brooklyn, N.Y. 104, 169, 170
Brown, Ann (Bruning) 173
Brown, Donald R. "Herky" 176
Brown, Don R. 176
Brown, Lt. 70
Brown, Lt. W.H. 51
Brown, Mahlon 40
Brown, Sandra Brome "Sandi" 177
Brown, Wilbur R. "Rap" 176
Brown, W.R. 176
Browne, Percy T. 102
Brown's Creek 40
Bruffey, George 21
Bruning, Ann Brown 129, 173, 178
Bruning, Charles 114, 168, 179
Bruning, Elizabeth (Robertson) . 124, 129, 168
Bruning Gilberta Hughes 129, 174, 178
Bruning Girls Candy Store 172
Bruning, Herman Henry, Jr. . 114, 127, 144, 171
Bruning, Herman Henry, Sr.
  (Henry Baedel) 169-171
Bruning, Lillie Turpin 168, 172
Bruning, Lizzie 168, 175, 178
Bruning, Louise Erb (Josephine) 179, 184
Bruning, Nellie Coe 168, 172
Bruning, Theresia (Zimmerer) 166, 170
Bruning, Willie 168
Bryan, Lt. F.T. 9, 36
"Buffalo Jump" 115
Buffalo, WY. 176
Bull Boats 5, 6
Bull Durham 114
Bunch, Henry 152
Bunker, Chloe Eller Robertson 187
Bureau of Land
  Management 90, 96, 100, 116
Burns, Robert H. 39
Burntfork, WY 8
Bush, Joe 45
Butterfield Overland Express Road 10

C

Cache la Poudre River 7, 9, 25, 26, 31, 58
Cache or Willow Valley 5
Caldwell, Corp. W.H. 50, 70
Calicott 152
California 8, 10, 12, 58, 99
California Hill Trail 20
California Trail 101
Camden, N.J. 88
Camp Collins 27
Camp on Snake River (Army) 152
Camp Rankin 18
Camp Walbach 36
Campbell, D.B. 133
Campbell, Mr. 50
Campbell, Robert 5, 7
Candlish Sheep Wagon 172
Carbon County Courthouse 105
Carbon County Historical Society 71, 77
Carbon County Journal . . . 104, 137, 141, 144
Carbon County Museum 171
Carbon County Wool Growers Assoc. 116
Carbon County, WY 9, 41, 66, 77, 90, 107
Carson, Kit 4
Casper, WY 11
Cassidy 43
Cassidy, Butch 127, 144
"Caster Pool" 31
Castle Gate 144
Centennial State 10
Central City, CO 77

Central Overland California & Pikes
    Peak Express 11
Central School, Rawlins, WY 105
Chadd, Fred 215
Chastain, Debbie 66
Cherokee Indians 31, 33, 34
Cherokee Station 31, 33, 34
Cherokee Trail 8, 30, 31, 83
Cherry Creek 9, 10
Cheyenne Indians 27, 46, 53, 60, 78
Cheyenne Pass 36
Cheyenne, WY 36
Chief Washakie 89
Children's Hospital Denver 184
Child's Station 25
Choteau, Pierre Jr. 4
Chug Creek 53
Church Buttes Station 101
Church's Station 25
Circus, John Robinson 26
Civil War 27, 58, 114, 169, 170
Clark, Capt. 54
Clarke, Lt. Thomas D. 52
"Clean Out of Cash and Poor Pay" 11
Clyman, Jim 7
Coal Mine Ford 208, 210
Coal Mine (Government) 181
C.O.C. & P.P. 11
Coe, George Jr. 172
Coe, George Sr. 172
Coe, Mary 172
Coe, Nellie (Bruning) 172
Collins, Lt. Col. Wm. O. 27, 52
Colona 25
Colorado 10, 109
Colorado Rawlins Stage Line 141
Colorado River 7, 73
Colorado State University 58
Colorado Territory 10, 11, 34
Colorado Territorial Legislature 11
Cofax, Speaker Schuyler 39, 65
Colter, John 6
Community of Virginia Dale 35
Comstock, William 41
Concord Coach 109
Concord, N.H. 12, 109
Conger, J.B. 132
Conness, Senator John 39
Continental Divide 5-10, 69, 73
Cooley, Sgt. 41
Cooper Cove Valley 42
Cooper Creek Station 41-47, 53
Corlett, A.T. 121
Corlett, Dad 142
Corona Pass 186
Corps of Topographical Engineers, U.S. Army . 9
Corson, Addie 146
Corson, Addie (Humphreys) 146

Cotterill 71
Cottonwood Springs 18
Council Bluffs, Iowa 10
"Council Tree" 25
Courtney 215
Courtwright, Frank 52
Coutant, C.G. 50-52
Cow Creek Ranch (JO Ranch) . 138, 195, 198
Cow Creek, WY 140
Craig, CO 106
Creed, Sgt. 57, 58
Creighton, Edward 13
Cremony, John C. 27, 29, 72
Crofutts, George 99
Crofutts Overland Tours 99
Cronin, Mike 179
Crow Indians 4
Cullen's Store 114
Curry, Kid 127
CY Ranch 213

D

Dacotoh Territory 87
Dad, WY 138-142
Daily Union Vedette, Salt Lake City UT 46
Dakota Territory 35, 39, 102
Dale Creek 31, 34
Daley 162
Dam Canyon 206, 211, 212
Darling, Maj. Daniel 87
Davis, Ella Mary (Mrs.) 66
Davis, John C. 66
Davis Roblin H. 66
Denmark 150
Dennison's Station 20
Dentz, Joe 137
Denver City 10, 11, 22, 27, 34, 51
Denver, CO 142
Denver Pacific Railroad 34
Denver Post 130
Deseret News 73, 91
Devil's Gate 50
Devil's Washboard 33
Diana 130
Dickson, John 98
Dinosaur National Monument 7
Dixon, Alvy 48
Dixon, Bob 144
Dixon, E.L. 42, 43
Dixon, Rawlins Stage 106
Dixon, William Hepworth 76
Dixon, WY 106, 144
Dobson 31
Dodge, Justice 137
Dodge, Maj. Gen. Grenville M. 102
Donald, William M. 66
Doty Brothers 138
Doty, Dow 137

Index

Doty, Gertrude Randleman 137
Doty, John 137
Doty, Mazie Newell 137
Doty, Stella 137
Double Eleven Ranch 144
Double Team Hill 31
Downing, Clara 141
Dow, Charlie 155
Drago Boy 57
Drake, Lt. 54
Dry Cow Creek 140
Dry Sandy 7
DuBois, Col. 9
Duck Lake Station 91
Duckett, Orlando 70
Dug Springs Station 92, 94
"Dutch" Fred 43
"Dutchman" Picture Man 54
Dutton Creek 43

E

Eagle's Nest Station 20
Eckler 43
"Elephant Corral" 84
Elk Mountain 7, 8, 36, 50, 61, 73
Elk Mountain Station 53, 60, 61
Elk Mountain, WY 50
Embree 43
Emerson, Alice Robertson 167
Emerson Ranch 186
Emigrant Ford 208, 210
Emigrant Fork 194
Enberg Place 215
Enos Jim 35
Erb, Lacey 185
Erb, Larisa 185
Erb, Lee Alan 185
Erb, Lester D. 185
Erb, Louise (Bruning) Josephine 185
Erb, Lynette Carol 185
Ernest, Frank 65
Eton, Isaac 83
Evans-Cherokee Route 36
Evans, Capt. Lewis 8, 83
Evans, Capt. William H. 27
Evans, W.L. 123

F

Fairfield, ID 178
Fairplay, CO 22
Fergusen, Ed 65
Ferguson-Hansen Mercantile 150
Ferris Rawlins Stage 106
Ferris, WY 106
Filmore Ranch 116
Finfrock, Dr. J.H. 41, 53-55, 58
Finfrock, William Edmund 58
First National Bank Rawlins 104

Fisk, Dwight 41
Fisk, Mrs. 41
Fitzpatrick, Thomas 4-7
Fitzpatrick, Val 186
Flame Spray, Inc. 184
Flaming Gorge 7
Flattop Hill 31
Fletcher 46
Ford, Harry 114
Fortification Creek 152
Forts
    Atkinson 7
    Bridger 9, 17, 27, 28, 101
    Buford 58
    Collins 26, 27, 33, 58
    Halleck 27, 41, 50, 53, 58, 70
    Kearney 18, 27
    LaClede 27, 28, 94
    Laramie 12, 27, 51, 53
    Lupton 25
    Sanders 58, 59
    Sedgwick 18
    Supply 101
    Union 9
    Washakie 106
Ft. Collins, CO 60
Ft. Collins Courier 26
Four Mile Creek 146
Four Mile Placer Mine 146
Fouts, Capt. W.D. 54
France 116
France, Mr. 162
Frandsen, Soren 116
Fremont, John C. 8, 10
Fremont's Orchard 20
French, Jack 25
Frenchman 152
Fresquez, Joe 129
Friend, John C. 51, 133
"Friendlies and Loafers" 52
Fullie, A.W. 153

G

Garrett, T.S. 111
Garwood, W.W. 132
Gates, Peggy (O'Neil) 116
Gatewood, Mary 99
Geddes Sheep Company 122
Germany 169, 170
Gerry, Elbridge 25
Gideon, George 121
Gideon, Mary 121
Goffar, Michael P. (Mrs.) 115
Goffar, Mike 115
Goffar, Millicent Miller 115, 150
Gold Hills, WY 170
Goldrick, O.J. 46
Goodwin, Raymond 25

Grand River 111
Granger, Lafayette 100
Granger Stage Station 99-101
Granger Station Controversy 100
Granger, WY 99
Grasse, James 154
Gray, Dr. John S. 87
Gray, William L. 54
"Great American Desert" 10
Great Divide Basin 7
"Great Medicine Way of the Whites" 5
Great Salt Lake 5
Greeley, CO 13, 24, 34
Green River 4, 5, 7, 9, 58, 98, 99
Green River Game & Fish Dept. 99
Green River Station 27, 94, 98
Green, Sam 114
Grieves, Tom 162
Griffiths, Corp. John 53
Gulf of Mexico 73
Gypsies 106, 179

H

Hahn's Peak, CO 106
Haines, Aubrey L. 99
Hale, Eddie (Grave) 30
Haley, Ora 162
Half-Way House 25
Hall, Flake 43
Halleck, General Henry Wager 51
Ham, Zacharias 7
Ham's Fork River 99
Ham's Fork Station 99, 100
Hancher, Pvt. David 52
"Hanging Tree" 25
Hansel, H.V. "Mack" 44
Hansen-Ferguson Mercantile Store 116
Hansen, Iver 150
Hansen, Jennie 118
Hansen, Jim 114
Hansen, John 118
Hansen, Karoline Miller 115
Hansen, Peter 141, 191
Hansen, Thyra (Jensen) Rasmussen 150
Hart, Bill 191, 193
Hart Island, N.Y. 170
Haygood, A.W. 110
Hays, Mrs. 195
Hay Gulch 155
Healy, Dan 121
Heenan, "What a Man" 66-69
Heink, Madam Schuman 193
Hemingray Telegraph Insulator 84
Henderson, Paul 100
Henry, Maj. Andrew 4-6
Henry's Fork River 7, 8
Hickman, Bill 99

Highway 30 .... 36, 99
Highway I-80 .... 42, 90, 98
"Historic Sites Along the Oregon Trail" 99
Historic American Buildings
   Survey (HABS) 99, 100
Hocker & Junquist 172
Hogg, W.T. 116
Hole in the Wall 127, 146
Holladay, Ben 11, 18, 20, 31, 39, 102
Holladay, Dr. 52, 53
Holladay Overland Mail
   & Express Co. 11, 36, 83, 87
Holladay's Losses in Colorado 37
Holladay's Losses in Wyoming 103
Hollingsworth, J.J. 51
Home Station 11, 16
Hoosier Pass 22
Hopper, Silas 36
Horse Gulch 194
Houghton, Bill 79
Hudnel, Pvt. Joseph 52
Hudson Bay Co. 8
Hughes, Colleen (Michie) 180
Hughes, Debra Black 180
Hughes, Douglas C. 180
Hughes, D.O. 131
Hughes Gilberta (Bruning) 178, 181
Hughes, Hillary "Hally" 180
Hughes, Katherine "Katie" 180
Hughes, Lewis "Mickey" 180, 181
Hughes, Melissa "Missy" 180
Hughes, Keeley 180
Hughes, Sharon Parr 180
Hughes, Teddy 130
Hull, Lewis Byrum 50, 54, 60
Humphreys, Maggie 110
Humphreville, Capt. Jacob L. 55
Humphreville, Lee 74
Hunter, John 66
Huntersville, WV 166
Hurt, Joe J. 66

I

Idaho 5
Immigrant Hill 42
Independence, MO 10
Ingman, George 72
Inn, W.R. 83
Iowa 152
Iscos 121
Italy 176
Iverson 195, 199

J

Jacobs, Mormon Elder Zebulon 73, 91
Jack Creek Land & Cattle Co. 88, 121
Jackrabbit 186
Jackson, David 4

Index

Jackson's Hole	5
Jacques La Ramie Chapter of DAR	59
Janis, Antoine	9, 25
Janis, Nicholas	25
Jankowsky, James & Martha	43
Japs	202
Jefferson Territory Legislature	10
Jennings, Bob	41
Jensen, Thyra Hansen Rasmussen	150
Jepps Canyon	36, 149, 150
Jerry's Place	109
Johns, Lt.	54
Johnson Island	65
Johnson, Millard	25
Johnson, P.M.	83
Johnston, Col. Albert Sidney	9
Johnstown, WY	106
Jones, O.W.	52, 53
Jones, "Tassel Pete"	113
"Josephities"	50
Jumbo Rest Stop	109, 143
Junquist & Hocker	172
JO Ranch (Cow Creek Ranch)	114, 138, 162

K

Kansas	22
Kansas City, MO	15
Kansas Pacific Railroad	34
Kansas Territory	10
Karstoft, James "Jim"	150, 154
Karstoft, Jessie (Alameda)	150
Kelly, Bus	191, 193
Kelley's or American Ranch Station	20-22
Kelsey	140, 141
Kelsey, F.H.	147
Kelsey's Gulch	211
Kennedy, D.M.	170
Kerfoot, Neelie	99
Kerr, Maj. John	11
Killpecker Creek	98
Kuykendall, Eva (Turpin)	168
Kuykendall, Dr. Fred	168
KC, WY	127

L

LaClede Station	94, 96, 102
Lake Creek, WY	177
Lamar, L.Q.C.	159
Lamb, Zeno	130
Lamprey Gulch	121
Lancaster, PA	172
Lander Clipper, WY	109
Lander Rawlins Stage	106
Lander, WY	106, 114
Laporte	9, 25, 26, 34
Laramie Plains	7, 9, 35, 36
Laramie Range	36
Laramie River	39
Laramie WY	39, 59
Larsen Oil Co.	132
Larsen, Hans	132
Latham, Dr.	42
Latham Stage Station	13, 20-25
Lawrence, Amy	40
Lay, CO	186
Layne, George	66
Leah	195
Leap, Ann (Robertson)	124
Leap, Dale	195
Leap, Harold	195
Leap, Walter E.	167, 188-215
Leap, Walter M/M	167
Leavenworth & Pikes Peak Express	10, 11
Leavenworth Times	35
Lemons, Cal	113
Lewis-Burt Command	65
Lewis, E.N.	41
Lewiston, WY	106
Lincoln Highway	36, 99, 107
Littlefield, Barrett	162
Little Laramie Station	36, 40
Little Snake River	73
Little Thompson	26
Livermore, CO	30
Livingston, Col. Robert	19
"Loafers & Friendlies"	52
Lodge Pole Creek	18, 36
Lone Tree Station	99
Loupe Pawnee Indians	7
Lovesay, G.H.	86
Loving, Col. W.W.	9, 36
Lozier Ranch	99
Luber, John and Mrs.	43
Ludlow, Fitzhugh	9, 62
Lundy, Scotland	166
L 7 Ranch	137
L.T.	83

M

MacIntosh Freight	113
MacIntosh, William	130
Mackey, Capt. Thomas L.	53, 54, 57
Mandel, Phillip	40
Marcy, Capt. R.B.	9
Maybell, CO	186
McClure, A.K.	72, 76, 90
McFadden, Sgt.	70
McIntosh, Mildred	147
McKeal, Earnest	179, 188-215
McMicken & Blydenburgh	132
McNeil, Mary	54
McPherson, KS	195
Meanea, Frank	170
Medicine Bow Butte or Mountain	10, 36
Medicine Bow Mountains (Snowy Range)	7
Medicine Bow River	46, 49
Medicine Bow Ski Run	177

Medicine Bow Station 48, 50
Medicine Bow, WY 50
Meeker, CO 51, 106, 115, 122, 166
Meeker, Josie 111
Meeker Massacre 51, 88
Meeker, Mrs. 111
Meeker, Nathan Civer 111
Meeker Rawlins Route 107, 126
Meldrum, Bob 145
Merino French Sheep 116
Merritt, General 111
Meschter, Daniel Y. 87
Mess Wagon 145
Michie, Colleen Hughes 180
Middlemas, Tom 116
Military Cavalry
    7th Iowa Cav. CO D 55
    9th Kansas Cav. CO B 27, 52, 53
    1st Kansas Volunteers 83
    6th Ohio Cav, COs A & C 50, 51, 52
    11th Ohio Cav, CO C 53
    11th Ohio Cav, CO F 53
    11th Ohio Cav, CO K 50
    11th Ohio Volunteers CO D 57, 94
    2nd U.S. Cavalry 18
    18th U.S. Regulars 18
    5th U.S. Volunteers 18
Milk River, CO 144
Milk River Rawlins Route 144
Miller, Chris P. 115
Miller Creek 69
Miller Hill 69
Miller, Karoline (Hansen) 115
Miller, Millicent (Goffar) 115
Millersville Station 101
Mills, Mr. 52, 53
Mills, W.P. 133
Miner's Delight, WY 106
Minnie Shank's Inn 145
Mississippi River 10
Missouri 10
Missouri River 4, 10, 17
Mizner, Cal 48
Moffat, J.B. 83
Moffat Railroad 186
Montana 23, 58
Morgan, Marian 110
Morisette, Oliver 25
Mormon Rebellion 9
Mormon Trail 88
Mormon Uprising 101
Mormons 10, 65, 99
Morrison, LeRoy W. 66
Morse, Maj. R.A. 78, 83
"Mountain Fever" 55
Muddy Bridge Post Office 141
Muddy Bridge Station 109, 141
Muddy Creek 6, 9, 73, 91, 126

Muddy Creek Canyon 9, 76, 78
Muddy Creek Massacre 78, 79
Muddy Crossing 106
Muddy Gap, WY 51
Murphy-Ready Bldg. 107
M.S. 83

N

Naestbed, Denmark 116
National Park Service 100
National Register of Historic Places
    Bridger's Pass Station 77
    Duck Lake Station site 91
    Dug Springs Station 92
    Ft. Bridger 101
    Ft. Halleck 59
    Ft. Sanders Guard House 59
    Granger Station 100
    LaClede Station 95
    North Platte River Crossing 66
    Pine Grove Station 73
    Point of Rocks Station 98
    Red Rock 91
    Rock Creek Station 48
    Sage Creek Station 72
    Virginia Dale Station 35
    Washakie Station 90
Nebraska City NE 170
Nebraska State Historical Society 20
Nebraska Territory 10
Neill, Capt. 18
Neilson, Bobby 42, 43
Neiman, Charley 137
New Mexico 9
Niel, Mr. 84
Nevada 58
Newcastle, CO 109
Newell, Mazie (Doty) 138, 139
Newell, Ralph 139
Newell, Dr. Robert C. 139
New York 25th Cavalry 169, 170
North Africa 176
North Platte River
    & Crossing 5, 7, 9, 34, 58, 61, 64, 66, 73
North Platte River Ferry 62, 63
Northern Colorado 147

O

O.C.T.A. 20
O'Ferrell, Maj. John 50
Ogden, UT 180
Ogilive, Jeannie 197
Oklahoma 8
Olsen, O.P. cabin 215
Olsen, Pete 150
Omaha, NE 150
O'Neil, Flora 116
O'Neil, Mary 116

O'Neil, Peggy Gates 116
O'Neil, Tom 116
Orange C.H., VA 166
Ordway, Edward 49
Oregon California Trail 10-12, 26, 36, 50
Oregon California Trail Assoc. 20
Oregon Trail 5, 9, 10, 12, 99
Osborne Cabin 190
Osborne Bridge 210
Oscaroose, Carl 71
Otis, Maj. 87
Outlaw Trail 127
Overland City 18
Overland Automobile 163
Overland Mail Stages 12
Overland Park Stage Station 31
Overland Stage and Mail Line 12
OVERLAND TRAIL 9-103, 126, 127
Overland Trial Markers 72, 77, 90
Owl Canyon 30
Owen, W.O. 66

P

Pacific Ocean 5, 73
Paden, Irene 20
Palm Livestock Company 59
Palm, Mr. and Mrs. Norman 60
Park Creek Station 31
Parmalee & Weld 183
Parr, Rick 180
Parr, Sharron (Hughes) 180
Parr, Stacey 180
Parr, Stephen 180
Pass Creek Ranch 61
Pass Creek Station 60
Patterson, E.H.N. 26
Peach Orchard Flats 143
Penitentiary, WY State 104
Percheron Horses 114
Perkins, Charley 140, 141
Perkins Dinner Stop 109, 140
Perry, Frank 113
Peterson, Jepp 114, 127
Pick Ranch 66
Pierson's Station 25
Pikes Peak 10
"Pikes Peak or Bust" 10
Pikes Peak Gold Rush 46
Pilot Knob 18
"Pin Ears" 150
Pine Grove Station 36, 67, 72, 73, 75
Pitcher, Goldie and Chet 45, 48
Platte River 7
Platte River Bridge 11
Platte, Upper Valley 106
Plumb, Col. Preston B. 58, 94
Pocohantas County, WV 135
Point of Rocks Station 98

Pony Express 10
Postmaster Brown 109
Post Office Dept. 21, 22
Potter, Col. C.H. 89
Powder River 4, 27, 77
Powell, John Wesley 7
Powell Train 76
Powell, WY 180
"Professor, The" 46
Provost Ferry 26
Provost, John B. 25
Puffing or Puffin' Bull Station 92
Pusch, A.F. 132
Putnam, Euvern 154

R

Randall, Todd 25
Randleman, Gertrude (Doty) 137
Rankin 131
Rankin, Joe 110
Rankin, WY 106
Rasmussen & Brodt 113
Rasmussen, Edna 162
Rasmussen, Fred 198
Rasmussen, H. 142
Rasmussen, Skerner 116
Rasmussen, Thyra (Jensen) Hansen 150
Rattlesnake Canyon 60
Ravofiere, A. DeBon 25
Rawlings, Gen. John A. 107
Rawlins Baggs Road 109, 127, 130, 137
Rawlins Boy Scout Troop #253 90
Rawlins Central School 105
Rawlins Colorado Stage 141
Rawlins Dixon Stage 106
Rawlins Ferris Stage 106
Rawlins Historical Museum 84
Rawlins Lander Stage 106
Rawlins Lions Club 66
Rawlins Meeker Road 107, 126
Rawlins Mercantile 137
Rawlins Milk River Route 109
Rawlins Red Paint 104
Rawlins Saratoga Stage 106
Rawlins Snake River Stage 104
Rawlins White River Run 110
Rawlins, WY 6, 7, 28, 51, 107, 109
Raymond, Sarah 30, 31, 94
Red Cabin (Willows) 211
Red Desert 9, 28, 89, 114
Red Rock 91
Reeves, 2nd Lt. John C. 52
Reid, H.M. 132
Remington, Fredric 47
Republican River 18
Reynolds, Adrian 97, 98
Richardson, Albert D. 65
Richardson, Margery 39

Riffenbergers	57
Rifle, CO	109
Riley, John	111
Rio Blanco County, CO	166
Rio Grande Railroad Company	109
Riverton, WY	179
Robbers' Gulch	143
Robbers' Roost	127, 144
Roberts, M/M Evan and Catherine	33
Robertson, Alice (Emerson)	146, 167
Robertson, Ann Leap	124, 128, 130
Robertson, Ann (Stewart)	167, 173
Robertson Chloe Eller (Bunker)	187
Robertson Elizabeth Ann "Beth"	186
Robertson, Elizabeth Bruning	124, 128
Robertson, George Edward	186
Robertson, Jack	135
Robertson, James "Jim"	2, 133, 141, 146, 167
Robertson, James Clay "Jim"	186
Robertson, Jean Tallman Stewart	124, 167
Robertson, John	116, 121, 128, 173
Robertson, Mary Beatrice Vassek	186
Robertson, Monty Bill	186
Robertson, Nellie (Braig)	113
Robertson, Richard, "Dick" Stewart	186
Rock Creek Station	43, 45, 46, 102
Rock Dale	45
Rock Point	98
Rock Springs Station	98
Rocky Ford	191, 194
Rocky Mountain News	41, 48
Rocky Mountain Rendezvous	7, 8
Rocky Mountains	4, 18, 33
Root, Frank A.	18, 21-23
Routt County, CO	122, 152
Rumsey	104
Rumsey, J.M.	132
Rumsey, J.R.	137
Russell, Charlie	6, 28, 115
Russell, Hod	41, 57
Russell, Horace	54
Russell, Majors & Wadell	11
Ryan, Ralph	137

S

Saddle and Harness Shop	171
Sage Creek	9, 69-71
Sage Creek Road	71, 72
Sage Creek Station	69-71
St. John, Sgt.	65
St. Joseph's Hospital	134
St. Joseph, Missouri	10, 65, 170
St. Mary's Station, Sweetwater County WY	170
St. Louis, MO	4, 5, 7
St. Vrain	26
Salisbury, George	162
Salt Lake City, UT	9, 12, 46, 58, 91
Salt Wells Station	98
Sand Creek	19

Sandstone Dugway	208
Sand Hills, WY	76, 194
Sanger, Millicent (Enberg)	121
Sanger Ranches, Inc.	121
Santa Fe Trail	10
Saratoga Lions Club	66
Saratoga Rawlins Stage	106
Saratoga Sun Newspaper	66
Saratoga, WY	66, 106, 121
Satiel	76
Savery, WY	215
Schloo, M.H.	33
Scotland	135, 166, 184, 186
Sears Roebuck Catalogue	177
Sedgwick County Historical Society	19, 20
Separation Creek	150, 152, 154
Seven Mile Creek	41
Seville, William P.	9
Shackelford, Frank	99
Shackelford, Ruth	31, 84, 99
Shank, A.T.	146
Shank, Mrs. A.T.	146
Shank, Minnie, Hotel	146
Sheep Mountain	69
Sheep Wagon	162
Shipley, Capt. Francis M.	50
Shoshone Indians	11, 89
Sierra Madre Range	73
Signal Hill	94
Signature Rock	33
Sioux Indians	4, 27, 53, 77, 78
"Sinks", The	40
Siskadee	5
Sixteen Mile Station	109, 114
Slade, Jack	11, 34, 35, 52
Slater, Bob	144
Slater, CO	130, 144
Slide Canyon	149, 153
Smead, Burton A.	132
Smead, Edward L.	132
Smith, Bill	113
Smith, Jedediah	4, 6, 7
Smith, Malcom E.	20
Smith, Perry	109
Smoke Signal Tower	29
Smoke Signals	28, 29
Smoky Hill Trail	10
Snake Indians	4
Snake River - Little	144, 150
Snake River Rawlins Stage	104
Snake River Valley	109, 139, 140
Snodgrass, Jerry	142
Snowy Range	7
Snowy Range Mountains	177
Snow Shoe Gulch	149, 153, 154
Soda Springs	189, 204
South Pass	5, 7, 10, 26, 99
South Pass City	98, 99

Index 229

South Pass Oregon California Trail 10
South Platte River 9, 10, 17, 22, 36, 58
South Bend Station 99, 100
Spotswood, Robert J. 35
Spring, Agnes Wright 100
Spring Creek 26
Spring Hill Station 20
Squaw 152
Squaw Canyon 149, 152
Stackhouse, Lee 181
Stanolind Oil Company 167
Stansbury, Capt. Howard 9, 10
State of Colorado 10
State of Wyoming 59, 102
Steamboat Rock 33, 34
Steamboat Springs, CO 139
Steele, Ft. Fred 111, 139
Stewart, Ann Robertson 165
Stewart, A.F. 183
Stewart, Dave 137
Stewart, James 72
Stewart, Perry 50, 70
Stonewall Creek 31, 33, 34
Stonewall Station 31, 33, 34
"Store" 43, 46
Stuart, Robert 5
Stock Growers National Bank, Rawlins . 132, 162
Stradivarias Violin 116
Stratton, Abe 162
Sublette, Milton 4
Sublette, William 4
Sulphur Springs Ranch . . . 6, 108, 109, 121-136
Sulphur Springs
    Station 66-72, 76-80, 83-88, 102, 103
Sutherland, NE 180
Sutler Store 52
Sutting, W.R. 83
Sutting, M.B. 83
Swan Land & Livestock Co. 144
Sweet, Mike 144
Sweetwater County, WY . 91, 92, 95, 96, 98-100
Sweetwater Livestock Co. 96
Sweetwater Mines 98
Sweetwater River 5, 7, 8, 50
Swing Station 11
Swisher, Dr. T.J. 179

T

Tallman, Clay 167
Tallman, Jean Stewart
    (Robertson) 80, 81, 83, 124, 146, 167
Talpey, Lt. 54
Tanner, Russel L. 39, 100
Tapers, Jack 150
Taylor, Robert 115, 116
Taylor, M/M William S. 35
Ted's Place 30
Ten Mile Station 31, 33, 34

Teton Reservoir 71
Thayer, M/M Bruce 73
Thomas, Rocky 40
Thornburg, Major Thomas F. 111
"Three Thousand Miles Through
    the Rocky Mountains" 72
Tie Siding, WY 39
Tierney, Ed. 76, 94
Tierney, Ed. M. 162
Tierney, Joe E. 162
Tierney, William 162
Timberlake Station, CO 111
Trotter, Col. 152
Truesdale, Jim 115
Tubbs, Pvt. Frank 61
Tug 34
Tulsa, OK 167
Turner, J.M. 83
Turpin, Eva Kuykendall 168
Turpin, Gilbert 168
Turpin, Lille (Bruning) 172
Turpin, Rollin W. 168
Tuttle, Burton 66, 77
Twelve Mile Station 25
Twenty Fifth Cavalry 169, 170
Twenty Mile Station 109, 115
"Twenty Years Among Our Hostile Indians" . 75
Two Forks Crossing 197, 208, 209
Two Forks Draw 197

U

Uinta County, WY 89, 101
Uinta Mountains 7
Union Army 169, 170
Union Pacific Railroad . . 6, 34, 36, 87, 96, 102,
    104,   107,   121,   126
University of Wyoming 59
University of Wyoming Library 79
Upper California Crossing 17
Utah 5, 99, 102, 127
Ute Indians 52, 53, 60, 70, 109

V

Valley Station 20
Vasquez, Louis 4
Vernon, Tom 147
Via, Alex M/M 121
Virginia 166
Virginia City, MT 35
Virginia Dale Station 9, 27, 33, 34, 90

W

Wagon Hound Creek 49
WAGON TRAILS and FOLK TALES 104
Walbach Cut-Off 36
Walcott Junction 61
Walker, L. 83
Wall, Calvin 75, 76, 86

Wallace, Mrs. 142	Wyoming University 59, 176, 184
Wallace, T.J. 141	
Wallis, M/M Dan 61	**Y**
Wamsutter, WY 114	Yalton Place, VA 166
Wanless, Asbury 71	
Ware, Lt. 19	**Z**
Warren, G.K. 5	Zeamer, J. 45, 46, 48, 60, 64, 70, 75
Warren Pole Creek Ranch 36	Zimmerer, Theresia Bruning ... 166, 169, 170
Washakie Station 89, 90	
Washie 89	
Waskie 89	
Washington 39	
Watts, Jo 75	
Weber 215	
Weber, Clint 147	
Weber, Matt "Dutch" 148	
Weber, Nina 146, 148	
Weber, Sid 140, 146, 148	
Weller, Dan 111	
Wells, Fargo & Co. 87, 100, 102	
Western Stage Co. 11	
Western Union Telegraph Line 13	
West Virginia 166	
Whiskey Gap, WY 51	
White, J.S. 66	
White River, CO 111, 128	
White River Rawlins Stage 110, 144	
White River Utes 110	
Wild Bunch 127	
Wilkes, Elizabeth 141	
Wille, Ron 127	
Williams, Bill 45	
Willow Springs Station 39	
Willows Stage Station 84, 108, 109, 121, 137-139	
Willow Valley 5	
Willows Post Office 138	
Wilson Bros. 152	
Wilson, George 52	
Wilson, Glen 141	
Wilson, Pvt. Wm. 50, 70	
Wilson, President Woodrow 159	
Windham, Kinnard 39	
Windsor, CO 25	
Wood, Mrs. Mildred M. 42	
Woods, G.K. 141	
Worland, WY 176	
World War I 179	
World War II 176	
Wyoming 4, 38-215	
Wyoming Centennial 8, 102	
Wyoming Daily Times 87	
"Wyoming's Pioneer Ranches" Burns, Gillespie and Richardson 43	
Wyoming Recreation Division (State) 115	
Wyoming State Historical Preservation Office . 36	
Wyoming State Landmark Commission 66	
Wyoming Territory 102	

Index